.

Flowing Through Time

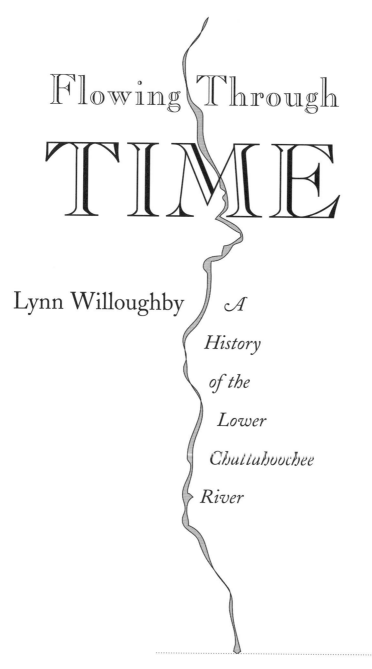

Flowing Through

TIME

Lynn Willoughby

A

History

of the

Lower

Chattahoochee

River

THE UNIVERSITY OF ALABAMA PRESS
Tuscaloosa and London

Published in Cooperation with
The Historic Chattahoochee Commission and
The Columbus Museum

1 2 3 4 5 6 7 8 9 • 06 05 04 03 02 01 00 99

∞
The paper on which this book is printed meets the minimum requirements of American National Standard for Information Science–Permanence of Paper for Printed Library Materials, ANSI Z39.48-1984.

Library of Congress Cataloging-in-Publication Data

Willoughby, Lynn, 1951–
    Flowing through time : a history of the lower Chattahoochee
River / Lynn Willoughby.
        p. cm.
    Includes bibliographical references (p.   ) and index.

    ISBN 0–8173–0934–9 (paper meets minimum requirements)
    1. Chattahoochee River—History. 2. Chattahoochee River
Valley—History. I. Title.
    F292.C4 W55 1999
    975.8—ddc21

                            98–19771

British Library Cataloguing-in-Publication Data available

To John Samuel Lupold

CONTENTS

ILLUSTRATIONS

ACKNOWLEDGMENTS

In the process of becoming, this book has been guided by many hands. I am grateful to the Historic Chattahoochee Commission and the Columbus Museum for commissioning this work. They envisioned creating a book that chronicled humankind's relationship with the Chattahoochee River over the centuries. My intention has been to make this work enjoyable to the general reader while informative to the professional. If I have succeeded, much of the credit goes to *the* experts in Chattahoochee River history, archaeology, and anthropology: the Historic Chattahoochee Commission's Chattahoochee Valley Legacy Series editorial board. It has been both a luxury and a pleasure to have Jerry Brown, Fred Fussell, Clason Kyle, John Lupold, Frank Schnell, and Billy Winn at my disposal for technical advice and the careful reading of each draft of this manuscript. Their comments and criticisms have vastly improved this work and saved me from a number of embarrassments. In particular, I wish to thank Frank Schnell for opening his personal library to me, sharing his expertise on the subject, and helping me reproduce photographs.

John Lupold, to whom this book is dedicated, has been a tireless supporter of both me and this book. He has generously offered technical assistance with computers, photographs, maps, and morale. He has taken me on tours of abandoned textile mills, river dams, and the more exotic of Columbus's restaurants. For the past nine years he has shared his encyclopedic knowledge of the Chattahoochee's history with me. His exuberance on the subject has inspired, challenged, and supported me. Both the book and I owe him a lot.

During the research phase of this project, I received help from many other professionals and friends. Among them were David Holmes, who patiently guided this computer-phobe in selecting a laptop computer; Lillianne Peterman of South Georgia Tech, who gave me technical assistance when the laptop broke; my parents, Broadus and Lib Willoughby, who sacrificed their log cabin for a summer so that I could be near my

xii   research; my sister Ginny Willoughby Bass, who graciously looked the other way when I stole squash from her garden to sustain myself; Carole Schuler, who fed my cat and probably an opossum while I was in Georgia; Craig Lloyd and Callie McGinnis at the Columbus State University's library, for cheerfully accommodating my sometimes irregular requests; Kaye Minchew of the Troup County Archives, for friendly assistance with research and photographs; Margaret Calhoon, archivist at Georgia Power, for opening the resources of the company's photographic collection to me; and Miriam Ann Syler of the Cobb Memorial Archives, for making my days of research there seem like an afternoon in her parlor. Copyeditor Jonathan Lawrence and the staff of The University of Alabama Press guided the manuscript to press with finesse and tact. The editors of the *Georgia Historical Quarterly, Apalachee,* and The University of Alabama Press have graciously allowed me to reprint material previously published.

As the writing phase of this project stretched out into years and most workdays felt like dog-paddling uphill, it would have been lonely going without the encouragement of my baby sister Windee Willoughby and my dear friends Pat Edmondson, Lynne Dunn, and Ginger Williams. Their love and support were appreciated most on the days they avoided asking me how the writing was going.

Thank you all!

Flowing Through Time

INTRODUCTION

Once upon a time (four hundred million years ago, or thereabout), the future site of Columbus, Georgia, had an ocean view. The original coastline of the American Southeast arced like a crescent moon southwestward from present-day Maryland to the vicinity of Charlotte, North Carolina, then on toward Augusta, Macon, Columbus, and Montgomery, before meeting what would one day be referred to as the Gulf of Mexico.

In that long-ago age, all the continents were drifting around on the earth's crust. North America floated northward from near the equator. A supercontinent now called Gondwanaland began to break up into the future continents of Africa and South America and drift westward toward North America. The triangle of land that today constitutes the peninsula of Florida and the coastal plain of Alabama, Georgia, and Carolina was originally a piece of Africa. It broke off from the mother continent and drifted westward until it rammed into North America about three hundred million years ago. The crash crumpled the coastline and thrust up a new mountain range. The peaks and volcanoes of these Alp-like mountains were so high that they would dwarf the present Blue Ridge.[1]

As dinosaurs stalked North America in the Triassic period, the South American and African continental masses drew away, opening up the Atlantic Ocean basin. A shallow sea settled over the latest appendage of the North American continent, the Southeast's Coastal Plain. Once again, the crescent-shaped line running through present-day Columbus, Georgia, marked the shoreline. Today this line is referred to as the "fall line." It represents the point of intersection of the ancient mountains (now whittled to foothills by erosion) and the old seashore. The difference in elevation between the Piedmont and the Coastal Plain is highlighted in the southeastern rivers by the waterfalls that mark the highest point that boats can run up the rivers from the coast without the aid of man-made locks or diversionary canals. North and west of this line, today's Piedmont Plateau is all that remains of the once-mighty mountain chain after millions of years of upheavals and erosion. Geologic stresses broke up the

2   mountains, and rains washed the pounded rocks away. Many of its minerals leached out of the crushed rock in the process, but the iron remained to stain the Piedmont clay a deep, rusty orange.[2]

The Coastal Plain which today lies south and east of the fall line lay under water for seventy-five million years or so. Gradually, over a period of probably another sixty-five million years, the waters receded to the present position of the coastline. As the ocean ebbed, the Chattahoochee extended farther southward from the Piedmont into the emerging coastal plain.

In modern times, the Chattahoochee River heads high in the Blue Ridge Mountains at about thirty-five hundred feet above sea level. As one writer described the headwaters over a century ago, "In less than a mile the Chattahoochee develops itself into a rippling rivulet; a few yards further down makes it a branch; next you find it a bold creek, and by the time the bottom of the pass is reached you find your way blocked by a swift little river."[3] The river plummets again for almost seventeen hundred feet before it reaches the Nacoochee Valley.[4] From there, the sparkling waters flow on southwestwardly, following the Brevard Fault Line to cascade down to the Atlanta Plateau, a tableland no more than fifty miles wide that stretches out one hundred miles in length to encompass present-day Gainesville, Atlanta, and West Point, Georgia. Through this plateau, the river has cut a deep trench as deep as four hundred feet and as wide as five miles. In the stretch above Atlanta, the water is cold and clear and considered "the best trout fishing for stocked rainbow, brown, and brook trout in the Southeast."[5]

At Franklin, in Heard County, the Chattahoochee steps down again to a lower plateau that extends from Meriwether County, Georgia, into Alabama. Between West Point and Columbus the river plummets headlong over boulders, throwing up foaming plumes of white water. Before the Chattahoochee was dammed in modern times, these rapids were a landmark. Humans—red, white, and black—were attracted to "the Falls of Coweta" where white men would one day build Columbus at the head of river navigation.

South of the rapids, the flatness of the terrain slows the Chattahoochee. At this point it is not only the character of the river that changes, but also that of the native flora and fauna, and even the climate. Through the earth, the river has eaten a ravine, creating high bluffs that stand fortress-like over the river at Phenix City, Eufaula, and Fort Gaines. At the southwestern corner of Georgia, the Chattahoochee weds the Flint River, a smaller but important stream that has been shadowing the larger one since it bubbled out of the Atlanta Plateau. Mingled together, the two enter Florida as the Apalachicola River, which has been described as having "the flavor of alligators, moccasins, and dank swamps, laced over with beards of Spanish moss."[6] Finally, at Apalachicola Bay, the Chattahoochee River broadens into an estuary. After 418 adventurous miles, the Gulf of Mexico swallows the tawny river and ends its travels.

Over this watercourse, humans have drifted for thousands of years. Generations of red, and later, white and black people have worshiped its power, marked the seasons of the year by its ebbs and flows, lazed on its sun-dappled banks, swum it, fished it, paddled it, drunk it, dammed it, and damned it.

This is its story.

CHAPTER I

The Ancients

RISING FROM THE BERING STRAIT THAT SEPARATED Asia from North America, a land bridge conducted the first humans into the Americas over ten thousand years ago. These ancient explorers wandered in search of a land where game was more plentiful and the weather more forgiving. Other groups followed. Some of the bands settled in the northern or western regions; others trekked eastward. Centuries passed in this manner before the first humans roamed into the Chattahoochee River valley.

Armed with their spears, the valley's first human residents stalked mastodons and mammoths in the forests above a roaring river, swollen by the melting snows of the Ice Age. These nomads followed the herds that sustained them. Since they made no permanent settlements, little was left behind as proof of their existence in the river valley except their heavy flint spearheads. Modern archaeological digs have uncovered mankind's first mementos at Bartlett's Ferry, north of Columbus, Georgia; at Fort Benning; on a creek near Seale, Alabama; and on a river bluff north of Phenix City.[1]

The warming trend that thawed the Ice Age continued over the next two thousand years, drying and warming the floor of the Chattahoochee Valley. By about 3,000 B.C. the climate had come to resemble our modern-day weather, and the valley brimmed with food. The people who lived in the Chattahoochee Valley between 8,000 and 1,000 B.C. were hunters and gatherers. They followed the food sources with the seasons. In the spring and summer they camped near the river to fish and gather clams and mussels. In nearby woods they foraged for berries, wild fruits, and roots. In fall and winter they roamed the forests in search of nuts and acorns. All year long they hunted game. Although the gigantic mammoths and mastodons had disappeared from the valley, other, smaller animals were now in abundance. Hunters manufactured smaller, lighter weapons to kill the white-tailed deer, raccoon, rabbit, squirrel, wild turkey, and black bear. At two places along the Chattahoochee, archaeologists have found the remains of the flint factories where the archaic artisans chipped away at pieces of flint and quartz to craft their spear tips.

Archaeologists have labeled the next period of human habitation along the Chattahoochee (which lasted from 1,000 B.C. to A.D. 700) the Woodland period. By around 4,000 B.C., the Indians had learned to make stone axes and other heavy tools used to clear openings in the forest and hollow out trees in order to fashion dugout canoes. Floating down the river, the archaic people transported loads too heavy to carry on foot. In this way they conserved the precious calories required to find food and shelter. During the Woodland period, the tribes of the Chattahoochee region were in regular contact with other peoples living in distant parts of North America. In their dugouts they floated downstream to the Gulf of Mexico, and by paddling to the mouths of other river systems they floated into the heart of other regions.

But the Chattahoochee waters served as more than a transportation artery. The river was also a natural trail marker for overland travel. Trails shadowed the river on both banks and also paralleled its tributaries. Travelers knew that any path that followed a creek downstream led to the river. By following a trail in an upstream direction one eventually came to the river's headwaters, which were not far removed from those of adjacent river systems. Short trails connected one waterway to another. This was the logical way to travel from the Chattahoochee region to the Flint River valley to the east or the Coosa/Tallapoosa/Alabama waterway to the west.

Following the trails that connected one river system to the next, the natives walked as far as the valleys of the Ohio and Mississippi Rivers. Through trade with distant people, the Chattahoochee Indians acquired exotic materials like marine shells and salt from the Gulf Coast, mica from the Appalachians, flint from the Flint River valley, copper from the eastern Tennessee region and even from the Great Lakes area, and obsidian from as far away as the Rockies. So whether or not they traveled by water, the Woodland people relied on the rivers to find their way in the wilderness.

By way of the flowing waters, the Woodland Indians communicated and traded with each other and also shared their spiritual beliefs and

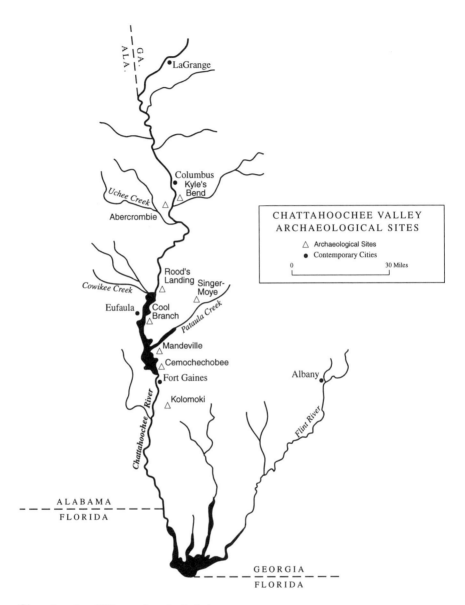

Chattahoochee Valley archaeological sites

culture. Around 1,000 B.C., the Chattahoochee people, influenced by Indians to their west, began to place great significance on the burial of their dead. The burial mounds that these people erected along the Chattahoochee Valley required thousands of hours of labor by the entire tribe.

On the banks of the Chattahoochee near present-day Fort Gaines, Georgia, Woodland Indians left a monument to a complex set of spiritual beliefs that they shared with Indians throughout the Midwest and South. Around two thousand years ago, these early Chattahoochee residents built what would become known as the Mandeville site, which is today covered by the impounded waters of Lake Walter F. George.[2] Before its watery interment, archaeologists found a burial mound with copper and silver trinkets buried along with the cremated remains of humans. A second mound was the site of religious and secular ceremonies. Inside the Mandeville platform mound, the archaeologists found a human figurine, a pipe with a bowl shaped like a bird, and pieces of exotic minerals, including copper, quartz crystals, and mica.[3]

Sculpture found in Chattahoochee Valley archaeological site. *Courtesy of the Columbus Museum.*

The huge Kolomoki complex, located on a tributary of the Chattahoochee River near the present-day town of Blakely, Georgia, provides further evidence of the complexity of the Woodland-period civilizations. Of the nine mounds that stand impressively today as a relic of the Woodland people, two have definitely been identified as burial mounds. These people apparently kept the burial and construction of these mounds in continuation over many years. Recent excavations have revealed a highly ritualistic manner of putting to rest the corpses of those whom they revered.

Fanning outward from an imposing platform mound measuring 56 feet high, 325 feet long, and 200 feet wide, as many as two thousand people lived at Kolomoki. Basket by basket, they piled up the earth to create their temples to the spirit world. Without draft animals to carry the loads of earth, the construction took dedication and organization. It is estimated that it took 875,000 man-hours to complete "Mound A"

8   alone. In addition to the earthworks at Mandeville and Kolomoki, Woodland people left a stone enclosure atop Pine Mountain and occasional stone cairns on both banks of the river.

The Woodland Indians lived in harmony with nature. Indeed, William Winn has deemed these people "the greatest naturalists the Valley has ever known": "They knew the river itself, and its many tributaries, better than we know the streets on which we live. They swam and fished in its waters, used it as a broad highway to travel throughout the Valley, stretched out on its banks to take in the warmth of the winter sun, listened to the hiss of rain striking its surface, and heard the strange, sad, rustling sound of wind in the cane that grew on its banks."[4]

It is unclear what became of the Woodland Indians, but after their passing, a final civilization would rise and fall on the banks of the Chattahoochee before the advent of the Europeans into the Southeast. The period from A.D. 700 to 1400 saw the flowering of the "Mississippian Culture," so called because it was related to the large mound complexes of this era found along the Mississippi River valley. Likewise, the Mississippian villages of the Chattahoochee Valley were usually located near the river or its larger tributaries. Like their predecessors of the Woodland period, the Mississippians constructed large, flat-topped platform and temple mounds. Encircling these seats of government and religion were wide, open plazas and extensive villages.

Although the Woodland people had raised some of their own food, their major preoccupation was in hunting and gathering. While supplementing their diet with game, the later peoples of the Mississippian period were the first in the Chattahoochee Valley to systematically cultivate the vegetables that were their mainstay: beans, squash, pumpkins, and, most important, corn.

Along the Chattahoochee there are no less than sixteen significant Mississippian sites. Most of these are still visible, although the river has reclaimed several. On the Georgia side of the river these include the late stages of Kolomoki and Mandeville, as well as two sites in Stewart County (Rood's Landing and Singer-Moye), one on Bull Creek near Columbus, and three near Fort Gaines (Drag Nasty Creek, Graces Bend, and Cool Branch). On the Alabama side, there are two sites in Houston County (Omussee Creek and Spann's Landing), three near Eufaula (Reeves, Lampley Mound, and Lynn's Fish Pond), and the Abercrombie Mound in Russell County. The Chattahoochee people shared such cultural traits with the other Mississippians as shell-tempered ceramics, multistage platform mounds, fortified towns, the first extensive cultivation of vegetables, and the production of effigy pottery and triangular projectile points, as well as a similar ethos.[5]

9

At Cemochechobee in Clay County, Georgia, three large mounds—a burial mound, a temple mound, and a house mound—represent the heart of this village that once covered more than 150 acres.[6] The Rood's Landing site in Stewart County, Georgia, has been described by archaeologist Frank Schnell as "the largest and most complex Mississippi Period site known on the Georgia Coastal Plain."[7] Its eight mounds, with associated residences and plazas and defense works, have convinced archaeologists that this site was probably the "capitol of a major, complex chiefdom which must have controlled a significant portion of the Lower Chattahoochee Valley."[8] From their vantage point on the Chattahoochee, the people of Rood's Landing could have influenced trade and transportation between the Gulf of Mexico and the Appalachian Mountains.

The mounds at Cemochechobee were abandoned about a hundred years before the coming of the first European explorers to the area. The settlement at Rood's Landing seems to have collapsed at about the time

Sculpture found in Chattahoochee Valley archaeological site. *Courtesy of the Columbus Museum.*

Dog pot found at Bull Creek archaeological site. *Courtesy of the Columbus Museum.*

Archaeologist Jack Tyler at Cemochechobee archaeological site. The Walter F. George Lock and Dam is in the background. Circa 1977. *Courtesy of the Columbus Museum.*

Drawing of a Mississippian-period platform mound by Cheryl Mann Hardin. Modern-day artist's conception. *Courtesy of William W. Winn and the Historic Chattahoochee Commission.*

of Hernando de Soto, who was, in 1539, the first European to explore the Southeast (although not the Chattahoochee region).[9] Archaeologists are not certain what happened to the Rood's Landing and Cemochechobee people or to the other Mississippian peoples of the Chattahoochee. Most experts today agree that their civilization probably was decimated by European diseases for which they had little immunity. The initial contact between the Spanish and the indigenous peoples of North America, Central America, and the Caribbean set off waves of epidemics of such diseases as smallpox and measles that ravaged the various regions of the Americas.

As the fevers raged in the villages of the Chattahoochee River, the chiefdom that centered around the Rood's Landing capital collapsed. Survivors from other areas moved into the depopulated areas over the next century or two. The newcomers included the Ocheesee people, whom de Soto had encountered near the falls of the Ocmulgee River; the Tomathly, Tuskeegee, and Chiaha, whom he met in eastern Tennessee; and the Kasihta (or Cusseta) of central Alabama, who relocated to the Chattahoochee in the 1600s.[10]

In Russell County, Alabama, just south of today's Phenix City, are the remnants of an Indian village that date back to this era of drastic upheaval along the Chattahoochee (approximately 1600) and provide concrete evidence of the presence of epidemic diseases soon after the de Soto entrada. Instead of the careful laying to rest of the corpses into burial mounds, a practice that required hours and hours of intensive labor, these graves are shallow and haphazard.[11] The people who lived here made their pottery in a very similar way to a group of people who lived on the Alabama River at about the same time, indicating the movement of the survivors from one area to another.

As the various refugee groups moved into the Chattahoochee Valley, they absorbed the local survivors. The diverse people were often unrelated to each other and even spoke different languages. Yet they formed an alliance that offered the sovereign towns a regional council in which ideas were exchanged, friendships forged, and mutual defense pacts made. This "confederacy" was dominated by speakers of Muskogean dialects. For that reason, the Chattahoochee people were known collectively as the Muskogee (or Muscogulgi, literally, "Muskogee people"). White men would later refer to all of them (Muskogean-speaking or not) as Creeks, probably because of their tendency to locate their towns on the banks of rivers and their larger tributaries.[12]

The influence of this "Creek Confederation" extended from the Appalachian Mountains southward to the Gulf of Mexico and from the Atlantic Ocean to the Mississippi River. Its nucleus was formed by the twin towns of Coweta and Cusseta, located on either side of the Chattahoochee near the waterfalls that divided the river into the Piedmont and the Coastal Plain. Coweta, the political capital for which the falls would be named, stood on the western bank of the river. On the eastern side sat the peace and religious capital of Cusseta. Associated with these two capital cities were other Muskogean-speaking Creek settlements, such as Coosa, Abihka, Hothliwahali, Hilibi, Eufaula, Tuckabatchee, Okchai, and Pakana. The Hitchiti and the Alabama spoke a dialect that was distantly related to Muskogean. The Yuchi and the Shawnee who migrated into the Chattahoochee Valley spoke languages unrelated to the others. When the Natchez fled the French invaders of their homeland to the west for the Creek Confederation in the 1730s, they brought with them a language that was related to Muskogean but unintelligible to the other Muskogees.[13]

The original towns agreed not to make war on each other, but to aggressively conquer others. Those whom they captured or subdued became allies. This period of conquest ended in the 1700s. As Europeans encroached, the Confederation took on a more defensive intent and grew stronger. The Muskogees continued to absorb newcomers, but the later Confederates were more than likely to be refugees from European aggression than the Creeks' defeated enemies.[14] Joining the Confederation was voluntary. As new towns were settled, they were welcomed as friends who helped each other the way neighbors do. There "were no mass armies of Confederacy warriors, no central policy, and no central government. There was only good will among friends and the realization that an invading enemy was a common enemy."[15]

During the eighteenth century, the names of over eighty Creek towns were recorded by various Europeans. The towns were spread near the heads of navigation of two different river systems: the Chattahoochee and the Coosa/Tallapoosa/Alabama to its west. The English traders of Charleston, South Carolina, probably were the first to refer to the people of the two rivers as living in either the "upper" or "lower" towns. Their trading path from Carolina forked in central Georgia. Taking the upper path led to the villages centered on the Tallapoosa River, while the lower path led to the Chattahoochee.[16] Thus the people of the Chattahoochee River became known as the Lower Creeks.

One means of uniting the Creek people of both river systems while simultaneously decentralizing power was the system of clan identity.

Drawing of a Creek square ground by Cheryl Mann Hardin. Modern-day artist's conception. *Courtesy of William W. Winn and the Historic Chattahoochee Commission*

Every Creek belonged to a clan whose members traditionally were related by blood. Creek clans were matrilineal, which means that descent followed the mother's, not the father's, line. Each person was born into and forever remained a part of his or her mother's clan. A Creek boy was guided and protected throughout his life by his mother's brothers, not his own father. Clan members were required to defend each other, share the responsibility of raising the children, and care for the old and infirm. Members of the same clan were forbidden to marry or have sexual relations.[17]

Since the clans were matrilocal, a young man who married left the home of his mother and went to live with his wife's people. Each Creek town was composed of several clan compounds, each headed by the oldest woman, who gathered her daughters and granddaughters with their husbands or unmarried sons. Clan elders were men related to the venerated woman. They supervised the family and were responsible for the education of the young, but they did so from afar, since they lived with their wife's family. At least fifty clans made up the Creek Confederation.

14   The most prestigious was the Wind Clan. The others were also named for elements of nature important to the Indians. Examples are Bear, Bird, Alligator, Deer, and Fish.[18]

The Creeks' judicial system was known as clan vengeance. In the fashion of the Old Testament's "eye for an eye," the males of one clan were required to exact a like punishment on anyone who injured one of their own. In practical terms, the rule of blood retaliation meant that "if a small boy accidentally put out the eye of a playmate, it was incumbent upon the injured child's clan to put out the eye of the other child. If a man lent his horse to a friend and that friend was thrown and killed, the clan of the dead man was required to kill the man who lent his friend the horse." If the person whose life was required could not be located, the offended clan took his next of kin to be punished in his place.[19]

Besides the unifying effect the clans had on Creek civilization, two traditions helped to bond the Chattahoochee tribes in spite of their decentralization and diversity. Ball games were one source of camaraderie. Every Creek town had a ball yard near the town square and meeting house. Local ball teams were organized into two leagues. Games were organized so that towns faced the teams in the opposite league, encouraging solidarity among league members. If a town lost four games in a row, it was required to switch leagues. In this way, a town's allegiance and friendships changed with time.[20]

Another tradition that united the Creeks was the Green Corn celebration, or Poskeeta, which was held every summer when the new corn crop was ripe. This festival had religious, as well as social, political, and recreational, aspects. Throughout the celebration, all satellite villages were required to attend the festivities of the central town, thus bringing the people together for several days each year. At such a time, the clans held meetings to evaluate the conduct of their people over the past year. The town council met to review the local laws, review the events of the past year, and devise a plan for the coming one.

During the Poskeeta, the men fasted every day for four days. At night they walked down to the Chattahoochee and washed themselves, then spent the remainder of the night dancing. During these four days the men did not go to their houses, and they were forbidden to have sexual intercourse. On the morning of the fifth day, the women brought in a meal of fresh corn. After bathing one last time in the river, they feasted and the annual celebration ended. These rites marked the year's end and required mental and spiritual preparation for the coming one. Old fires were extinguished and new ones lit, symbolizing the renewal and rebirth of each individual and of the tribe as a whole.[21]

The Poskeeta was also a time of forgiveness. Old sins were erased, "crimes short of murder were forgiven, and all were made pure and innocent."[22] If, during the year, a man ever brought up an old resentment that dated back to a time prior to the last festival, his peers castigated him.[23]

> By wiping the slate clean every year, the Creeks kept their society in harmony. By remembering the sacred sources of their power, they kept their lives in spiritual perspective. And by ending the Busk [Poskeeta] with the green corn feast, they looked ahead to the living of a new year. Like the fire, the corn symbolized the renewal of life. Corn came from the ground, and through it the land nourished the people. By focusing on the produce of the land, the Creeks celebrated their past and their future life in the place where they were. They could never forget that they were uniquely the people of that place.[24]

No matter what language the villagers spoke or which clan commanded their loyalty, all the peoples of the Creek Confederation shared at least two important daily customs. One ritual for men only was the drinking of the "black drink." At least that is what the white people called it because of its dark hue. "Ah-cee," as the Creeks pronounced it, was brewed from the toasted leaves of the common yaupon holly bush. The Indians called it the "white drink" because of its aid in purification and peace. It actually looked similar to the foam-capped cappuccino so popular in the coffee bars of the 1990s, and like the latter, it contained the stimulant caffeine. The Indians considered the drink both mind-and spirit-altering, especially when taken with tobacco.

Though consumed daily by the important men of the town, the black drink was not taken casually. A-cee was drunk by the town elders in their order of importance while a singer chanted "Yaa-hoo-laa," holding each note as long as possible. Each drinker pressed the cup to his lips until the singer stopped. The singer and server was designated as the "A-cee Yahola" ("black drink singer"). The English corrupted this phrase to "Osceola." Since the drink was an emetic, when the men drank a lot of it they vomited the a-cee in a great show which resulted in the spewing of the liquid six or more feet in the air. Because of this practice, the scientific name of the yaupon holly is *Ilex vomitoria.*[25]

Bathing was another daily ritual that the Creeks' custom and religion required. Water was a sacred element of life to the Creeks. First thing every morning, summer and winter, every able-bodied man, woman, and child went to the river and plunged under the water four times. An early white traveler recorded this account of the custom:

> In the coldest weather, and when the ground is covered with snow, against their bodily ease and pleasure, men and women turn out of their warm houses or stoves, reeking with sweat, singing their usual sacred notes, *Yo, Yo,* etc., at the dawn of day . . . and thus they skip along, echoing praises till they get to the river, when they instantaneously plunge into it. After bathing, they return home, rejoicing as they run for having so well performed their religious duty, and thus purged away the impurities of the preceding day by ablution.[26]

To the Indians' way of seeing the universe, there were spirits in the waters, in the animals and plants, and in the rocks. The Creeks made sense of both miraculous and mundane occurrences by explaining them in terms of the spirit world. There were no coincidences and no accidents. Therefore, if a hunter lost his knife, he believed a spirit must have taken it, and if one became ill, it was probably because he had offended the spirit world in some way.[27] The Chattahoochee was more than a river to these people. It was a spirit and a conduit of creatures from the underworld. In the Chattahoochee swam beaver, otter, and water snakes who linked the physical and spirit worlds.

Besides these animals, fantastic creatures were fabled to live in the river. One was the feared "tie snake," which lived in deep holes in the water and in the falls of the Chattahoochee and drew its prey down into its den. Another water creature, the "horned snake," believed to have antlers like a stag, was held in particularly high esteem. The creature did not seem to harm humans, but it had a magnetizing effect on game. Drawn by its power, wildlife walked into the river and drowned. Of its prey, the horned snake ate only the end of its nose.[28]

But the Chattahoochee was more than a spiritual conduit. The waters may have been the habitation of magical serpents, but they also were home to the fish that gave the Muskogees sustenance in summer. During spawning season, the fish that swam upstream were halted at the fall line, making the rapids of the Coweta Falls one of the richest fishing sites in North America.[29] In the summer, when the water was in its lowest stage, fishing was especially easy. Word was passed around the neighborhood that all should meet at a certain time to spend the day catching fish. The fishers used "devil's shoestring," or buckeye roots, to poison the fish. When released in the water, the plants, which contained a rotenone-like chemical, stunned the fish. Using bows and arrows and other weapons, the fishers speared or clubbed the fish that floated to the surface. The catch was roasted, baked, or fried and served as the main course for a moonlight feast and dance.[30]

The towns of Coweta and Cusseta, on either side of the river, claimed fishing holes on their respective sides of the river just below the waterfalls that mark the present-day city of Columbus. Fishermen also caught fish using gill nets, trotlines, baskets, and rock traps. At night they built fires in their canoes to attract the fish to them, then speared the fish or shot them with arrows as they swam toward the light. By these methods, the Indians caught bream, bass, catfish, drum, sturgeon, and shad.[31]

Like the Indians of old, the Creeks used the Chattahoochee as a highway. They devised portable leather boats to ferry across the river. These were made by cutting poles on site and stretching animal skins over them. When they reached the other side, they threw away the poles, rolled up the leather, and took it with them to use the next time they needed a ferry. Dugout canoes were made from elm, hickory, or cypress logs, sometimes with the bark left intact. When the Indians paddled them to the point where they wanted to leave the river, they simply turned them over. Because the canoes resembled fallen, rotting logs, the Indians could conceal them from passersby who might want to steal them.

In the eighteenth century, Coweta Creeks and other Muskogees paddled and sailed all the way to Havana, Cuba, and Nassau, Bahamas, in their twenty- to thirty-man canoes. Once the Cowetas invited a white trader to join them on a trading sortie to Nassau. "He agreed—until he saw their dugout. Then he paled." But Indians did not think it extraordinary to cross the Gulf of Mexico in their converted trees. They ventured to the Caribbean "again and again."[32]

Besides serving as a boating thoroughfare, the Chattahoochee beckoned swimmers to enjoy its coolness on a midsummer's day. A white missionary of the early nineteenth century was scandalized when he found Creek women, girls, and boys swimming together in "naked naughtiness" at Coweta.[33]

Part recreation site, part food source, part transportation artery, part trail marker, part spirit, the Chattahoochee was more important to Native Americans than modern man can ever appreciate. The Creeks may have named the river for the rocks along its banks that they also held sacred.

18   "Chat-to" may have meant "a stone"; "ho-che," "marked or flowered." Even though modern society has lost its collective memory of the sanctity of its waters, the Chattahoochee still bears the name of reverence that the natives bestowed on it centuries ago. Today the river eats into the sacred resting places of these people and washes their bones downstream.

> And yet they left their names on our waters
> And we may not wash them out.[34]

§

The Scramble for Muscogee

STRUNG LIKE BEADS ALONG THE CHATTAHOOCHEE, thirteen major Lower Creek settlements flourished in 1674 when a European recorded their names.[1] The inhabitants of these villages had no way of knowing that their civilization sat squarely on the epicenter of what would become an international contest for not only the Chattahoochee Valley, but all of the Southeast and even beyond.

The southern tribes—such as the Cherokee, the Yamasee, the Chickasaw, the Choctaw, and the Creeks, as well as many minor groups—had through warfare and diplomacy established the limits of their people well before the Europeans arrived. Their sometimes bloody history caused them to be wary, at best, of each other. To exacerbate the natives' distrust of each other, strangers soon encircled them, drawing the cord ever tighter until the Indians were forced to stand and fight—among themselves and against the very source of the guns they would need for protection. As a three-way competition for Creek loyalty materialized among the Spaniards, the English, and the French, the Indians soon found themselves pressured to ally with each. Dangling the carrot of European-made goods before Creek eyes, the newcomers could not be ignored. And whoever dominated the trade in Indian buckskins would dominate the Indians as well.

From the outset, England, Spain, and France had different interests in the Creeks' lands. The Spanish adventurers found silver in Mexico and Peru in such abundance that Spain became the wealthiest country in Europe. Though they searched for such riches in "La Florida," they found none. Several attempts to plant large-scale colonies in what became the southeastern United States also failed. These disappointments

20 reinforced Spain's focus on the New World southward, and the future United States became of secondary importance.

The value of "La Florida"—the southeastern quarter of North America—lay neither in precious metals nor in advanced Indian civilizations, but as the post from which Spain could guard the route of the annual silver fleet from Havana through the Straits of Florida across the Atlantic to Seville. Although colonization was not their primary focus in Florida, the Spaniards used Catholic missions to win the loyalty of the native population in the region. For a century after the establishment of St. Augustine in 1565, a handful of friars, primarily Franciscans, controlled thousands of Indians: the Guale along the coast of what became Georgia, the Timucua across Florida, and the Apalachee at the mouth of the river named for them. They learned to mumble their prayers in Latin while producing foodstuffs and other supplies for the priests and the small military garrisons.

Although the Spaniards maintained hegemony over the strategically important coast, they never attempted to control the Indians in the inte-

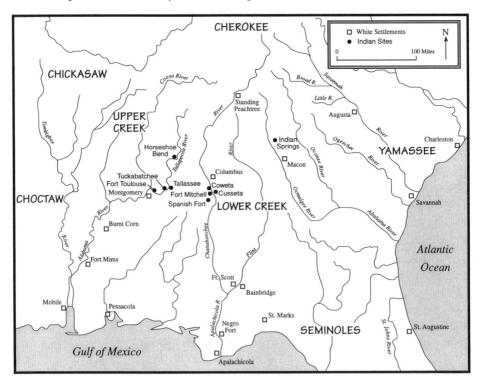

Indian sites and white settlements

rior, including those in the Chattahoochee region. Nor did the Spanish develop any extensive trade with these Indians. Expanding capitalism with its aggressive, independent merchants—the hallmark of England—never evolved in Spain or her colonies. For a myriad of reasons, Spain remained a more medieval society than northern Europe, and what the Spanish found in Mexico and Peru (enormous quantities of precious metal and sedentary, exploitable natives) reinforced their traditional society and allowed them to transfer feudalism to the New World. Merchants seeking new markets, especially on the perimeter of the empire, never became a feature of Spain's colonial world.

England's colonization was handled differently from the start. Merchants arrived with the first Englishmen at Charleston in 1670. British capitalism was much more dynamic than Spanish Catholicism. English and Scottish traders quickly began penetrating potential markets in the interior, an area Spain had claimed but ignored for a century. Alarmed at the close proximity of the English to their claim, the Spanish set about to outflank them by advancing up the Chattahoochee.

Within four years of the founding of Charleston in 1670, Spanish priests had constructed three missions near the juncture of the Chattahoochee and Flint Rivers. Of these, Sabacola el Menor was probably located near the site of present-day Chattahoochee, Florida. North of Sabacola were San Carlos and San Nicolas, whose ruins are probably buried today under the impounded waters of Lake Seminole.[2] At the upper end of the chain of Creek villages, near the fall line, the natives did not tolerate the missionaries as neighbors. A Coweta chief ordered two Franciscan friars to leave his people's land in 1679.[3]

Unlike the Spaniards, the Englishmen combined colonization of the New World with capitalism from the very beginning. Parliament chartered individual companies to settle their North American claims on the condition that they be financially successful. This practice was based on the belief that business would benefit everyone. The colonists would have their chance for wealth in the New World; the company that sponsored the colony would reap a profit; and the Crown would tax both.

Therefore, as soon as the Charlestonians settled into their new environs, they sent out traders to the Indians. The English traders, unlike the Spaniards, were more than willing to trade guns and shot and powder to the Indians. Originally, the English preferred to trade for Indian slaves. The Carolinians encouraged neighboring tribes to bring in captives of rival Indian groups to be exchanged for luxuries such as colored cloth, rifles, ammunition, beads, blankets, pots, tools, and rum. The English

22 learned that Indians did not make good slaves. They converted the Indian trade to a deerskin trade, and business flourished.

Once the Indians exchanged their earthenware bowls for copper kettles, their stone tools for iron ones, and their bows and arrows for muskets, there was no turning back. Luxuries became necessities in the blink of an eye. The Creeks preferred trading with the Englishmen over the Spaniards for three reasons: English traders offered the Creeks better prices for their buckskins; they provided a steadier source of trade goods; and they did not try to Christianize them. When it came down to it, "the tolling of church bells . . . [was] no match for a calico petticoat."[4]

In 1685, about the time the Spaniards were erecting their forts on the Chattahoochee, a Carolina trader named Henry Woodward, with his packhorses loaded with goods, became the first Englishman to reach the Coweta Falls. When news reached the Spanish garrison at the Gulf of Mexico that an English interloper had arrived in Creek territory, Commander Antonio Matheos hurried northward to defend the Chattahoochee.

Woodward did not have enough men to stand and fight the Spanish, so he and his fellow countrymen slipped into the woods. Matheos burned down Woodward's half-finished blockhouse above the falls. But no sooner had the Spaniard returned to the coast than he learned that Woodward had returned to the Chattahoochee. This time, Matheos turned his ire on the Creeks.

The Spaniard spared the southernmost Creek villages, who promised allegiance to Spain, but he burned to ashes Coweta and Cusseta and two neighboring Creek towns, then paddled back down the Chattahoochee to his post at the Gulf coast. Five weeks later the burned villages called for Matheos to return so that they could repent, but to the Spaniard's way of seeing things, this was only a ruse. As soon as the satisfied Spaniard stepped into his southbound canoe, the Cowetas called Woodward out of hiding and the English trade continued. The Indians did not understand why they could trade with only one group. Later, when Woodward became ill, the Creeks bore him on a stretcher all the way to Charleston, his escorts laden with deerskins.[5]

Although Woodward never returned to the Chattahoochee, the next season other English traders replaced him. For the next several years, the Spaniards raided the Chattahoochee hoping to rout the English peddlers, but their mission was as useless as trying to stop the flow of the Chattahoochee. Commerce follows the route of least resistance. The English trade flowed like the river for the next century.

Realizing the folly of Matheos's tactics in trying to make friends of the Lower Creeks, the Spanish governor of St. Augustine, Diego de Quiroga y Lasada, journeyed to the Chattahoochee to apologize to the inhabitants of the burned-out towns in 1687. He encouraged the Indians to resume trade with the Spaniards and "to make the river once again a friendly pathway between the two provinces."[6] Governor Quiroga was so impressed with the richness of the land along the Chattahoochee that he wrote the king of Spain suggesting that the monarch dispatch farmers to settle there. The cumbersome Spanish bureaucracy never answered Quiroga's letter. Instead of fathering a thriving Spanish farming civilization in the New World, Quiroga built a fort on the western bank of the river, south of Coweta, approximately sixteen miles south of present-day Phenix City. Forty Spanish soldiers and Indian allies from the coast manned it. The Spanish colors flew over the parapet of this stockade for two years.

The Coweta Creeks had no intention of becoming Spanish protégés. Rather than make enemies, they and some of their neighbors quietly packed up their belongings and moved eighty miles eastward to the Ocmulgee River, where they could be nearer the preferred English trade. The Spaniards were left with a useless fort in a virtually uninhabited wilderness. When the garrison was needed in St. Augustine in 1691, they burned down the stockade so that the English could not make use of it and then left. With its destruction, they abandoned forever the idea of maintaining a military post on the Chattahoochee.[7] In the first decade of the eighteenth century, the Creeks allied with the Charlestonians to attack, enslave, and decimate the ill-armed Apalachee Spanish mission Indians near the Gulf coast.

Frenchmen soon completed the encirclement of the Creek lands. Determined to keep up with their European rivals, they first drove their North American claim into Canada. While the Spanish soldiers hammered away on their Chattahoochee stockades, the French explorer Robert Cavelier became the first European to sail the entire length of the Mississippi River from Canada to the Gulf coast. From the mouth of the Mississippi, Pierre Le Moyne made a series of French settlements in the Biloxi and Mobile area of the Gulf of Mexico between 1698 and 1702.

The insertion of French claims into the western Gulf region spurred the Spaniards to establish a settlement at Pensacola in 1698. But that did not prevent the lieutenant governor of French Louisiana from trekking all the way to the Chattahoochee in 1714 to pay respects to the head towns of Coweta and Cusseta.[8] By 1717 the French had also befriended the Upper Creeks, who asked the French to build a fort among them at the juncture of the Coosa and Tallapoosa Rivers in order to give English traders some competition. But that overture came only in the wake of the great Yamasee War of 1715 against the English.

When the English moved into Carolina, the Yamasee tribe moved near the Charlestonians to become their primary trading partner. Over the years, these Indians came to regret their proximity to the English. They ran up debts too high to pay off in captives or deerskins. The Carolinians collected their debt by seizing their wives and children and selling them as slaves. No matter how much they needed the English guns, the Yamasees could not stand for this. When they revolted, they asked the Creeks to join them. The Creeks were persuaded by both the Yamasees and the French. The fact that they had been cheated by several English traders also influenced their decision. The natives' combined stand against Charleston represented the only significant pan-Indian war against whites in the colonial era. The Yamasees were routed, but the Creeks continued the fight. They appealed to the Cherokees to join them, but the Cherokees decided not to side against their trading source. Instead, they allied with the English and attacked the Creeks. This doomed the Creeks' war. When the fighting ended, the Carolinians rewarded the Cherokees for their loyalty and broke off relations with the Creeks.

The failed Yamasee revolt changed the Creeks' attitude toward the English. Instead of relying solely on them for trade, the Creeks now sought to distribute their dependency among all the European colonies. The first step in keeping their distance from the English was to physically move away. Some of the Lower Creek towns which had previously moved to the Ocmulgee to be closer to the English packed up and returned to their old village sites on the banks of the Chattahoochee. Once they settled in, the Creeks opened the door to new commercial and diplomatic relations with England's rivals. The Upper Creeks eagerly sought the presence of the French in the heart of their country, resulting in the erection of Fort Toulouse at the head of the Alabama River in 1716. The Lower Creeks, too far removed from the French to sustain communications, befriended the Spanish, who, in 1718, built Fort San Marcos (St. Marks) on Apalachee Bay, sixty miles east of the mouth of the Chattahoochee River system.

Since the Creek Confederation remained decentralized, there was no active, central Indian government to treat with each European colony. Instead, each town was free to make its own deals, though they often negotiated collectively as lower or upper towns. The actions of the two groups tended to counterbalance so that no European could take the loyalty of all the Creeks for granted. On significant matters affecting the entire tribe, the National Council met, but unilateral decisions were not always the result.

The primary Lower Creek headman was Brims of Coweta. The English and French called him "Emperor." Though the Indians did not regard him as such, as the headman of the most important Lower Creek town, Brims was "as close to a true monarch as the Creek political organization was capable of sustaining."[9] He developed a doctrine of neutrality that served the Lower Creeks well throughout the colonial period. He demanded independence from each of the European groups while simultaneously using their fears of each other to extract the best possible deal.[10] As long as the three European powers remained close by, Brims and his descendants were able to maintain neutrality, dominate the other southeastern tribes, and prosper.

Soon after the Yamasee War brought the Cowetas back to their old home site on the Chattahoochee, Emperor Brims sent his son Sepeycoffee to Pensacola to ask the Spanish to build a fort at Coweta. The Spanish presence at the falls of the Chattahoochee would not only serve to hold off the English who breathed down on them from the east, but would also serve as a counterbalance to the French fort among the Upper Creeks to the west. The Upper Creeks also cooperated with Brims's plan to solicit the Spanish, since they needed a counterweight to the French.

In September 1716, representatives of the entire Creek Confederation swore allegiance to the Spanish monarch. The Spanish were delighted with this sea change and immediately invited the Upper Creek deputies to travel to Mexico to be received formally by the Viceroy of the Americas. They also began outfitting an expedition to Coweta the following year to build a fort. However, by the time the Spanish arrived with Sepeycoffee to mark out the fort site, the winds had changed again. The Spaniards found twelve Englishmen at Coweta seriously discussing sealing a peace between them. While his son was in St. Augustine, Brims had found a way around becoming a dependent of Spain by resuming trade with the English and concurrently keeping the peace with the Spaniards.[11]

Though the Spanish captain fumed at his spoiled chances and plotted his revenge on the Englishmen, his safety was endangered by a particularly pro-English faction of the Creeks. So down the Chattahoochee the Spaniard paddled to report to superiors that the only Spanish fort

26   that feasibly could be built on the Chattahoochee would have to stand on
the lower river where friendly refugees from the Yamasee War had settled. After the Spanish were gone, representatives of both the Upper and
Lower Creeks traveled to Charleston and concluded the first Creek/En-
glish treaty of record. Not surprisingly, the subject of it was trade: setting
fixed rates and promising to trade in good faith.

Though the Creeks promised by this document to have "no further
correspondence with the Spaniards," Emperor Brims never took this provision seriously. Spanish agents were welcomed and protected in most
Creek towns. There was always a faction that leaned heavily on the Spanish, just as there was always a majority faction composed of Anglophiles.
Thus the Creeks of the Chattahoochee began to walk a slippery slope of
friendship to all and servitude to none.[12] This diplomatic duality in relations with the two most prominent Europeans was personified in Emperor Brims's sons. Sepeycoffee became Brims's envoy to the Spanish;
Ouletta, another son, was his hand to the English. Even after the three
of them were dead, the Creek policy of maintaining independence from
all the Europeans was carried on by their successors for as long as the
English and Spanish lived nearby.[13]

Trouble moved onto Creek lands in 1732 in the form of General Edward Oglethorpe. The Creeks' lands extended eastward all the way to the
Atlantic coast. The Charlestonians were not willing to raise the ire of
either the Creeks or the Spaniards at St. Augustine by settling south of
the Savannah River, but they asked London to establish a buffer colony
between them and Florida. Oglethorpe spearheaded the establishment
of the colony of Georgia, which would eventually be the undoing of
the Creek Confederation. But instead of immediately seeing the Georgia
colony as a threat, the Indians viewed it as a way to undercut the trading
monopoly of the Carolina Englishmen. To the Indians, not all Englishmen were the same. The natives were fed up with the Carolina traders'
abuses and assumed that a new faction of Englishmen would only improve their bargaining power. Since the Yamasee War, they had been
at war with the Cherokees (and would continue to be until 1754). They
needed ammunition. They also had become wary of the French, who in
1729 obliterated the Natchez Indians living west of the Chickasaws in
present-day Mississippi.

With these developments influencing the Creeks, Oglethorpe and
his settlers easily secured from Emperor Brims's descendants permission
to settle in the tidewater region of Georgia; in return, the Englishman
vowed to conduct a fair and honest trade with the Indians. To seal the

agreement in 1735, the Creeks passed a bundle of eagle feathers from town to town along the Chattahoochee, then sent them with their emissary to London to be presented to the king "as a sign of everlasting peace."[14] For the next generation, the Muskogee nourished a neutrality among the various European groups while drawing to them as many gifts and as much trade as they could. Over the Coweta square, the English, French, and Spanish flags were raised and lowered frequently.

With the coming of the English to Georgia, the Spanish gradually withdrew southward from the Georgia coast to the St. Johns River, to just north of St. Augustine. But since Spain did not relinquish claim to the Georgia coast until 1763, intrigue and open warfare broke out from time to time between the Georgians and the Spaniards. Each group encouraged the Creeks to join their side against the other. It was for that purpose that General Oglethorpe made the long journey from the Atlantic coast to Coweta in 1739.

Chigelly, Brims's brother and successor, met Oglethorpe on the pathway leading to Coweta bearing an English flag and accompanied by an honor guard of Creek headmen. The Englishmen fired a salute. The Indians solemnly returned it, then escorted Oglethorpe and his entourage into the Coweta town square, where they drank the black drink, feasted, and observed the ritual dances around the ceremonial fire.

Oglethorpe stayed in Coweta for almost a month, holding talks with the headmen, hearing complaints about the English traders in their country, and promising reforms. By the time he left, relations between the two groups were warm and trusting. The resultant Treaty of Coweta granted Oglethorpe the tidewater lands along the Atlantic Ocean from the Savannah River to the St. Johns. In return, Oglethorpe promised that his people would not take any lands other than those expressly granted to Georgia. Oglethorpe left Coweta believing he had made a Creek military alliance. The Lower Creeks did give limited aid to him in his forays onto Spanish territory. But a faction of the Chattahoochee Indians continued to send envoys to St. Augustine to receive their seasonal gifts and to work for peace between the Europeans.

In spite of the Coweta agreement that Georgia's western boundary would be the high-tide mark of the rivers flowing into the Atlantic, this nebulous line did not hold back the Georgians. The English colony continued to spill westward. Before long, the Creeks were calling the interlopers "Ecunnaunuxulgee," which meant "people greedily grasping after the lands of the red people."[15] As white intrusion escalated and trade abuses mounted, relations between the Creeks and the Georgians

28   deteriorated. Though the Creeks intended to maintain the peace with all their neighbors and keep the flow of trade goods open, events outside the Southeast were beyond their control. In 1763, at the end of the European Seven Years War, England took possession of Spanish Florida and held it for the next twenty years; Spain grabbed French Louisiana; and France temporarily was kicked out of America entirely.[16]

Until 1763, Spanish and French garrisons had intimidated the English enough to keep them crowded near the Atlantic coast. But the effect of losing the Spanish and French presence on the population of Georgia "was like pulling the cork from an upturned bottle."[17] While only six thousand whites were living in Georgia in 1760, by the eve of the American Revolution the colony of Georgia had mushroomed to almost fifty thousand non-natives.[18] Since the Creek population was also thriving—even though it was probably one-quarter the number of the non-natives—competition for the open land between them was inevitable. In the next ten years, five of the six official meetings between the Creeks and the Georgians resulted in land cessions, and Georgia quintupled in size.[19]

The British administration tried to forestall any conflict by limiting the participation of the colonials in Indian affairs through their Proclamation of 1763. A British agent was appointed to supervise the southern Indians. While the Creeks came to respect the British agents, their regard for the colonials only lessened with time. The Georgia and Carolina traders were often greedy and dishonest. Their disrespect for the proud natives resulted in insults and injuries. Therefore, when the American Revolution broke out in 1775, most of the Creeks sided with the British.

As the war opened, the Americans hoped the natives would stay out of the affair, while the British hoped the Creeks would fight alongside them. Both were disappointed. Though their sympathy lay mostly with the English, the Indians had reason to be guarded. Since 1765 the Creeks had been at war with the Choctaws, and they resented the English for arming their enemies and generally encouraging the war. There was also the example of the Cherokees' fate during the Revolution to cool the Creeks' toward openly fighting the Americans. In 1776, Carolina and Virginia militia invaded the Cherokee Nation and demolished their towns and fields. The Creeks did not wish to invite such retaliation.[20]

Instead, Alexander McGillivray, an Upper Creek headman of the Coosa River with solid British ties, organized an "unofficial" war against the Americans.[21] Several hundred Creeks served with the British commander in raids into South Carolina and in searches for deserters in the swamps fringing Creek lands. Some Upper Creeks even attacked Savannah, but the raid was meaningless since the British evacuated Savannah and Charleston within weeks. With the British evacuation from Georgia and the Carolinas, the Indians, still in need of guns and powder, were left with the choice of making peace with the Americans or following the British into Florida. While the Cherokees and Chickasaws chose the former course, the Creeks chose the latter.[22]

Traveling to St. Augustine for supplies was inconvenient but imperative. By the last months of the Revolution, the streets of St. Augustine were flooded with more than two thousand warriors, mostly Creeks. Then came even more dispiriting news. When Creek envoys tramped into St. Augustine in the summer of 1783, they found the British packing to leave St. Augustine permanently. England had given up the will to fight the Americans. By the treaty ending the war, she released her claim to all lands east of the Mississippi River. Without a thought as to providing for her orphaned allies, the British were gone.

So in 1783 the Creeks found themselves hemmed in by a new pair of neighbors: the Spanish in East and West Florida and Louisiana, who had never been able to provide the Indians with a satisfactory supply of trade goods, and the Americans of Georgia and Carolina, "whose trading capacity was unproved but whose land hunger was notorious."[23] The Creeks stood alone against the new consolidated nation of the United States, and the Georgians took advantage of the friendless Creeks to press them to sign over their tribal lands east of the Oconee River as compensation for opposing them in the late war.[24]

A small faction of the Creeks, led by the Fat King of Cusseta and the Tallassee King of the Coosa River, had remained loyal to the Americans throughout the war. In 1783, 1785, and 1786 this group signed three treaties that bound all the Creeks to give up their hunting lands east of the Oconee River. The fact that the treaties were not accepted by most Creeks did not stop Georgians from pouring into the new lands. The Indians had never felt as insecure as they did now. They desperately needed a strong leader.

McGillivray was, by birthright and ability, the logical Creek headman to take over the reigns of leadership. He was born to a wealthy Scottish Indian trader and a mestizo mother of the revered Wind Clan. Young McGillivray had spent his youth in Savannah, where he received at least a rudimentary English education. When the Revolution broke out, his father fled back to his homeland, leaving the son out of favor with the colonials in Savannah, so he returned to the Coosa River to live among

30 his mother's people. Since Creek culture was matrilineal, McGillivray was welcomed home. Since he claimed both his father's business associations and his mother's lineage in the most prestigious of the clans, he was the obvious one to become the Creeks' voice to the British.[25]

Though he was an Upper Creek, McGillivray had earned the respect of many Lower Creeks during the Revolution when he had masterminded Creek strategy. Standing unilaterally on any issue ran counter to Creek tradition, yet he pressed the reluctant Lower Creeks to join him. In the post-Revolutionary circumstances, he knew that the Creeks must unite if they were going to save themselves from the land-voracious Georgia frontiersmen. McGillivray's one hope was to arrange a "marriage of convenience" with the only remaining foreign power in the Southeast.[26] By the peace treaty that ended the American Revolution, Spain regained Florida. McGillivray counterbalanced the Americans by leaning toward the Spaniards.

McGillivray worked out a trade arrangement with a St. Augustine business called Panton, Leslie and Company. The firm was actually owned by Scotsmen and had been situated in Charleston and Savannah before the end of the Revolution. Afterward, Spain allowed it to relocate in East Florida to supply the Indians on behalf of the Spanish, since the latter could not produce the goods needed to keep the Creeks' friendship. Through his contacts with Panton, Leslie, McGillivray controlled who within the Creek Nation received gunpowder. This influence won the loyalty of some Lower Creeks. A more heavy-handed tactic was his use of a private force of "constables" to ride herd on Lower Creek dissenters.

However, McGillivray did not want absolute rule over his kinsmen. He rarely issued direct orders to the Nation at large. Instead, he rested behind the power of the Upper Creek faction of the National Council. With enough time, McGillivray may have pushed the Creeks into centralizing their government even more, but the Georgians gave him precious little.[27] And because of his governance style, he was not universally popular among his people. The farther one rode southeast from McGillivray's home on the Coosa, the more mavericks one found.[28]

Georgians were trespassing on Creek lands between the Ogeechee and Oconee Rivers. In 1787 the Creeks convened at Coweta to decide what actions to take against them. They welcomed a United States commissioner to meet with them since he was not a Georgian. To him, the Indians explained why they must keep their vast hunting lands that stretched eastward from the Chattahoochee. Since the Creeks made their living from hunting, and since hunting required vast acreage, they could not continue to sell off pieces of it without dooming themselves to future poverty. Since "there was no vacant wilderness behind them into which they could retreat," the Chattahoochee Indians would have to stand firm. The Hallowing King of Coweta told the U.S. official, "Our lands are our life and breath. . . . If we part with them, we part with our blood. We must fight for them."[29]

McGillivray echoed the sentiments of the Hallowing King. At his bidding, Muskogee war parties, using Spanish muskets, raided the illegal white settlements. In the fall of 1787 the Creeks killed thirty-one Americans. In all, between 1787 and 1789 the Creeks killed seventy-two whites.[30] Even the pro-American faction joined in the raids on Georgia pioneers after Georgians murdered six Cussetas in a particularly gory fashion with no apparent cause.[31]

Creek attacks on the Americans made the Spanish nervous. Picking a fight with the United States would give the new, but stronger, nation a reason to strip Florida from the remnants of Spain's once great empire. Spain clamped down on the flow of gunpowder into the Chattahoochee Valley and urged the natives to make peace with Georgia. McGillivray was stymied. It was obvious the pioneers would only respect military might, but without Spanish powder the Indians were only paper tigers.

Just as hope was dimming, William Augustus Bowles strode into the Coweta town square. Bowles introduced himself to McGillivray there and bragged that he could deliver a continuous supply of arms via the British Bahamas. The dream of having an unlimited supply of weapons without promising obeisance to the Spanish delighted every Creek. Only later did McGillivray learn that Bowles "represented a rival trading company bent on breaking the Panton monopoly and undermining McGillivray's influence."[32] Bowles was never able to deliver much in the way of trade goods, but his promises did undermine McGillivray's authority. Those who lived on the Chattahoochee, far removed from McGillivray's influence among the Upper Creeks, and who groaned under the high Panton prices, formed a new faction which threatened the slowly developing unity McGillivray was trying to forge.[33]

Bowles was an English adventurer who at sixteen had left the British outpost at Pensacola to join a party of Lower Creeks who had come into town for presents. He remained with the Indians for several months and later went back to live among the Lower Creeks on the southern end of the Chattahoochee in the village of Chief Perryman, a mestizo. When

32 Bowles married the chief's daughter, he ensured his acceptance among the Lower Creeks of the lower river valley. After the American Revolution made it unhealthy for Loyalists to remain in America, Bowles fled to the Bahamas. Periodically he visited his adopted family on the Chattahoochee, and on one of these visits he was made a chief. From this time forward, Bowles was usually garbed as an Indian chief. He donned a silver half-moon gorget and a cloth turban accented with an ostrich plume. Though he wore a white man's shirt and breeches, he carried the "ceremonial silver pipe tomahawk signifying he was a war chief."[34]

In the Chattahoochee Valley, Bowles envisioned his very own Indian nation which would have the unofficial backing of the English. He intended to supersede McGillivray as the leading Creek spokesman. He titled himself "Eastajoca," or "Director-General of the Creek Nation." He knew the British hoped to regain a presence in America south of Canada. England still controlled the Indian trade north of the Ohio River. An inroad with the southern Indians was their next objective. Though the British were not fool enough to openly support an adventurer such as Bowles, he presumed that official backing would follow his private success. He lured British merchants in Nassau with the profits to be made in the Indian trade and hinted to the Indians that he had the support of the Crown.[35]

With the blessings of the entire Creek Nation, Bowles and eight other Creek officials sailed to Nassau with a petition from the Coweta council which expressed their continued loyalty to England, denounced the Spanish and the abuses of the Panton store, and urged "an open trade with Britain via free ports to be opened and defended by the Indians."[36] Bowles had an ensign made for his supply ships. This flag of the Muskogee Nation had a blue cross on a red background. In the upper left-hand corner, a sun's face "resembling both an American Indian and Bowles himself" shone defiantly.[37] This ensign was destined to fly over some impressive places before long.

While Bowles was thus employed, McGillivray dealt with the diplomatic challenges of the day. He became convinced that it was too late to recapture the lost lands between the Oconee and Ogeechee Rivers. Realizing that the United States government was less rabid on the subject than the Georgians, who had everything to gain from taking Indian lands, McGillivray traveled to New York to treat with U.S. officials. By the 1790 Treaty of New York, the Creeks conceded Georgia ownership to the three million acres of hunting lands lying between the Oconee and Ogeechee. Though this looked like an Indian loss, McGillivray did not give up anything the Georgians had not already taken. However, his adversary Bowles would use the treaty to discredit McGillivray.

When Bowles returned to "Muscogee" with presents for the Lower Creeks, his father-in-law and other local chiefs greeted him warmly, and Bowles called a meeting of the Nation in Coweta in the autumn of 1791. At that gathering, Bowles told the elders that McGillivray must go. He said the recent treaty proved McGillivray was in the pay of the Americans. Bowles claimed he was the only one who could protect the Nation from the land-grabbing Americans, the greedy Panton store, and the two-faced McGillivray.

The Creek Confederation was now divided in their choice of leader. McGillivray still commanded great respect. McGillivray's brother-in-law also vied for the position, and there were other rivals. If Bowles wanted undisputed leadership, he would have to produce the trade goods he boasted about. When his supplies did not arrive, he took drastic measures. He robbed a Panton warehouse near St. Marks, Florida. The theft brought Bowles nothing but trouble. It caused his in-laws, the Perrymans, to forever distance themselves from him, and worse yet, it convinced the Spanish to arrest him. Years passed before Bowles returned from his imprisonment. In the meantime, the Creeks lost the only true leader they had. McGillivray died in 1793 at the age of only thirty-four.

His death was a great blow to the survival of the Creek Confederation. Theodore Roosevelt wrote in *The Winning of the West* that McGillivray's "consummate craft" and "masterly diplomacy" allowed the Creeks "for a generation to hold their own better than any other native race against the restless Americans."[38] There was no one left in the Nation with "equal education, position, and imagination to continue his work."[39] Within two generations of his death, the Creeks lost all their lands along the Chattahoochee.

Bowles never lost hope of establishing an Indian state protected by the British. Instead of seeing the Spanish as saviors, as McGillivray had done, Bowles saw them as the chief obstacle in making his dream come true. Since they would not allow the Muskogee navy to enter Florida legally, Bowles determined to capture the Spanish fort at St. Marks on Apalachee Bay, which was the Spanish gateway to the interior from the Gulf of Mexico. The most amazing part of this audacious act was that he was successful. The Muskogee capture of the Spanish fort in April 1800 was one of the very few successful Indian sieges in history. The victory raised eyebrows all over the United States. U.S. Indian agent Benjamin Hawkins, who witnessed how the Lower Creeks celebrated the news at Coweta, was quite disturbed. Georgia governor James Jackson stood ready to send five thousand state militiamen onto Creek lands. President Thomas Jefferson so feared an official Indian alliance with the English that he considered sending U.S. troops to expel Bowles from the fort.

All of this turned out to be needless worry. With injured pride, the Spanish returned to Apalachee Bay and retook the fort in only an hour and a half. As the Muscogee ensign was lowered from the St. Marks flagpole, Bowles's influence among the Lower Creeks also plummeted. He was never able to produce the steady supply of guns needed to stave off Creek enemies. In 1802, twenty-two principal chiefs of the Lower Creeks and Seminoles of Florida agreed to trade with the Spanish and to have nothing to do with Bowles. With that, he faded from history.

Bowles had never visualized the future of his "Muscogee" as being independent from white men. He had envisioned an Indian nation "dominated and eventually colonized and exploited by whites."[40] He had anticipated that intermarriage with whites would continue to dilute Creek blood, and that the Indians would disappear as a separate people. While the Americans would never allow an adventurer such as Bowles to build his own nation within their boundaries, the more enlightened whites of the United States did agree with him that the best the Indians could hope for was to become "white" in culture and lighter in skin color.

Official U.S. policy encouraged the Indians to become yeomen farmers by laying down their hunting rifles and taking up the plow. As authorized by the Treaty of New York, the government gave the Indians farm implements. Jefferson continued this Indian policy when he moved into the executive mansion. He believed that if the United States could make farmers of the Indians, they would not need their hunting lands. Instead of being removed from their lands, the Creeks simply could be absorbed into the United States as individuals who posed no threat to white civilization.

Benjamin Hawkins was the embodiment of the U.S. Indian policy. Appointed U.S. agent to the Creeks in 1796, he would live among them until his death following the War of 1812. Hawkins's job was to serve as the liaison between whites and reds. He was assigned to be the Indians' advocate in any negotiations between the two groups, and he would serve the Creeks in this capacity as well as any white man could have. But underlying his beneficence was the belief—shared by Jefferson—that the only chance for survival the Indians really had was to become "white."

When Hawkins established his headquarters in the midst of the

Creeks, he set about to impose a "civilization program" on them. He passed out free plows and farming implements. He gave them spinning wheels and looms. He schooled any Creek who would listen on the techniques of husbandry and horticulture. He encouraged them to fence their lands, plant fruit trees, and build barns.

Ironically, this white man replaced McGillivray as the dominant leader of the Creek people. These two very different men shared a determination to strengthen Creek government, but for strikingly different reasons. Whereas McGillivray had worked to centralize the Creek Confederation in order to preserve the Nation's independence, Hawkins now intended to centralize it so that his control of it would eventually dissolve its separate identity.[41]

Hawkins's civilization program drove a wedge into the Creek Nation that would terminally divide it. The Chattahoochee's Lower Creeks tended to see the value of adopting white ways. Living closer to Georgia than their Upper Creek associates gave them more incentive. From their vantage point on the Chattahoochee, the Lower Creeks could see with better clarity the ever-approaching white tide. Living "behind" them, many Upper Creeks of the Coosa and Tallapoosa Rivers clung to their traditional lifestyles and resented Hawkins's meddling. The split into these opposing factions later evolved into a civil war with enormous costs to be paid by all the Creeks, but especially those of the Chattahoochee River.

In order to dominate the Creek decision making apparatus, Hawkins revamped the Nation's organization so that it more closely resembled a white government. Under his leadership, the Confederation became more centralized. Hawkins divided the Nation into legislative districts, each with appointed delegates. He insisted on the establishment of an executive committee. He demarcated Tuckabatchee and Coweta, the head Upper and Lower towns, as the twin capitals from which the National Council would hold all meetings. At each capital he installed a subagent. In this way he could keep his hand on the pulse of both spheres of the Nation. Hawkins delivered a "state of the Nation" address annually. This practice gave him the opportunity to elaborate his civilization program.[42]

Once he had established a governmental machinery, Hawkins installed a new legal system patterned after the white one. He removed the traditional duty of crime control from the clans and put it into the hands of the National Council. A body of "law menders," similar to McGil-

36 livray's constables, enforced the laws. The ancient Creek tradition of using clan vengeance to keep the peace was greatly weakened by this action.

Hawkins's policy of assimilation perhaps worked too well. It split the Creek Nation into factions. Because of their closer proximity to white men, the Lower Creeks had begun to assimilate the white culture at a faster pace than the more distant Upper Creeks. As traders and other white officials took wives among the natives, a gradual paling was taking place. Indeed, a significant majority of the Creek leaders were themselves part white. The homesteads of many Creek headmen looked no different from those of their white neighbors. These prosperous Indians were resented by the others. As the natives felt the pressure to change, the people divided into those who embraced the changes in order to survive and those who would rather die than live like the people they so detested.

As the Creeks divided among themselves, the whites became more united. When the United States had been formed, Georgia claimed that her territory extended all the way to the Mississippi River, just as it had in the colonial period. The newly formed federal government had countered that the lands west of present settlement belonged to the United States collectively. In 1802 the state of Georgia and the U.S. government reached an agreement by which Georgia sold to the United States all lands lying west of the Chattahoochee, extending to the Mississippi. In return, the federal government promised to "extinguish Indian claims" to all of the land that remained within the boundaries of Georgia.[43] Although it would take two bitter decades to accomplish this feat, the Creeks' hunting lands east of the Chattahoochee effectually were taken from them by an agreement to which they were not even a party.

The first subsequent Creek treaty was the Treaty of Washington, which sold off lands around the Ocmulgee River and granted the United States the right to build a horse path through the heart of the Creek Nation. The pathway was part of a postal route planned to extend from Washington to New Orleans. It crossed the Chattahoochee near the Coweta Falls. Over this route more and more white settlers would filter through Creek lands, some becoming illegal squatters.[44]

The 1805 treaty, with its provision for a federal road to be built through the lands of the Upper Creeks, caused an uproar among the towns of the Coosa and Tallapoosa Rivers. The westernmost Creeks did not want to invite more whites to tramp over their lands, cutting down their trees, killing their animals, and coming into contact with their headstrong youth who might too easily resort to violence. The older townsmen understood that any violence that erupted along the road could be used to extort a further land cession. Because of their opposition, the completion of the road was delayed until 1811.[45]

What alarmed the conservative group of Creeks most about the federal road was that whites were not just passing through Creek lands. Though it was illegal, whites began to settle in Alabama south of most of the Upper Creek settlements. The sight of scores of wagons daily spewing dust into the Chattahoochee Valley convinced many that the white man's frontier was not isolated only to the east of the Creek Nation. It was beginning to surround them. But instead of blaming the whites, resentment focused more on the assimilated Indians and mestizos.

The festering bitterness that now divided the Creeks into progressives and reactionaries was ripe for the exploitation of a Shawnee leader named Tecumseh, who rode into Creek country in October 1811. It is believed that Tecumseh's parents were born in a Shawnee town on the Tallapoosa before moving north to the Ohio territory. Tecumseh came from the North to enlist the help of his distant kinsmen in forming a pan-Indian military alliance to run the whites out of their country. Tecumseh and his Shawnee brethren struck an impressive pose as they marched into the town square of Tuckabatchee. They were naked except for their breechcloths and war paint. Eagle feathers adorned their hair, and buffalo tails swung from their belts.

Hawkins was present to witness this sight, but he did not take the Shawnee seriously. Tecumseh waited until Hawkins and his men had left before addressing the crowd of five thousand Upper and Lower Creeks who crowded into the town square. All five thousand stood spellbound for the visitor's hour-long soliloquy. Tecumseh began by appealing to the Creeks' proud history as warriors and inheritors of the Chattahoochee Valley:

> The pale faces trembled at your war-whoop, and the maidens of my tribe, on the distant lakes, sung the prowess of your warriors, and sighed for their embraces. And when our young men set out on the war-path the Shawnee sachems [chiefs] bade them "be brave like the Muscogees!" But now your blood has become white; your tomahawks have no edge; your bows and arrows were buried with your fathers. You sleep while the pale face ploughs over their tombs, and fertilizes his fields with their sacred ashes. . . . Oh, Muscogees! Brethren of my mother! Brush from your eyelids the sleep of slavery, and strike for vengeance and your country! The red men have fallen as the leaves now fall. I hear

their voices in those aged pines. Their tears drop from the weeping skies. Their bones bleach on the hills of Georgia. Will no son of those brave men strike the pale face and quiet these complaining ghosts? Let the white race perish! They seize your land; they corrupt your women; they trample on the bones of your dead! Back whence they came, upon a trail of blood, they must be driven! Back—aye, back into the great water whose accursed waves brought them to our shores! Burn their dwellings—destroy their stock—slay their wives and children, that the very breed may perish. War now! War always![46]

His speech especially roused the young. Tecumseh then told them that he was leaving, but for them to look for signs from the heavens when it was time for all Indians to rise up in unison. Apparently making use of some astronomical information he learned from the British, which predicted that a comet would soon appear in the southern skies, he promised them: "Soon shall you see my arm of fire stretched athwart the sky. You will know that I am on the war-path. I will stamp my foot and the very earth will shake."[47]

With these promises, Tecumseh departed. But he left behind his "prophets" who had been trained by him to "catch the bullets of their enemies," as well as bundles of sticks painted red.[48] When his disciples saw the comet, they were to throw away a stick every day until the sticks were gone. Since each bundle held the same number of sticks, the various villages could coordinate their attack.

Tecumseh's followers would ever be known as the "Red Sticks." They believed it was up to them to attack those who embraced the white man's ways in order to save their people from destruction. Since the gods were on their side, they could not be hurt by the white man's bullets. Many young Upper Creek men, in particular, were swayed to join them by prophets such as Josiah Francis, who was reputed to spend days at a time underwater, communing with the river gods. Other prophets amazed onlookers by their ability to go into trances and convulsions during their war dances.

A few weeks after Tecumseh left Muscogee, an earthquake wrecked the town of Tuckabatchee. Sometime later, a comet burned its way across an autumn night, beckoning the Creeks to the warpath. Creeks unwilling to support the war party were murdered in mysterious and painful ways. As Tecumseh had commanded, his followers destroyed the plows and looms of the progressives. By the spring of 1813—amidst the War of 1812, which added the British to the Americans' list of worries—Red Stick depredations mounted.

On the Chattahoochee, the Lower Creek towns were surprisingly quiet. Most of the Chattahoochee Indians were not convinced that starting a war against the whites would bring them relief from white encroachment. The Lower Creeks began to ask Hawkins for ammunition to quell the Red Sticks. Since the latter constituted only a minority of even the Upper Creeks, Hawkins believed the Indians could put down their own troublemakers. But when the Red Sticks besieged the Upper Creek capital of Tuckabatchee, he began to lose confidence that the situation could be settled internally.[49] When the Red Sticks destroyed Tuckabatchee and Kialigee, two Upper Creek towns which had tried to remain neutral, those inhabitants fled to Coweta.

The Red Sticks rode down to Pensacola and received powder and shot from the Spanish. Rumors spread from the Indian towns to the white settlers, who began to fear for their lives. Militia rode out to check the hostile Indians returning from Pensacola. A skirmish at Burnt Corn Creek, just north of Mobile, in which the outnumbered Red Sticks fought off the whites, gave the hostiles more faith in Tecumseh's promises of invincibility. The Indians then set out to attack a white settlement at Fort Mims on the lower Alabama River. There the Red Sticks slaughtered 250 to 275 whites, friendly Indians, and mixed-bloods. An authority of the Creek War has written, "No fort of this size and strength had ever been captured by the Indians,"[50] Perhaps Tecumseh's magic really did work. Fewer than forty people escaped Fort Mims to tell of the atrocities committed. Like wildfire, the news burned across the land, and panic consumed the white settlers.

The fall of Fort Mims in the summer of 1813 convinced even Hawkins that the Americans must launch a full-scale campaign against the hostiles before the latter could join forces with the British. Had it not been for the Fort Mims massacre, it is possible the plan of Hawkins and Jefferson would have eventually worked and the peaceful Chattahoochee Creeks could have remained forever on the banks of their beloved river, gradually growing paler through continued intermarriage and assimilation by white society. Until Fort Mims, most white people were not in favor of the drastic act of bodily removing the Indians by force.

Andrew Jackson heard the news of the Creek civil war at his home in Tennessee, where he was recuperating from a wound he received in a duel. Like his fellow Tennessee frontiersmen, he believed the Creeks

40 stood in the way of their access to the Gulf of Mexico via the Alabama River system. Jackson got up from his bed to lead a band of Tennesseans southward to defeat the Indians.

Several white armies converged on the Red Sticks. While Jackson's men drove down from the North, Georgia troops under Major General John Floyd set up a base camp at Fort Mitchell on the western side of the Chattahoochee (ten miles south of present-day Phenix City). From Fort Mitchell, Floyd was to march west to meet Jackson and the Tennessee militia at the confluence of the Coosa and Tallapoosa Rivers. Floyd worried that his army was not up to the task and spent extra time in training and gathering supplies. The only offensive action taken against the Red Sticks before Floyd was ready was actually made by friendly Creeks.

Three chiefs led the friendly faction. Big Warrior had replaced McGillivray as the principal speaker of the Upper Creeks. Like his predecessor, he was a mestizo who made his fortune in the deerskin trade with Pensacola. William McIntosh, the son of a Scottish father and a Coweta mother, was the principal speaker of the Lower Creek towns. Little Prince was chief of Broken Arrow, a village on the Chattahoochee about twelve miles south of Coweta, and was regarded by whites as the Indian in highest authority among all the Creeks.[51] In October 1813, a month before Floyd moved his force to the Chattahoochee to build Fort Mitchell, Big Warrior, McIntosh, and Little Prince rode out of their base at Coweta to burn down several villages of Red Stick towns. They prevailed over 150 Yuchis who were on their way to join the hostile group.[52]

During the Creek civil war, a scarcity of food plagued both sides. The Indians' fields were destroyed as a war tactic. Since the whites could not live off the land any more than the reds could, George Gilmer, a future governor of Georgia, was ordered to build a fort at "Standing Peachtree" on the banks of the Chattahoochee River near present-day Atlanta to supply Floyd's army. From there a quartermaster floated a barge down the river to Fort Mitchell. The first one hundred miles of the journey were fairly easy going, but it is unknown how the army dealt with the thirty-five miles of rapids and waterfalls that divide the Chattahoochee at the fall line. Since Fort Mitchell was south of the treacherous waters, the goods were probably portaged overland and the watercourse resumed. At any rate, there is record that the trial barge reached its destination, and five other barges were sent downstream to supply Fort Mitchell.[53]

As Floyd left for the Alabama River, he was joined by three or four hundred friendly Indians. The Lower Creeks who fought on the American side in the Creek War were generally from the middle and upper parts of the Chattahoochee and Flint Rivers. Most of the Indians living on the lower Chattahoochee took advantage of their remoteness to remain neutral. The friendly Indians, combined with Floyd's force of 950, were able to rout the Red Sticks from their encampments. The hostiles began to drift westward ahead of Floyd, congregating at a horseshoe-shaped bend in the Tallapoosa River.

After months of fort building and forays, the U.S. armies commanded by Jackson converged there at Horseshoe Bend, and with the aid of the allied Lower Creeks led by the mixed-bloods Timpoochee Barnard and William McIntosh, the Americans defeated the Red Sticks. When it was over, almost nine hundred hostiles lay dead. In contrast, the Americans and allied Creeks lost only forty-nine. The defeat of the Red Sticks was timely for the Americans. Within two months the British would land on the Gulf of Mexico with plenty of shot and powder for the Indians. Had the Red Sticks not been so soundly defeated at Horseshoe Bend, the history of the southern theater of the War of 1812 may have been written differently.

Those Red Sticks who survived the final battle drifted south to become an important faction of the Seminole tribe of Florida. As they retreated, they sent a note to Hawkins vowing that they would never surrender: "We have lost our country and retreated to the sea side, where we will fight till we are all destroyed."[54]

The Battle of Horseshoe Bend signaled the end of organized resistance of the Red Sticks against the combined white and Creek armies. But even before this fray, Hawkins and another U.S. official discussed with the friendly Creeks the terms of ending the war. The Lower Creeks realized that even though they had fought on the American side, they would be punished for the actions of the restless young Red Sticks. However, the terms offered them were fairly generous, and they were ready to agree to give up as an indemnity enough of the "conquered territory" as was necessary in order to pay for the expenses of war.[55]

However, Jackson soon replaced the earlier government representatives, and his intention was to strip from all of the Creeks—no matter on which side they fought—lands on every side of them. The Jackson version, as written into the Treaty of Fort Jackson, which officially ended the hostilities between the Red Sticks and the United States, included a confession of war guilt and required the Creeks to give up all their lands west of the Coosa, north of the Alabama, and a wide band across their southern extremity at the Florida boundary. From Jackson's point of view, the treaty had the desirous effect of separating the Creeks from the Choctaws and Chickasaws to their west and barring the Creeks from communication with the Spaniards and the Seminoles of Florida.

The Lower Creeks' protector, Indian agent Hawkins, protested that the treaty provision to strip away the southern Creek lands on either side of the Chattahoochee River would punish the very people who had helped the Americans to win. But Jackson did not see it this way. He told the Lower Creek leaders who gathered at Fort Jackson for the signing of the treaty that they were just as guilty as the Red Sticks for allowing Tecumseh to enter their nation and arouse their youth to raise their arms against the United States. Then with reverse logic, Jackson argued that when the friendly Indians joined his army they were guilty of trying to destroy their own people and, therefore, must be treated as traitors to their people.

The Lower Creek chiefs were shocked by their treatment, but when they realized they could not persuade Jackson to change his mind with reason, they attempted to shame him into decency. Magnanimously, the Creek chiefs gave Jackson personally a three-mile tract of land, with equal amounts going to Hawkins and other "friends," although these grants were not approved by Congress. Instead of being a treaty between the vanquished and the victors, thirty-five Lower Creek chiefs and only one Red Stick leader signed the Treaty of Fort Jackson. Lower Creeks signed on the condition that their original agreement be attached to the treaty when it went to Washington.

At the stroke of a pen, the Creek Nation lost over twenty-two million acres of land, which constituted over half their holdings. From the land sales to whites over the next forty years, the U.S. treasury would profit over eleven million dollars. The Treaty of Fort Jackson left the Creeks as an isolated island "surrounded by a sea of politically organized and rapidly growing white settlements."[56]

Just as things looked their bleakest for the Native Americans, the British arrived. The action of the War of 1812 had been centered on the northeastern United States, but as the war neared its conclusion, England changed its focus to the Gulf of Mexico and expected to use Creek fury to its advantage. In May 1814 two royal ships landed supplies near the mouth of the Chattahoochee River system at the Gulf of Mexico. From there the redcoats moved up the Apalachicola River about thirty miles to Prospect Bluff, where they built a fort. They intended to attract as many Red Sticks and escaped slaves as they could enlist to fight against the United States. It was hoped that British-inspired harassments would force the United States to reassign troops to Florida and away from the Canadian campaign.[57]

Even after the betrayal of the Treaty of Fort Jackson, the Lower Creeks who had fought for the Americans remained ready to aid them again. Hawkins raised a troop of one thousand friendly Lower Creeks and set off to thwart the British and their Indian allies at Apalachicola. Hawkins set up a base camp at the confluence of the Chattahoochee and Flint Rivers. From there at least one skirmish occurred between the two groups before Hawkins learned that the War of 1812 was officially over. With that knowledge, he ordered his red and white troops to return to their homes.[58]

Following Jackson's defeat of the British at the Battle of New Orleans, the British colonel Edward Nicholls was assigned to the fort on the Apalachicola River to gather three thousand Indians and three to four hundred escaped slaves and continue the war as long as possible from there. Nicholls found some malcontents among the Lower Creeks at the southern end of the Chattahoochee and on the Apalachicola. It was this group of Lower Creeks who stood to lose their lands by the Treaty of Fort Jackson, even though they had remained neutral during the Creek War. Nicholls told the Lower Creeks and the Red Stick refugees there that the Treaty of Ghent which had just concluded the War of 1812 guaranteed to return the lands taken from them by the Fort Jackson treaty. This news gave the Indians hope that if they could continue to resist the Americans until the British enforced the Treaty of Ghent, their lands would be returned.[59]

However, the Creeks had little time. The Spaniards ordered the British out of Florida in 1815, and the Americans were already building a fort at the juncture of the Flint and Chattahoochee Rivers to protect some fifty white families who had rushed into the newly ceded lands. Though the redcoats intended to return, they sailed from Apalachicola Bay in August 1815, leaving behind a gang of runaway slaves and a few Red Sticks "in possession of a well-constructed fort, with plenty of provisions, arms, ammunition, and even cannon."[60]

General Edmund Gaines at the American Camp Crawford (later called Fort Scott) at the Flint and Chattahoochee juncture dispatched Lieutenant Duncan Clinch to destroy the "Negro Fort." With the support of the ever loyal William McIntosh of Coweta, Clinch descended the Apalachicola River with 150 friendly Lower Creeks. At their rendezvous point with American gunboats coming up from the Gulf of Mexico, the Indians surrounded the fort and opened fire. The gunboats fired heated shot into the fort. A fireball hit the powder magazine and the fort exploded, killing nearly everyone inside. McIntosh's men scalped and then hanged the black commander.[61]

Following the War of 1812, the Creeks were broken and dispirited. Their ardent defender, Benjamin Hawkins, died in 1816. White people crowded them on all sides. Alabama became a territory in 1817 and a state in 1819. Georgia pressed the Creeks for more land cessions. In 1821, by the Treaty of Indian Springs, the Creeks sold off their lands east of the Flint River.

With the loss of much of their hunting lands, many of the Chattahoochee Indians lived in poverty and despair. Their old way of living had been destroyed, but they were unprepared for a new one. The progressive chiefs believed that their only hope of remaining on the Chattahoochee lay in acquiring the white man's culture. In 1822 they allowed white missionaries to enter their country and teach their young. The Baptists, after promising not to preach to adults, established a school at a place on the Chattahoochee later called Withington; the Methodists established Asbury Manual Labor School near Fort Mitchell.[62] A new Creek agent soon reported to Secretary of State John C. Calhoun, "It is now no new thing to see ploughs in use in different parts of the country." The Indians were producing enough to sell vegetables at way stations along the federal post road.[63]

McIntosh, as head chief of Coweta, was still recognized as the most influential Lower Creek leader. He encouraged the Indians to make a written record of the laws they now lived under. These were adopted by the National Council in 1817, and they reveal that the Creeks had begun to practice a modified form of white justice, with trials for the accused.[64]

Even as the Native Americans scurried to build a legal and social defense to protect them from further losses, the whites were coming to the conclusion that wholesale removal of the Indians was preferable to gradual absorption. McIntosh began to council his people that since their fate in the East looked doomed, they should prepare to emigrate beyond the Mississippi River, where they could live unmolested. The Cherokees had purchased land in the West in 1817 and a number of their people had already emigrated, while the majority of the Cherokees intended to remain by embracing white ways.

Following their example, the Creek National Council met in 1824. Young, educated Cherokees were there as council. These Cherokees probably wrote down the declaration that the Creeks formalized there. It stated that since their "crazy young men" had gone to war against the

United States, resulting in the loss of most of their property, the only way they could support themselves was through agriculture. They resolved to learn the skills necessary to remain in the home of their ancestors. And they vowed not to ever sell another foot of their land.

The declaration ended with a warning to the headmen: "We have a great many chiefs and head men but, be they ever so great, they must all abide by the laws. We have guns and ropes: and if any of our people should break these laws, those guns and ropes are to be their end."[65] The document was signed by Little Prince, Menewa, and twelve other leaders.

U.S. commissioners ignored such pronouncements and pressured the Creeks for still further land cessions. When the natives refused, the federal officials handpicked a few chiefs who were known to be sympathetic to the whites to meet them at Indian Springs in the closing days of 1824. The treaty site was probably chosen because of its proximity to the home of McIntosh, the foremost friend of the whites among the Lower Creeks. He and Etommee Tustennuggee, who was also sympathetic, were the only leaders who came to Indian Springs to make a deal. Opothle Yahola was sent by Menewa to observe. At the moment when McIntosh and Etommee Tustennuggee took the white man's pen to sign a new land cession, Menewa's messenger reminded them that death would be their fate for disobeying the National Council declaration.

The federal commissioners downplayed the threat, promising the protection of the U.S. government, and signatures of "McIntosh, Etommee Tustennuggee, thirteen lesser chiefs, and about fifty men of no rank whatever were affixed to the fatal document."[66] By this legally questionable agreement, the Creeks lost all their lands east of the Chattahoochee. A supplementary agreement paid McIntosh personally $25,000 plus 1,640 acres of land in the western tract for his Georgia property.

When Opothle Yahola reported to the rest of the Nation how McIntosh had betrayed them, the National Council pronounced a sentence of death on McIntosh and Etommee Tustennuggee. With one hundred warriors, Menewa rode to McIntosh's home and surrounded the house. After allowing the women and children to leave the building, the avenging Creeks set fire to the house and shot the two traitors as they tried to flee.[67]

When President Adams learned of the fraud committed in obtaining this treaty, he insisted a new one be made. Menewa and Opothle Yahola were called to Washington. Believing that they had no choice but to accept the conditions of the McIntosh treaty, the duo relinquished all of the Creek lands east of the Chattahoochee (the lands between the

46   Chattahoochee and Flint Rivers) for $217,600 plus a perpetual annuity of $20,000. The United States agreed to pay the McIntosh faction $100,000 for emigrating to the West. Those Creeks who remained in the East were required to move west of the Chattahoochee by January 1, 1827.[68]

A few months after McIntosh's death, the Revolutionary War general Lafayette toured the Southeast. Following the federal road that crossed the river at Fort Mitchell, Lafayette and his party were greeted on the Alabama side of the river by McIntosh's son Chilly. The son had taken over leadership of the emigration party which now lived near the protection of Fort Mitchell until it was time to go west. Chilly was described by Lafayette's secretary as being "about twenty eight years old, of medium height only, but the symmetry of his body was perfect; his face was noble, his expression sad. When he was not talking, he cast his great, dark eyes toward the ground and his lashes covered them."[69] The white man noted, "He understands the true position of his nation; he sees it growing weak, and he foresees its approaching destruction. . . . [H]e seems to hope that the treaty which sends them into an uninhabited region will restore and strengthen the old tribal organization or at least will preserve what is left of it today."[70] Chilly, dressed as a white man, traveled with the Frenchmen to Montgomery. The Indian's business was to escort his ten-year-old brother to a school where he would be educated by whites.

By the end of 1828, thirteen hundred Creeks of the McIntosh party had arrived in Oklahoma to begin their new lives. Though the trip west was arduous, in general these were affluent "mixed bloods who began with their slaves to lay out plantations along the rich river valley. . . . They soon began to prosper."[71] The remaining, less progressive Georgia Creeks crossed over to the western bank of the Chattahoochee and crowded into the lands of their Upper Creek kinsmen. In 1828 an English traveler described the Creeks he saw on the western bank of the Chatta-hoochee River as "miserable wretches" who "wander about like bees whose hive has been destroyed."[72]

CHAPTER 3

૨

Along the White Frontier

THE CREEKS VENERATED THE CHATTAHOOCHEE RIVER as a spirit, a source of food, and a means of travel. But to the white people who followed them into the valley, the river symbolized wealth. Without it, they could never hope to be more than subsistence farmers. But along this natural highway to the Gulf of Mexico, they would clear their fields and send off their cotton to market. The coastal port of Apalachicola at the river's end would, one day, be as familiar to British textile manufacturers as New Orleans or Savannah. But those glory days were two decades off. In the meantime, the pioneers who settled in the Chattahoochee Valley dreamed of the future but lived off their pluck.

By the spring of 1819, a few hundred Georgians had already settled illegally along the banks of the Chattahoochee. The settlement of the valley increased as the Creeks released their lands south of Fort Gaines, Georgia, in 1814 and east of the Chattahoochee in 1825. A further impetus to settlement came when Spain ceded Florida to the United States in 1821. When Georgians no longer found their river outlet to the Gulf of Mexico blocked by a foreign power, there was nothing to hold back the onrush of settlers into the river valley.

In the early nineteenth century, virtually all travel and commerce was dependent on rivers. Overland transportation amounted to following a narrow Indian trail through the wilderness. The public "roads" were merely slightly widened paths so narrow that two wagons could not pass each other. The heavy southern rainfall melted the Georgia red clay into a sticky mire that sucked in wagon wheels and left deep ruts when it dried out again. The more wagons that traveled along these former walk-

Chute de la Chattahoutchie, an 1838 painting by Francis de la Porte of the falls of the Chattahoochee before the river was dammed. *Courtesy of the Columbus Museum.*

ways, the more impassable the routes became. If an oxen- or mule-drawn wagon could make ten miles in a day, it had done very well.[1]

Roads were used only to augment river travel by connecting one river system to another. Floating downstream was much easier than riding a wagon, and watercraft could manage a much larger load than a mule-drawn cart could haul. Pole boats, rafts, and flatboats (often called "boxes") were used to carry the first cotton from Georgia and Alabama downstream to Apalachicola Bay. These craft usually moved in only one direction: downstream. At the coast they were unloaded and the boats knocked apart and sold for their lumber. The crew walked home.

In the spring of 1822, the very first Apalachicola exports of cotton (266 bales) were loaded at the river's mouth aboard the *William and Jane* for New York. A United States customhouse was established at the mouth of the river in March 1823, but its collections hardly paid for expenses in these early years. (In 1824 the office netted only $126.58.) However, in 1827 the Florida legislature formally established the settlement of

West Point, soon to be renamed Apalachicola, and named five trustees "to regulate the harbor, provide quarantine, erect wharves, regulate streets, and 'restrain and punish vagabonds.'"[2]

While the Florida legislature acted to establish the town of Apalachicola at the mouth of the waterway, Georgia lawmakers encouraged white settlement of the former Indian lands lying between the Flint and Chattahoochee Rivers by holding a land lottery.[3] Georgia residents drew lots for free homesteads in the Creeks' former homeland. Naturally, land lying along the rivers was the most prized, and the acreage at the head of navigation of the Chattahoochee was so valuable it was not included in the land giveaway. There, at the ancient Coweta Falls, a city was planned that would be a commercial center. This strategic location would take advantage of the river that ran southward to the Gulf and of the falls capable of powering mills and factories.[4] The lawmakers named this trading town Columbus.

Even though Apalachicola and Columbus were separated by over three hundred river miles, they were joined symbiotically by the Chattahoochee. Clear passage between them was necessary for their very existence. As soon as the settlements were established, a pole boat named the *Rob Roy* moved up and down the river, taking down cotton and then, loaded with groceries, pushing its way back up against the current to Columbus.[5] But the river's merchants needed a quicker and easier form of transportation on which to build their businesses.

The steam-powered boat had been perfected in 1807 by Robert Fulton. As soon as there was enough Chattahoochee commerce to merit the considerable investment of a steamboat, it became the preferred form of transportation. One Georgia historian has commented that "steamboating on the Chattahoochee and Flint was more picturesque and stirring than on the other Georgia streams, because . . . those rivers virtually marked our frontier."[6] The men who first ventured up the river were true pioneers.

The first to attempt to run a steamboat up the Chattahoochee from the bay was John Jenkins, one of the Florida trustees appointed to develop Apalachicola. His eighty-nine-foot boat, *Fanny*, began the journey in the spring of 1827. While ascending the Chattahoochee, Jenkins ran up against a massive dam of fallen trees and other debris. He managed to cut a twenty-foot swath through it and to proceed as far as Fort Gaines by the end of July. But there the *Fanny* had to wait for the winter rains before continuing upstream. On January 28, 1828, she became the first steamboat to arrive at the Coweta Falls.[7] Jenkins found there a tiny settlement surrounding Kinard's Tavern and ferry. Several stores traded with the Indians, now living across the river.

Following closely in the wake of the *Fanny* was the 117-foot *Steubenville*. It traveled from Mobile to Fort Gaines in only four days in the summer of 1827, and did so, thanks to Jenkins, "without meeting with any delay of consequence and but few obstructions in the river."[8] At Fort Gaines the *Steubenville* turned around, her pilot intending to return when the winter rains made it possible to proceed all the way to the falls at Columbus. She eventually reached the future site of Columbus on February 6, 1828, only nine days behind the first boat. Both of these vessels arrived just as a state-employed surveyor arrived to lay out the proposed town of Columbus.

To celebrate the *Steubenville*'s arrival and court some business, its captain took a group of local boosters down to Woolfolk's Mound (an old Indian mound located on Woolfolk's plantation about five miles downstream) on a pleasure excursion. However, the venture turned out to be a negative advertisement for the efficacy of steam travel. On the return trip the boat could not make headway against the current, and many of the passengers got off and walked home.

Overlooking this inconvenience, the board of commissioners in charge of laying out the town and selling lots was still very appreciative of the *Steubenville*'s appearance at the falls, for they understood the reliance their town would have on the river. They gave the captain a commendation for successfully navigating the Chattahoochee, an achievement that "will produce results important in [its] influence on the future prospects of this town."[9]

By the summer of 1828, surveyor Edward Lloyd Thomas had roughly laid out of the forest the future city, which was to consist of nine streets running parallel to the river and thirteen cross streets. The parallel streets were all 132 feet wide (except Broad Street, which was 164 feet across), and the perpendicular streets were 99 feet wide. These expanses gave the future town "an elegant and airy appearance." Thomas reserved a wide expanse along the river "for a promenade, which . . . will form one of the handsomest and most romantic walks in the State."[10] The view of the river from this vantage point was breathtaking. Crystal-clear water foamed and splashed over the falls, which dropped 125 feet in two and a half miles. The high banks supported great groves of virgin timber, and a dozen springs spilled out of them and plunged to the river below.

Into this stark beauty was laid the rough handicrafts of men who had

Pont de Columbus, a painting by Francis de la Porte in 1838 showing the steamboat dock and Dillingham Street Bridge. *Courtesy of the Columbus Museum.*

come to cast their lot with this yet-imaginary town. "[My husband] says that he has seen a town without inhabitants, but that he never before saw inhabitants without a town," wrote Mrs. Basil Hall, who accompanied her English sea captain husband over the federal road and through Columbus, not long after the surveyor had completed the task of laying out the lots of the town in 1828. Her husband also recorded his impressions of the place:

> After threading our way for some time amongst the trees, we came in sight, here and there, of huts made partly of planks, partly of bark, and at last reached the principal cluster of houses, very few of which were above two or three weeks old. . . . There were three hotels, the sign belonging to one of which . . . was nailed to a tree still growing untouched in the middle of the street. Another had glazed windows, but the panes of glass were fixed in their places, merely for the time, by a little piece of putty at each corner. Every thing indicated hurry. As none of the city-lots were yet sold, of course no one was sure that the spot upon which he had pitched his house would eventually become his

own. Many of the houses were in consequence . . . built on trucks, . . . such as cannon are supported by, for the avowed purpose of being hauled away when the land should be sold. . . . [E]ven in the most cleared streets some trees were left standing. . . . Anvils were heard ringing away merrily at every corner; while saws, axes, and hammers, were seen flashing amongst the woods all round.[11]

The contagion of the building fever on land spilled over into the river. Planning a future city based on the river trade obviously meant looking to the future of river navigation as well. At about the time of Basil Hall's visit to Columbus, residents prevailed on state authorities to send in the state engineer to investigate how to improve the navigability of the river in some problem spots just below Columbus. Engineer Hamilton Fulton suggested that the state construct three "wing dams" at locations just south of the future city. By damming the river on the Alabama side of these bars, they could force the water to scour out a deeper channel through these sandbars in the eastern half of the river. The engineer vowed that there was no possibility of the sand reaccumulating, and he compared the Chattahoochee favorably to the Savannah: it had fewer logs to clear, fewer shoals, and was straighter.[12]

Columbus residents also planned to open navigation above the town by pole boats. From the falls at Coweta northward for the next twenty miles there was a series of treacherous rocks and falls, but once above them, it was believed one could pass another two hundred miles. When the river was swollen, as during the winter months, many of the rapids were covered so that one traveling downstream could get within four miles of Columbus. As proof of this, one pole boat built in 1828 made at least two round trips to Gwinnett County (northeast of present-day Atlanta) to buy corn. Cotton from the upstream regions was the first to be sold in Columbus in the fall of 1828.[13]

Most of the year, however, the falls acted as a great wall to separate the two ends of the Chattahoochee. Above Columbus, white settlers at the village of West Point, Georgia, traded with the Indians across the waters and with other whites upstream. Colonel Reuben Thornton ran barges and flatboats from West Point to Standing Peachtree, about sixty miles upstream (and southwest of present-day downtown Atlanta). His boats delivered groceries mostly to the isolated settlements of north Georgia. Once, though, he set aboard a load of flour and pointed the bow downstream. The boat bucked wildly over the falls but made it all the way

to Columbus. Once it arrived, there was no hope of returning by water.   53
Instead, he probably sold his battered boats at Columbus and hired a
wagon to transport his purchased sugar and coffee over trails to West
Point, then built new boats to convey the groceries from there to Stand-
ing Peachtree. From there he wagoned the supplies yet farther to eastern
Tennessee markets. Such was the nature of transportation in the 1830s.[14]

Daniel Duncan and J. M. Harrington ran flatboats between Franklin
and West Point as early as 1838. But the river residents above the falls
were more apt to ride their wagons overland to Savannah or Augusta
than to trek to Columbus for their supplies.[15]

In 1829 three steamboats reached Columbus from the Gulf of
Mexico. Their arrival was reason for the entire town to drop their work
and run to the river to enjoy the spectacle. After visiting Columbus, the
same boat, the *Robert Emmett,* turned downstream to call on other communities. At Bainbridge, situated just north of the juncture of the Chattahoochee and Flint Rivers, a crowd had gathered by the time the boat
rounded the last bend. A writer for the first edition of Bainbridge's *Southern Spy* described the boat's arrival: "With rough clinkings of iron, foaming of water, rolling of black smoke, and the red blaze of the large fire on
the fore part, . . . [it] came rushing with an irresistible impetuosity and in
a few minutes was still and alongside the bank within a few feet of the
shore."[16]

The arrival of the first steamboat owned by river residents must have
been equally thrilling. In January 1831 a crowd waited at the Columbus
wharf for the *Georgia* to steam into view. The Columbus merchants who
owned her had inaugurated "competition in boating" against the other
five boats that ran the river in that year.[17]

As Columbus and Apalachicola, at opposite ends of the river, developed, so did the hinterland between them. Fort Gaines was one of the
earliest settlements along the river. A fort here served as a refuge for
whites living on both sides of the Chattahoochee as early as 1818. A ferry
here funneled travelers through the town. Tradesmen located here to ac-
commodate those passing through. The storekeeper with the most lon-
gevity at this spot was John P. Dill, who originally came to the area
as military aide to General Edmund P. Gaines, for whom the fort was
named. In 1821 Dill formed a long-lived partnership with John W. Sut-
live. The duo prospered here, eventually adding a tannery and cotton
warehouse to their general store.[18]

Even earlier than the settlement of Fort Gaines was that of Franklin,

Painting of H. T. Hall's antebellum side-wheeler *Lowell* at Mary Freeman Landing near the southern limits of Columbus. *Courtesy W. C. Bradley Co.*

Alabama, just across the river. In 1817 a white family headed by James Hughes moved there on the fringe of Creek lands. This early pioneer was not welcomed. Indians kidnapped his nephews. Two years passed before Hughes learned their whereabouts from a white trader. He then poled down the Chattahoochee and ransomed A. C. Gordon and his brother for fifty dollars in silver. When they returned to Franklin, young Gordon took advantage of his fluent Muskogee tongue to work at the Indian trading post at Franklin.[19]

The town of Irwinton was incorporated by the Alabama legislature in 1830. It was named for William Irwin, who eventually would own mile after mile of land on the west side of the river. White settlers moved in there to compete with Columbus for the Chattahoochee river trade. However, they were a bit hasty in their plans, since the land still belonged to the Indians. "Roughnecks and hooligans" stole the homes of the Eufaula Indians and drove them into the woods.[20] The trespassers built a cotton warehouse and waited for the steamboats to call. A man named Aaron Packer established a ferry across the river. He charged one dollar for a wagon and four horses to cross, twelve and a half cents for a man and a horse.[21]

Williamston, Alabama, was settled nearby in 1820 by a Williams family from South Carolina. Another white settler, Green Beauchamp, rode across the river from Fort Gaines on the ferry in 1818 and set up a trading post on the west bank at Franklin and later at Williamston.[22] Also on the west bank, about four miles north of Franklin, was the trading post known as Prospect Bluff.

The town of West Point, Georgia, was originally known as Franklin as well. It was settled the year following Columbus's founding, and by 1831, when it was incorporated under the name of West Point, it had a population of one hundred. Its annual business was estimated at between forty and fifty thousand dollars.[23]

By 1832, only four years after the founding of the trading towns on either end of the river, a remarkable amount of development had taken place on the Chattahoochee. The *Columbus Enquirer* applauded the changes there, saying, "Well done, Columbus! Four years ago, a howling wilderness; now a handsome town with a population of 1800 souls." These residents did not need reminding that the Chattahoochee was their lifeline to prosperity. A visitor in 1832 commented that the Chattahoochee "has been of such infinite advantage to [Columbus], that it may already be called a flourishing town."[24] The population had by then exceeded two thousand. However, the same visitor also noted the town's hand-hewn character:

> Streets, which in 1828 were only marked out, were now so filled with loaded waggons that it was next to impossible to pass. The principal street which traverses the city, following the course of the river, is, like the rest, not paved, but has so many shops filled with a variety of goods, ... and in the mornings such a concourse of people, Christians and Indians, that it can hardly be believed that it is the same street which was only marked out in 1828.... The hotels are, perhaps, the worst building[s] in the town: I resided in one, the staircase of which bore a strong resemblance to a fire-ladder....
>
> The proximity of the Indian territory on the other side of the river contributed not a little to the toleration among the inhabitants of a certain number of loose persons.... Opposite the town, on the Alabama shore ... [s]carcely a day passed without some human blood being shed in its vicinity; and, not satisfied with murdering each other,

they cross the river clandestinely, and pursue their bloody vocation even in Columbus. Peaceable citizens are thus often attacked . . . which obliges every one to carry arms about his person.[25]

On the "Indian side of the Chattahoochee," the declining state of the once-proud Creeks attracted traders, whiskey sellers, and speculators. The several thousand refugees who emigrated across the river after the Treaty of Indian Springs could not easily be absorbed by the rest of the Creek Nation. Clearing fields for growing the food the Indians would need to sustain themselves would require several years of work. Many of them were already in a wretched condition upon entering Alabama. Some were so gaunt that "their bones almost wor[e] through their skin."[26]

Creek civilization was slowly disintegrating. Many Lower Creek towns never reorganized on the other side of the river. Without the support of their communities, Native Americans faced the white men and the wiles of nature alone. In search of food or whiskey to drown their woes, the generally harmless and entirely pitiable Indians wandered about in Columbus until dark, when they were required to return to the other side of the river. Within the city limits the Indians usually posed no more than a nuisance to the newcomers. They were often seen marching down Broad Street in single file, looking neither left nor right, in the dust or the mud. When they walked up to the doors of the new residents to beg for food, they stacked their guns at the door.[27]

Although relations between the races were strained, they were often respectful. When Dr. Edwin deGraffenreid, a physician who cared for the Indians, lay dying at his home in Columbus, a large group of Creeks paddled across the Chattahoochee in their canoes to keep vigil throughout the night in his backyard, where they lit candles and waited silently until he died. Afterward they returned to their side of the river, fired guns, and beat pans "to frighten away the old man's ghost and start his soul on his journey to the darkening land in the west."[28]

Steamboat captains in need of fuel paid the Indians a dollar per cord of wood. The Indians stacked it at the landings and helped the stevedores stow it. Once they were on board, it was difficult to get them to leave. They were so fascinated by the paddle-wheelers, they inspected every inch of the vessel. The boat captains eventually learned that the easiest way to get them ashore was to blow the boat's whistle long and loud. The blast so startled them that they ran to the gangplank or even jumped into the river and swam ashore.[29]

Once a traveling theatrical troupe used the local Indians as extras in a Columbus performance. The natives earned fifty cents plus a glass of whiskey, the latter being paid in advance. At the moment in the play when the cast broke out into chorus, the Indians erupted in their own songs and dances, which drowned out the scripted music. Ad-libbing, the traveling actors hopped around with the Indians in their endless dance until, dripping with sweat and tired to the bone, one motioned for the curtain to be dropped. Even this did not stop the Creeks, who continued their dance for several more minutes. Only after the Indians were paid and ushered from the building did the itinerant players dare continue. The troupe opted not to rehire them for the following night's performance.[30]

A later theatrical season brought Irish actor Tyrone Power to Columbus. He was fascinated by the stark contrasts of the town:

> Along the river-front of the town, a situation wildly beautiful, I observed several dwellings of mansion-like proportions, and others of a similar character in progress. I should say, that nowhere in this South country have I yet seen a place which promises more of the prosperity increasing wealth can bestow than this; or one that, from all I learned, is more wanting in all that men usually consider most worth possessing,—personal security, reasonable comfort, and well-executed law. In place of these, affrays ending in blood are said to be frequent, apprehensions few, acquittal next to certain even in the event of trial, and the execution of a white man a thing unknown.[31]

Yet according to Power, travelers had no cause for concern; the bloodletting was usually among friends—or, at least, acquaintances. He blamed the violence on a combination of alcohol, boredom, and the ever-present weapons. As the population increased, Power believed, more law-loving inhabitants would push the lawless to wilder areas, such as the Mexican territory. Time would prove him right.

In the year Columbus was born, Andrew Jackson became president of the United States. This development would have dire consequences for the Creeks crowded west of the Chattahoochee. Jackson intended to use his office to make the lives of those Indians still in the East so uncomfortable that they would voluntarily emigrate west of the Mississippi. White settlers were beginning to move into the reserved lands of the Creeks west of the river. The government did little to dispel them.

Alabama declared that the Creek Nation fell within its legal jurisdiction, and Creek laws that ran counter to state laws were nullified. Jack-

58 son publicly blessed this policy. In 1830, at the president's bidding, Congress enacted the Indian Removal Bill, which marked a sea change in U.S.-Indian policy from the long-practiced program of encouraging gradual absorption of the red people into white civilization to outright removal of the Indians as soon as possible.

Just three weeks after moving into the White House, Jackson wrote the Creeks a letter, saying that the only way they could escape the prosecution of Alabama law was by moving to the West. There, he promised, they would be free of white molestation, and they could live there beyond the Mississippi in the "care of your father, the President . . . as long as the grass grows or the water runs, in peace and plenty."[32]

The white frontiersmen continued to pressure the Creeks into leaving. Alabama passed a law prohibiting the testimony of an Indian against a white man in a court of law. Horse thieves and criminals roamed the Creek Nation with impunity. The Indians counted fifteen hundred white squatters in their territory in 1831.[33]

With what seems, in hindsight, like amazing innocence, the natives memorialized Washington to keep their earlier promises: "Murders have already taken place, both by reds and whites. We have caused the red men to be brought to justice, the whites go unpunished. We are weak and our words and oaths go for naught; justice we don't expect, nor can we get. . . . [T]hey daily rob us of our property; they bring white officers among us, and take our property from us for debts that were never contracted. . . . We are made subject to laws we have no means of comprehending; we never know when we are doing right."[34]

Washington refused to protect them. Government officials told the Creeks that the only way they could promise them security was for the Indians to move westward. Without government protection, the Creeks were powerless to fend off the constant deprivations made upon them. When this realization sank in, they agreed to sign another treaty in 1832. The Treaty of Cusseta was the last agreement signed by the Creek people while living in the East. It ceded to the United States all Creek lands east of the Mississippi River that were unoccupied—dissolving, in effect, the Creek Nation as a political entity.

Ostensibly, this was not a removal treaty. It guaranteed to individual heads of families a half section of land which they could remain on and farm in the manner of their white neighbors. But the treaty was written to encourage the Indians to sell their individual holdings and move west. The government promised to pay moving expenses as an added inducement. In return, all white intruders were to be expelled from Indian lands for five years, or until the Creeks sold their individual holdings to them. The failure of the United States to uphold this last treaty provision set in motion a tumbling line of dominoes that ended with the Creeks' being forced to leave what was left of their former empire.[35]

If the government had set out deliberately to decimate and demoralize the Creek Nation, they could not have planned a better instrument than the Treaty of Cusseta. Its division of Creek lands into individual holdings left each family head at the mercy of the myriad of land speculators who rushed in to buy up or trick away the Indians' allotments.

The Columbus Land Company sent agents among the Indians with supplies of goods and whiskey which they sold to them on credit. As security, the Indians signed their names to legal documents they did not understand. These were their land titles. Since blacks could not testify against whites, speculators sent their slaves into the Nation to hunt down the Indians still holding their allotments. These agents hounded the Creek men wherever they went until, in frustration, they sold their land for a song. If a native refused to sell his land, another Creek was paid to impersonate the reluctant one before a government officer who notarized the land sale.[36]

The federal government did attempt to live up to its promise to expel the illegal white settlers, but there was never a sufficient force dedicated to accomplish this. In July 1832 a company of soldiers from Fort Mitchell burned down the illegal white settlement of Irwinton and stabbed the local sheriff who stood against them. "Rough men require tough treatment," the marshal explained to superiors who exonerated him.[37] But no sooner had the troops left than the settlers rebuilt. The federal marshal complained to superiors that he needed ten times as many troops as he actually had in order to enforce the treaty.

The Creek National Council met at the Lower Creek town of Witumpka at the falls of Uchee Creek in September to discuss the growing menace. A horde of federal officials—census takers, land commissioners, and emigration agents—swarmed around the meeting, repeating again and again the necessity of the Indians' selling their holdings and moving west. The Creeks told the whites emphatically that they had no intention of selling out and did not understand why the government had supposed they would.[38]

Illegal settlers continued to spill over the river into Creek lands. One of the worst criminals to move into Alabama was Hardeman Owens. He drove an Indian from his home and moved into it. He robbed a young Creek girl from another farm and broke her arm. He dug up Indian

60   graves and stole their silver ornaments. When the Fort Mitchell troops arrived to oust him, Owens tried to shoot his way out, but a soldier's bullet killed him.[39]

When news of Owens's death reached the other squatters, they exploded in anger and indignation, believing they would be the next target. The soldiers were indicted for murder, and whites formed volunteer militia to resist further expulsion. As district attorney of Washington, D.C., Francis Scott Key was sent down to effect a compromise. When the Alabama authorities agreed to drop charges against the Fort Mitchell "murders," the federal authorities promised to suspend removing settlers from the Indian reserves, in spite of the fact that the Cusseta treaty had promised the removal of white squatters as soon as they had harvested their 1832 crops.[40]

Meanwhile, the first bridge to cross the Chattahoochee ushered still more white settlers into Alabama. The city of Columbus advertised for proposals to build this four-hundred-foot-long covered bridge in 1832. John Godwin of Cheraw, South Carolina, won the job, bidding $14,000. The city charged tolls to pay for it. The only problem was that Alabama residents felt that since the western abutments rested near the town of Girard (later Phenix City), they wanted to share in the profits from the bridge. Early in 1834 the Alabama legislature granted to private Girard citizens the ownership of the land under the western abutment. The lawmakers claimed that these private interests were entitled to half of the bridge tolls. Columbus did not agree to share the profits of their bridge. The affair ended up in court.

Predictably, the Georgia courts decided in favor of the rights of ownership of the Georgians to both sides of the river, while Alabama courts decided in favor of its citizens' interests. Eventually, the U.S. Supreme Court ruled that Georgia had jurisdiction to the high-water mark on both sides of the river.[41] By this decision, the Girard businessmen were excluded not only from any income from the bridge but from other riverside enterprises as well. Inability to use the river retarded the economic development of the Alabama settlements across from Columbus for many decades.

The river was potentially valuable in other ways as well. In 1830 someone discovered gold in the riverbank at Columbus, and one can only imagine the sensation that this news created. Since the river crossed through the gold-rich territory of north Georgia, some of the ore must have washed downstream. As little more was found, a gold rush in Columbus never materialized. Even so, Dr. S. M. Ingersoll obtained permission from the Columbus city council in 1838 to wash the loose river sands 61 in search of the yellow ore.

With every new farmer who moved into the valley, tens of acres of timberland were cleared for growing cotton. The river no longer ran clear. Erosion washed the iron-rich soil into streams that fed the river, staining it red. By 1830 cotton exports from Apalachicola had soared to five thousand bales.[42] This level of commerce was exactly what was needed to sustain a healthy steamboat trade. Cotton and the steamboats augmented each other; prosperity shone down like the sun on the white people of the Chattahoochee.

In Columbus at Christmastime in 1834, the evidence of the thriving state of business was witnessed at the wharf: "Our town . . . has presented quite a businesslike appearance. Bales of cotton have rolled down one street, whilst up another, sacks of Salt and Coffee, hogsheads of Sugar, barrels of strong drink, and boxes of all manner of merchandise have moved to their place of deposit on every known and conceivable vehicle, from the strongest road waggon burdened with its thousands to the humble wheelbarrow, ratling [sic] under the weight of a solitary flour barrel. Every body and every thing seemed at times to be moving to and from the boat landing."[43]

There at the wharf, seven steamboats queued up, "some giving up their cargoes to the industrious draymen, whilst others were receiving the bales of short staple bound to foreign lands, where manufactured into divers cambricks, calicoes and muslino, they will soon seek again . . . this self same port. . . . We hail them all, old and new, as evidence of present prosperity, and as signs indicative of brighter days yet to come. As long as there is freight to give them employment, we shall gladly see these seven and as many more loading and unloading at our wharves."[44]

In contrast to the thriving white civilization, the Creek people struggled merely to keep what they had. Resentments against the other erupted infrequently in violence. Occasional murders of whites were followed by isolated killings of reds. Most of the trouble centered on the Lower Creek refugees along the Chattahoochee, who, by virtue of living closest to white speculators, were the first to be stung by the land frauds. Landless, penniless, hungry, and hopeless, they finally came to the end of their tolerance in 1836.

The "Creek War" of that year exploded just as the cotton plants were sprouting in Chattahoochee fields once owned by the Indians. Warriors hailing primarily from the lower towns of Eufaula, Hitchiti, Yuchi, and Chiaha (Chehaw) attacked white travelers and the mail stage on the fed-

62   eral road and burned down the town of Roanoke on the banks of the Chattahoochee in Stewart County. From behind the trees that lined the river, the Indians fired at armed steamboats.[45]

White settlers, fearing for their lives, poured into Columbus for safety. Every day brought rumors of burnings, robberies, and murders, as well as exaggerated tallies of the number of hostiles. The citizens formed militia troops who "present[ed] a glorious array of dirks, pistols, and Bowie knives, with no scarcity of dirt."[46] Mayor John Fontaine of Columbus wrote to Georgia governor William Schley for aid, believing an attack on Columbus was imminent: "We are without soldiers Arms or Munitions of War, & the amount of property being exposed is so great—when taken into connexion with our confessedly defenceless state as to hold out such strong inducements to the enemy that we can scarcely hope to escape their early and most especial notice."[47]

Major General Winfield Scott moved into headquarters in Columbus directly from his campaign against the Florida Seminoles. Within a few weeks, the rebellion was put down. Even though the Creek War was prosecuted by a minority of Creeks, it was just the excuse needed by the white authorities to force all of them to move west. Eventually, 14,609 Creeks marched out of Alabama for the West in 1836. Of that number only 2,495 were believed to have raised their guns against the white man.[48] The following year another 5,000 Creeks were transported westward after they returned from serving with the U.S. Army against the Seminoles' resistance to removal in Florida.

On July 2, 1836, sixteen hundred Creek prisoners—men, women, and children—trudged westward from Fort Mitchell. The men were handcuffed in twos, and a long chain joined the pairs to one another. The U.S. troops force-marched the captives to Montgomery, ninety miles away. If they had any personal effects, they were obliged to carry them on their backs. The Yuchi were so destitute they had almost nothing to carry. Behind the manacled men rode the old and wailing women, the sick, and the children in a long train of wagons and ponies. As these defeated souls neared the waiting steamboats at Montgomery that would take them away from the only land they had ever known, one warrior drew a knife and slit his own throat. Another killed a guard with a hammer, then was shot dead in his tracks. A third Creek was stabbed with a soldier's bayonet.[49]

At Mobile, twenty-three hundred collected Indians were crowded into two steamboats bound via the Gulf of Mexico for the Mississippi River. The second night at sea, a storm blew up. The terrified and sickened Creeks were battened below decks until the gale passed. At some point in their journey, the men's manacles were removed and packed in barrels. One night some Yuchis silently rolled the barrels into the water. The chains were lost forever.[50]

As the Creeks traveled up the Mississippi, their muddy drinking water and their green fruit gave them dysentery. Fevers also spread among them. Fifty children under the age of ten died of disease en route to the West in the first emigration party alone.[51]

The travails of a subsequent Creek emigration party were recorded by an accompanying officer. During the overland leg in Arkansas, he wrote, "The flies are most distressing; a horse can hardly be controlled from lying down to roll, such is the torment. The heat is excessive and the water of the worst description; some forty-five sick, and constantly dropping; the ox-teams breaking and carts tumbling to pieces."[52]

The most telling evidence of how the Creeks suffered in their removal to the West lies in the statistics. In 1832 the Creek Nation numbered 21,792. In 1859, when a subsequent census was taken in the West, only 13,537 Creeks remained.[53]

A survivor recounted the heartbreaking trail to Oklahoma:

> Many fell by the wayside, too faint with hunger or too weak to keep up with the rest. . . . A crude bed was quickly prepared for these sick and weary people. Only a bowl of water was left within the[ir] reach, thus they were left to suffer and die alone. The little children piteously cried day after day. . . . Death stalked at all hours, but there was not time for proper burying or ceremonies. My grandfather died on this trip. A hastily cut piece of cottonwood contained his body . . . [which] was placed along a creek. . . . Some of the dead were placed between two logs and quickly covered by shrubs, some were shoved under the thickets, and some were not even buried but left by the wayside.
>
> There were several men carrying reeds with eagle feathers attached to the end. These men continually circled around the wagon trains or during the night around the camps. These men said the reeds with feathers had been treated by the medicine men. Their purpose was to encourage the Indians not to be heavy hearted nor to think of the homes that had been left.[54]

The Cowetas brought with them the ceremonial conch shells they had used from time immemorial in their black drink ceremony. Town elders carried the ashes from the campfire of the old town square with

64   them all the way to Oklahoma. On the trail to the West, these trusted men observed strict rules of abstinence from sex. They ate only "white food," or hominy with no seasonings. When the Creeks finally arrived in Oklahoma, town members circled around their chief, who laid the old ashes beneath their new communal fire. With this ceremony, the surviving Creek people began their new lives in an alien land, far from the banks of the Chattahoochee.

CHAPTER 4

A Land of Cotton

ROM THE YEAR THAT THE CHATTAHOOCHEE RIVER valley exported its first cotton bales until railroad lines pierced the valley in the 1850s, the Chattahoochee River coursed through a separate and secluded land. Dense forests isolated it from other river cultures, and, like the other southern waterways, the Chattahoochee represented its valley's only practical avenue to the outside world. With the clearing of the forests to make cotton fields, its waters no longer ran clear. But as its rusty waters flowed southward from Georgia and Alabama to the Florida port of Apalachicola, the river linked cotton merchants with cotton growers, wagon roads with steamboats, and industry with trade.

Even though valley residents relied on the river for transportation, they learned to be patient with it. In the dry summer months, the river dwindled to a thread in many places. Every summer commerce slept. With this inconvenience forgiven, the river usually rose again just as it was needed most. In the autumn, as farmers ginned their newly picked cotton to remove its seeds and pressed the remaining fluff into bales, the rains came again to swell the river. By Christmas the river was usually full and frolicky, ready and willing to shoulder the bounty of the autumn's harvest and deposit it at the coast. From there, creaky ships set their sails to capture the ocean breeze and headed out to sea loaded with Chattahoochee cotton.

Each fall, the crude wagon roads that radiated out like spokes from the hub of each riverside community conducted wagon after wagon loaded with cotton from the surrounding fields. Columbus, Georgia, was the largest commercial center on the river. By 1845 the city had two hundred businesses to serve the burgeoning wagon trade, including twenty-six dry

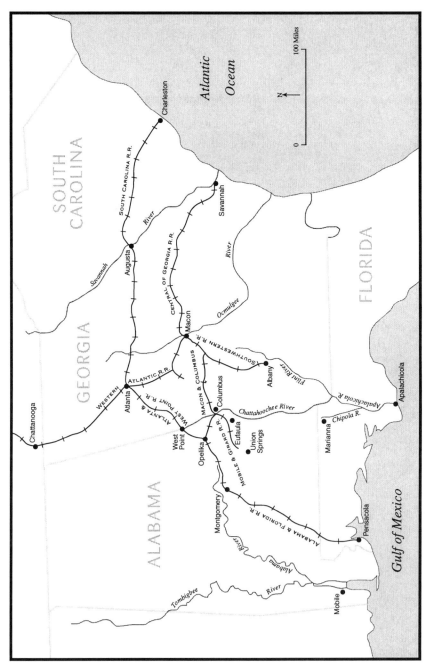

Antebellum railroads and the Chattahoochee Valley

goods stores, fifty-seven provisions stores, and five cotton warehouses.[1]
Though primarily a cotton marketing center, Columbus also capitalized
on its location at the fall line of the river to become a major southern
manufacturing center. Here local cotton was spun into thread and cloth.

The value of the falls was appreciated even before the town was settled. In 1827 the U.S. Army Corps of Engineers surveyed twelve sites
nationwide as possible locations for a federal arsenal. The army's plan for
the Chattahoochee was to build a dam at the falls and a canal that would
channel the rapids past four water-powered establishments. There was
only one problem. The high cost of transporting raw materials overland
to this location was prohibitive. The engineers decided to build their arsenal elsewhere, but other plans for using the power of the waterfalls
followed closely behind.

In 1828, the same year commissioners auctioned the first lots in the
proposed town of Columbus, Seaborn Jones, a wealthy Georgia planter,
built the first (albeit unimpressive) dam across the river. Jones's City Mills
dam diverted the flow of the water sufficiently to turn the waterwheel
that pushed a gristmill. Four years later, as the town was taking on a look
of permanence, Ephraim Brown used the river to turn the machinery of
his cotton gin factory.

In 1834 a Captain Johnson commenced the construction of the first
textile plant in the area, three miles north of Columbus. His original dam
was quite crude. He simply laid a felled tree over a gorge and nailed some
planks to it. This apparently worked well enough to force a portion of the
river into a natural raceway. Because of the Creek Indian War of 1835–36,
this "Columbus Factory" was not completed until 1838. However, once in
operation it provided local residents with not only thread, sheeting, and
osnaburgs (a tough, unbleached cotton), but also meal, flour, and tanned
leather.[2] In the 1840s other investors bought and operated the plant, and
it became known as Clapp's Factory. Many people commented on the
"beautiful and romantic" setting of this mill. The workers who lived at
the site were treated to the sound of the constant "splattering and rushing
of swift currents over the rocks."[3] Just below the mills lay Magnolia Islands, a lovely picnic spot that was accessible by wooden bridges from
both banks of the river. So popular was this area that as many as five
hundred people would visit the island in a single day.

These first steps at industrializing did not come close to tapping the
potential of the falls of the Chattahoochee. Just as the Columbus Factory
was beginning operations, an editorial in the *Columbus Enquirer* urged
further development: "I see a great source of wealth looming up to the

68   people of this section. . . . It would well compensate any one to go [look at the falls] and behold what nature has done, and what art and the superior genius of man permits to lie idle and waste."[4]

The "genius of man" did not permit this resource to "lie idle" for long. Within twenty years of the founding of Columbus, industry was thriving there, thanks mostly to John H. Howard and Josephus Echols, who bargained with the city of Columbus to develop industry along the river in return for control of the industrial riverfront lots. The two constructed a dam that extended five hundred feet to the center of the river. This structure funneled much of the river into a raceway that paralleled the eastern bank of the river. Howard and Echols also erected water-driven machinery at the head of this canal. Echols sold out to his partner after most of the development was completed, and Howard intended to sell off his industrial lots along with water rights.[5] But Howard himself became the first to construct a factory at these "water lots." In 1844 his Coweta Falls Factory began producing textiles on a limited scale just below the Fourteenth Street bridge. The following year he assured the city council that the water rushing through his race could turn as many as 200,000 spindles. His optimism attracted other investors.

In 1845 one of Georgia's wealthiest planters, Farish Carter, bought an interest in the Coweta Falls Factory and purchased a lot south of this concern for constructing a six-story brick textile plant. He planned to use slave labor to operate the ten thousand spindles and two hundred looms.[6] However, creating an industrial center dependent on the wiles of the river was chancy.

"The work [was] doing splendidly in the factory until we met with the . . . dam breaking down at the sluice . . . we shall start again on Monday *without fail* not to stop again forever," wrote Howard to Carter in 1848.[7] But other hardships followed. Floods, mechanical breakdowns, lawsuits, and red ink plagued the industrial pioneers. When the Coweta Falls company nearly folded, Carter lost interest in manufacturing cotton goods. He could make more money producing and selling raw cotton on his plantations. His new factory building remained unoccupied until the Civil War.

Others were not so easily dissuaded. William Brooks built the Variety Mills on an island on the western side of the raceway. He sawed and planed lumber there and also ran a three-thousand-spindle textile factory. Simultaneously, John G. Winter opened his Palace Mill at the very end of the canal. This business ground wheat and corn and housed a machine shop as well. Winter also inaugurated the Rock Island Paper Mills at about the same time to produce printing and wrapping paper. The paper mill sat on a picturesque point on the Alabama side of the river, about a quarter of a mile above "Lover's Leap," a spot fabled to have been the site of a double suicide of star-crossed Indian lovers. Factory workers lived nearby. Although isolated, they were often visited by pleasure seekers who came to spend the day enjoying the romantic scenery and watching the mill in operation.[8]

A different sort of industry, the Columbus Iron Foundry, was turning out mill irons, wrought irons, iron doors, and steamboat machinery as early as 1847. In 1853 the business was reorganized as the Columbus Iron Works. It was destined to play an important role in the Confederacy.[9]

The last two factories to be built along the canal prior to the Civil War were the Howard Factory (named for the industrial developer, even though he had no money in it) and William H. Young's Eagle Mill. Young came to Columbus from New York via Apalachicola, where he made a fortune as a commission merchant for Chattahoochee planters. He soon became the first president of the Bank of Columbus.[10]

Young and the other factory owners had their share of headaches in relying on the Chattahoochee. At low-water stages there was not enough water to turn the machinery. At high water the unstable dam and raceway were ever breaking or leaking. At one point, the Howard and Eagle mills threatened to give up on the river and install a steam engine.

In order to improve the reliability of river power, the dam was extended all the way to the Alabama side in the early 1850s. However, owners on that side of the river felt they should be compensated for such and sued the Georgia owners. Eventually, in 1855, the U.S. Supreme Court ruled that Georgia owned both sides of the river to the high-water mark. That decision made it possible for Young to build an improved dam south of the original one which eliminated much of the water volume problems. Just before the war, Young's Eagle plant absorbed the Howard Factory to become the second-largest textile mill in Georgia, having eleven thousand spindles.[11]

In 1854, Frederick Law Olmstead, who later gained fame as the designer of New York's Central Park, was hired by the *New York Times* to tour the South and record his opinions of conditions in the slave states. He was impressed enough with Columbus's industry to call it "the largest manufacturing town, south of Richmond."[12] By 1860 some 667 textile workers ran the looms and spindles of Columbus, and the surrounding county of Muscogee ranked second among all southern textile-producing counties.[13]

Industry and commerce were also budding just north of Columbus along the fall line. In Troup County, cotton trading centers popped up along the river at West Point (then known as Franklin) and Vernon. In 1850 the county boasted ten flour mills, eleven sawmills, fourteen gristmills, and four textile mills. Troup Factory manufactured nine hundred yards of osnaburgs a day.[14]

South of the falls, people were more focused on the growing or selling of cotton than on its use in manufacturing. At the coastal port of Apalachicola, hundreds of bales of cotton spilled out of the warehouses and clogged the streets during the commercial season. The auction bell clanged as draymen rushed the bales from the wharves to the compresses to the warehouses and back again. Cotton factors held court in their counting rooms where samples were laid out for prospective buyers. Here they dashed off letters to their associates in New York and Europe notifying them of an ensuing shipment. They arranged for the bales to be mended or repacked, insured, and stored, haggled over the lowest ocean freightage, and arranged financing so that neither they nor their clients had to wait for the cotton to reach the English textile mill before they received their payment. They sent other letters upriver to the farmer who waited to hear what his year's labor would bring. All day long their clerks bent over the precious accounting books that brought order to the entire operation. Long into the night, lights glowed from the upstairs windows of the counting rooms.

At opposite ends of the river, both Columbus and Apalachicola owed their existence to the hinterland lying between them. The triangle of land between the Flint and Chattahoochee Rivers in Georgia and the Chipola and Apalachicola Rivers in Florida and Alabama was prime cotton land. By 1850 there were 185,000 people living in the river valley, and a majority of them made their living growing or trading cotton.[15] Between the marketing centers on either end of the river system were dozens of lesser trading towns. In Alabama there was a brisk wagon trade at Eufaula, Otho, Abbeville, Columbia, Franklin, and Seale. In Georgia there were markets at Fort Gaines on the Chattahoochee and Bainbridge on the lower Flint. But a local market existed wherever one found a riverside warehouse and steamboat landing. In the 1840s there were about twenty-five such establishments between Apalachicola and Columbus.[16]

In the lonely pine forests of Georgia, Alabama, and north Florida, these wharves served as gathering places for farmers, travelers, and the idle daughters of nearby plantations. The sporadic arrival of a steamboat, announced by the blast of a whistle or the firing of a gun, brought people

scurrying to the landing to watch the slaves load and unload the steamboat. Since many of these landings were located on steep bluffs, this
process was quite interesting to observe. Long wooden slides which extended from the top of the bluff to the river's edge conducted the cargo
down the hill. Bale after bale of cotton, as well as other heavy freight
(even pigs), was sent tumbling down the steep incline to be stored in the
lower decks. When at last the freight was stowed and the shouting had
stopped, the steamer noisily pulled away from the dock and disappeared
around a bend in a cloud of smoke, leaving the onlookers to return to
the relative quiet and isolation of their work until the next steamer announced itself.[17]

Each watercraft that plied the cool Chattahoochee waters had its
own idiosyncracies in appearance, yet all had similar design charac-
teristics. Each was propelled by a steam engine pushing a paddle wheel.
The paddle wheels were ideal for the often shallow water of southern
rivers and were preferable to a screw propeller. Paddle wheels extended
less than a foot or two into the water and were thus less vulnerable to
the snags and debris floating in the river. Another advantage of paddle
wheels was that they could operate equally well in reverse as in forward.
Landing at the rough-hewn docks along the river required maneuverabil-
ity. By placing the two paddle wheels on either side of midships and turning them in opposite directions, a boat could turn on its axis.

The side-wheel arrangement had an advantage over placing the
wheels at the stern. Since the heavy machinery needed to power and steer
the boat was located at midships, the integrity of the hull was not jeop-
ardized. Early boatbuilders realized that if they placed the heavy wheel
at the stern of the boat they ran the chance that the unevenly weighted
vessels would break or bow from the strain.[18] For that reason, during the
first two decades of Chattahoochee steamboating all but three steamboats were side-wheelers.[19]

By the 1850s this problem of "hog-backing" had been overcome by
using a series of chains and trusses that extended from bow to stern, and
more and more stern-wheelers appeared on the Chattahoochee. These
had several advantages over side-wheelers. Since the machinery was all
placed in back, there was room for more cargo. And since the hull of the
boat protected the wheel, there was less chance of floating debris damag-
ing it. Lastly, the stern-wheeler was more suitable for narrow rivers.[20] In
the 1850s, ten of the paddle-wheelers that swam the Chattahoochee had
stern wheels.[21]

Antebellum steamboats were impressive in size. Chattahoochee paddle-wheelers ranged in size from the 27-ton *Edwin Forest* (1836) to the 372-ton *America* (1852). They ranged in length from the 79.5-foot *Robert Emmett* to the 175-foot *Music*.[22] The early boats were usually built in Pittsburgh, Pennsylvania, or in Steubenville or Cincinnati, Ohio. Once launched, they floated down the Ohio River to the Mississippi River to the Gulf of Mexico, then up the Chattahoochee. In 1834 the first steamboat ever built on the Chattahoochee was launched at Fort Gaines, Georgia. She was appropriately named the *Native Georgian,* and her owners boasted that she was built of Georgia timber by Georgia craftsmen.[23]

Although the Chattahoochee was never renowned for its boatbuilding, quite a few were built on its banks. In the antebellum period, twenty-one steamboats (or 17 percent of all the craft that stopped along the river in those years) were built locally. While Apalachicola craftsmen created half of the boats built along the river system, four were built in Columbus, two in Eufaula, two in Fort Gaines, and two on the adjoining Flint River. Most of the boatbuilding along the river was done in the 1840s.[24]

The more boats that plied along the Chattahoochee, the more there was need to improve the river's navigational potential. The three proposed jetties planned by the state engineer to be built on the stretch of river just south of Columbus were completed by 1838. Work was also done to clear the Apalachicola River below the Georgia/Alabama boundary, but navigational difficulties persisted. During six months of the year the river was too shallow for the boats to pass as far north as Columbus. Even after boats of lighter draft were introduced, they still could not make the trip during many summer and early fall months.

Besides the dangers of running aground, there were other hazards. In early 1834 the *Columbus Jr.* was the first Chattahoochee steamboat to sink after hitting a snag.[25] A few months later the *Van Buren,* loaded with cotton, caught fire. A recaptured runaway slave was alleged to have committed the arson. The vessel and all its contents were destroyed as passengers leapt overboard to save themselves.[26] The *Eloisa* was also consumed by fire on her maiden voyage from Apalachicola. And so it continued. After three losses in about as many weeks in 1835, a Columbus journalist commented, "Hardly a week passes . . . scarcely a paper is issued from our press, without bearing with it some such melancholy tidings. . . . Can nothing be done to render more safe the navigation of the Chattahoochee?"[27]

Because of the high incidence of destruction on the Chattahoochee, insurance rates were correspondingly steep. For example, it cost as much to insure goods shipped from Apalachicola to Columbus as it did to ship freight all the way from Boston, Massachusetts, to Tuscaloosa, Alabama, on the Tombigbee River system.

By 1839 some folks, disturbed over having to pay the highest insurance rates of any comparable river in Georgia or Alabama, suggested that iron-hulled boats might be the best solution. This idea was not pursued seriously, however, and accidents continued to plague the Chattahoochee River boats. In fact, of the forty-three vessels that are known to have operated along the river before 1853, at least twenty were wrecked or burned.[28]

From the steamboat stevedores to the cotton planters, virtually everyone in the valley made their living in some way connected to cotton. The mechanization of the English cotton industry, culminating with the invention of the cotton gin in 1792, intensified the cultivation of cotton in the South. Until then, cotton was generally grown only for domestic use. But once a machine was contrived that could speedily remove the little seeds that clung fast to each lock of cotton, the American South became the world's largest supplier.

From the outset of cotton's commercial history, the cultivation of cotton was intertwined with the institution of slavery. Those farmers who could afford to buy a slave did so. And those who could not afford to do so saved their money until the day they could. The farmer labored in the fields along with his few slaves until he could afford to buy a sufficient labor force. With this force came the possibility of earning great wealth, and who would not want to live like a planter?

As a rule of thumb, a farmer became a planter when he was wealthy enough to own twenty slaves. At that point he became more a manager than a field worker/supervisor. There was time for the arts, sports, and entertaining, all of which southern planters were renowned for doing in grand style. In a 1930s WPA interview, a former slave of Theodore Fontaine, whose plantation was six miles above Florence, Georgia, recalled that his master "had grand parties all de time, folks from Columbus, Atlanta and everywhere, dancing all night and they drunk enough liquor to float de creek, den next day dey would have de horse race. Marster had his own race track."[29]

While life was certainly not one continuous party for the planter, his position of wealth and power was revered by all, black and white. This class of elites was small. In 1860 there were only seventeen men in Muscogee County, Georgia, who owned as many as fifty slaves. Only 40 percent of the white families owned any slaves at all, and of these, half owned less than six each.[30]

The cotton plantations spread along the banks of the river and up the fertile hillside. Stretching out to the south of Columbus, the plantations of Anderson and Charles Abercrombie, Robert Flournoy, Forbes Bradley, Duncan and Alexander MacDougald, and John Woolfolk were only a few of the landmarks.[31]

Farther south, the grand homes of the wealthy adorned communities such as Cuthbert and Fort Gaines, Georgia. The grandeur of Eufaula's antebellum architecture speaks eloquently of the wealth that cotton brought to that town. Eufaula's most noted planter was General William Irwin, for whom the town was originally named until 1843. Irwin is reputed to have owned fifty thousand acres of land between Shorterville and Eufaula, Alabama. But in 1850 the general was returning to Eufaula on the steamer *H. S. Smith* when it caught fire. Irwin jumped overboard just before a plank was run ashore, and he drowned.[32]

It was said that he had come to Columbus to settle his accounts at the end of the cotton season, and that he was carrying $60,000 in gold in a money belt. Had it not been for the weight of his fortune, the story goes, he would not have lost his life. His grieving widow penned these words for his marble epitaph:

> Roll on, roll on, Chattahoochee—mad river.
> For I thought thou wert created too free
> To rob others of a brave friend forever,
> And sink all on earth that's dearest to me.[33]

In the final line the widow was referring undoubtedly to her husband, not the gold, for it is not likely that he carried such a fortune on him. A withdrawal of that size would have bankrupted an antebellum southern bank, where most transactions were made on or with paper. Even if he had been able to find that amount of coin, he would not have been able to wear it all in a money belt. It would have weighed over two hundred pounds![34]

John Horry Dent was a distinguished neighbor of the Irwins'. He moved to Barbour County from South Carolina in 1837. On his "Good Hope" plantation Dent concentrated on growing cotton, but he also raised his own food. Within four years he had done well enough to pay off his mortgage on the plantation.[35]

Dent's meticulous farm journal illustrates the rhythm of plantation life along the Chattahoochee. Dent planted his cotton in early April after the soil had been thoroughly prepared, and he planned for fifteen acres to be planted per hand. After planting, his slaves kept busy hoeing or "chopping" the ground around each plant to keep down the weeds, and "topping" the cotton, which forced it to branch out and produce more.

Dent wrote that cotton was most vulnerable to drought at the end of the growing season in August. But there were constant plagues that kept him nervous throughout the year. Rains and winds from summer gales occasionally flooded or flattened his cotton. Insects and worms cut down the cotton stalks. A reader of Dent's farm journal can sense his relief when the harvest was finally completed in late October.[36]

However, it was not the planters, such as Dent and Irwin, but the slaves who actually worked the cotton, and their influence on the culture and economy of the Chattahoochee River valley is notable. On every plantation lay the quarters where the slaves lived an isolated life. Slave houses were usually built of pine poles with red clay chinking. Most houses were only one room. Beds were set into the wall. Their burlap mattresses were stuffed with hay. Except for benches and a table, there were usually no other furnishings.[37]

The cooking was done in the fireplace. A slave's dietary staples consisted of corn, corn, corn, and bacon. Salted fish sometimes substituted for the pork.[38] Ash cake, or corn bread, was a mainstay. It was made of cornmeal, salt, and water or sour milk. The stiff pones were poured into either corn shucks or collard leaves before being covered with glowing ashes. When smoke rose from the ashes it was time to remove the bread from the fire, brush it off, and eat it.[39]

During the summer, the first bell rang out at 3 A.M. on a Russell County, Alabama, plantation. That was the signal for the slaves to rise and get their breakfast. When the second bell rang an hour later, the slaves walked out of their cabins and down the road to the cotton fields. There they labored until dark. A slave's work life was said to extend "from can to can't"—in other words, from such time as they could see to work until they could not.[40] Rarely did they catch a glimpse of the outside world.

However, the bigger the plantation, the more the slaves were able to preserve their African heritage. The land of the Chattahoochee was only a couple of generations removed from the forests and farms of Africa. The "Africanness" of the captives was reflected in their religion, their recipes, the drums they beat, and even in the way the women tied their kerchiefs. Whether white southerners owned a slave or not, they were greatly influenced by the African culture and the accompanying markets where slaves were bought and sold. Eufaula had a brisk business in slave trading. The local newspaper noted that groups of slaves were imported there from Virginia and Maryland to be sold to the highest bidder.[41] Three slave traders operated in Columbus in 1858. The extant records of one firm show that dealers made a profit of approximately 10 percent on sales. Only their sick slaves were given beef to eat. One slave named Rachel inexplicably received two bottles of whiskey and a chicken.[42]

The most famous slave of the Chattahoochee Valley was bridge builder Horace King. He learned his trade from his owner, John Godwin, and from the schooling he received in Ohio. Godwin brought King to the Chattahoochee from South Carolina in 1832 in order to build the first bridge over the river at Columbus. The duo was very successful in the Chattahoochee Valley; Godwin secured the public contracts, and King eventually constructed as many as a dozen bridges across the river at communities such as Fort Gaines, West Point, and LaGrange, Georgia.

The first covered bridge that spanned from Dillingham Street in Columbus to Girard (later Phenix City) was carried away by the flood of 1841. "Never was there a more majestic sight than the departure of that noble bridge on its remarkable voyage," wrote a witness. "The bridge floated uninterrupted for eight miles to Woolfolk's plantation where it took up new moorings in the center of a large cotton field."[43] King immediately set out to rebuild it.

Godwin gave King his freedom in 1846. Within a few years the former master failed in business, and his black friend kindly swapped houses with him. King moved into Godwin's smaller house, explaining that he did not need the room that Godwin's large family required. When Godwin died in 1859, King paid for his burial monument and helped out his widow. After the Civil War, a reluctant King was elected to the Alabama legislature. After rebuilding the bridges that Wilson's Raiders destroyed during the war, King moved his family to LaGrange. He taught his sons to continue the tradition of bridge building, and after his death they built some of the last covered bridges ever to be erected in Georgia.[44]

In addition to the slaves and farmers who produced the cotton, other workers made their living in making thread and cloth from cleaned cotton. The textile factories that clustered at the fall line hired women (60 percent) known as "Cracker Girls" to run the spindles that the river turned. Their wages varied from twelve to seventy-five cents per day, according to their skill.

Merchants of various kinds—among them retailers and brokers, auctioneers and warehousemen—relied on cotton for their livelihood as well. The most central of all the middlemen was the cotton factor or commission merchant. Technically these terms connote two different occupations. The factor was the agent employed to sell the planter's cotton; the commission merchant purchased the grower's supplies for a fee. In practice the grower's cotton factor was often his commission merchant as well, purchasing the necessary supplies for the planter on credit and paying for them when the merchant sold the cotton crop.

Commission merchants usually based their business in the largest marketing centers and catered to the planters and large farmers. Smaller growers dealt with smaller merchants who set up shop in the outlying areas. These country store owners joined the smaller producers to the commercial network by providing credit and a market for the production of smaller quantities of cotton. Virtually every occupation in the valley was at least tangentially related to the cotton culture: buyers for textile mills, insurance agents, gin and compress operators and manufacturers, bankers, hoteliers, warehouse proprietors, dry goods store owners, gin manufacturers, and steamboat captains.

The river that ran alongside the plantations, floating the bales along to sea and connecting the dots of commerce, was challenged in the 1850s by a new form of transportation. Railroads had many advantages over water travel. Generally rail travel was faster. Most steamboats seldom traveled faster than fifteen miles an hour, while trains by the 1850s maintained speeds of twenty to thirty miles an hour.[13] Additionally, trains could travel on a schedule that was not dependent on the seasonal level of the river and, therefore, were more dependable. And trains ran where rivers did not go. Most people thought these advantages offset the substantially higher freight rates that rail lines charged. It was only a matter of time before the railroads would compete with the steamboats and win.

As the iron horse puffed its way across the Georgia wilderness, it brought revolutionary change with it. But change in the name of progress threatened to destroy the river towns. Not everyone was ready for this new age, but the railroad epoch came to the Southland much the way dominoes fall: one river valley at a time. It all started in Charleston. For many years, the South Carolinians had been suffering from an economic decline as the older fields became less and less productive. Cotton farmers constantly abandoned their worn-out fields and moved to new lands to the west and south. Charleston businessmen were desperate to find a means of redirecting cotton back to them. As soon as word arrived from England that railroads were reconfiguring the economic landscape across the Atlantic, the Charlestonians seized the idea of constructing the very first southern railroad, which would run near to Augusta, Georgia, in 1833.

Augusta lay at the head of navigation of the Savannah River, and its trade with upriver farmers made it the preeminent inland Georgia market in the 1830s. By building a road there from Charleston, the South Carolinians diverted to themselves the cotton trade of the Savannah River and of their rival port of Savannah, Georgia. Now Savannah became alarmed. In self-defense the Georgia city built a railroad (completed in 1843) to tap the next river system to the west. By doing so, Savannah built an artificial corridor directly to the cotton of the Ocmulgee River system, whose upriver market town at the head of navigation was Macon.[46] Eventually this Central of Georgia line connected with Georgia's state-owned railroad network which stretched across northern Georgia to Chattanooga, Tennessee.

As rail lines extended into the upper reaches of the Mississippi and Alabama River systems, cotton receipts dipped at the preeminent Gulf of Mexico ports of New Orleans and Mobile. In response, these ports began their own railroad projects which would connect themselves to other river systems.[47]

Columbus initially welcomed a railroad project that would have connected it with the road between Savannah and Chattanooga, but the economic depression that descended on the country in 1837 killed it. In the 1840s steamboat travel on the Chattahoochee increased phenomenally with the advent of an improved shallow-draft hull design. Columbus became a bustling trade center that eclipsed Augusta as Georgia's premier inland trading town.

So when a new wave of railroad enthusiasm washed over Georgia after 1845, Columbus met it with a "noticeable lack of enthusiasm."[48] Merchants feared they would lose their wagon trade if the railroad extended from Savannah to the Chattahoochee. All the cotton to the east of Columbus which now was hauled by wagon into town to catch a boat downstream could move directly to the railroad and thence eastward to Savannah, cutting off Columbus altogether. Many thought of the railroad as an "iron boa" that would "eat up the wagon trade, and break down the business of the town."[49] The people took heed of the diminishing trade that Augusta and Macon witnessed after the rails connected those towns with Charleston and Savannah. Indecision gripped Columbus. "In every direction around us we perceive the utmost urgency and activity in the prosecution of public improvements, designed to divert trade from its natural channel—from Columbus—and to secure it for other points," wrote a Columbus editor in 1845.[50]

But if the railroad was to join the Chattahoochee River at another location, Columbus would be bypassed altogether. The *Columbus Times* warned its readers that if the rails from Macon did not come to Columbus, Eufaula might replace it as the most important cotton market on the Chattahoochee, in which case "every pull of the Locomotive will remind Columbus of her folly, and echo the laugh of our sister city of Macon, at our simple-minded gullibility."[51]

Eventually, Columbus businessmen realized they would have to bring the railroad to them to prevent its being built elsewhere. Indeed, historian Milton Sydney Heath wrote that the line from Macon to Columbus "may hold the unique distinction of being the only railroad ever to have been located with a view to avoiding traffic."[52]

Savannah was the driving force behind the Georgia railroad movement. With its location on the Atlantic Ocean, it could offer a more direct route to market for west Georgia cotton than via the Chattahoochee or Flint Rivers to Apalachicola, thence around the long Florida peninsula to its ultimate destination. Savannah's city corporation sponsored the Central of Georgia line, which joined the state-owned Western and Atlantic road at Macon in 1843. From there Savannah badly wanted to tap the rich cotton lands lying between the Flint and Chattahoochee Rivers. For that purpose the city of Savannah, in conjunction with the Central of Georgia Company, organized the Southwestern Railroad to build two lines into southwest Georgia. One line from Macon would extend westward to Columbus on the Chattahoochee. In association with this project, the city of Columbus sponsored the Muscogee Railroad Company in 1845, which was to simultaneously build eastward from Columbus to join the Southwestern line. The second Southwestern line would turn southward from Macon to Albany, at the head of navigation of the Flint River.

The rail lines that crept toward each other from Columbus and Savannah finally met in 1853. On that day the isolation on the Chattahoochee River valley was forever dissolved. A speaker at the jubilee that celebrated the occasion emphasized the significance of the day when he said, "[Today] is the day that unites the waters of the Gulf with the Great Atlantic. It is the day which unites the commercial relations of Columbus with those of Savannah. It is the day that binds those cities together with iron bands; and we trust they are not stronger than the silken cords of kindness and feeling, which are wound around our hearts."[53] At the end

80 of the ceremony, the mayor of Columbus symbolically mixed a vial of water from the Chattahoochee River with one from the Atlantic Ocean.

The advent of the railroad disrupted the southern economic order and set formerly amicable communities in competition with each other in order to retain their market share of the cotton trade. Fierce rivalries developed among port cities for each other's trade. Further inland, towns situated on different river systems conspired to steal the trade from one another. The alarm that one Columbus editor felt over the changing circumstances is obvious in this admonition to his fellow citizens: "We are surrounded by enterprising, active, go-ahead rivals, and we shall have to struggle for the prize of prosperity and advancement, if not of existence, if we hope to win it from the *Athletoe* who are our competitors."[54]

Even before the railroad was completed in Columbus, Savannah merchants began advertising in the Columbus papers. Before long, Macon, on the Ocmulgee River, competed with Columbus and Albany on the Chattahoochee and Flint Rivers. Montgomery, on the Alabama River system, contended with Columbus and Macon. Albany fought back by urging the improvement of the Flint River to keep open its Gulf of Mexico outlet while courting the Southwestern Railroad, which eventually extended its road to this Flint River port in 1857.[55]

Even more astounding was the competition for trade that developed among the communities of the same river system. After Columbus was connected with the railroad to Savannah in 1853, she jealously guarded this advantage from Eufaula. If Eufaula was to lure a railroad connection that bypassed Columbus, some feared that the latter's "prosperity would melt like the mists of the morning."[56]

Eufaula made early overtures to Columbus to link the two cities by rail, but many Columbus businessmen feared Eufaula could siphon off some of its cotton trade in this way. Eufaula then set its sights on securing a more direct connection with the Atlantic. When it was finally successful in gaining the promise of an extension of the Southwestern Railroad, Columbus citizens suddenly became very generous toward their southern neighbors. Their supercilious sneers made before the former secured a commitment from the Southwestern Railroad evolved into magnanimous gestures of goodwill after Columbus's superiority was challenged. The city now urged Eufaula to build a railroad to Columbus which would indirectly link the Alabama town with the Atlantic.

Columbus had been slow to realize the consequences of inaction, but once it shook its lethargy it worked faithfully, if somewhat fitfully, to retain its position as a major inland market. After the line to Macon was laid, city leaders turned their sights on the vast cotton lands of southern Alabama. In May 1853, the same month that the tracks were completed to Savannah, Columbus leaders approached Mobile about a joint railroad project between their cities. This would give the Georgians the advantage of having rail connections to both the Gulf and the Atlantic, and Columbus's leaders hoped the plan would also thwart the construction of a rival road being planned to extend from Montgomery to Mobile. Since Montgomery had already completed a rail line to the Chattahoochee River at West Point, thirty miles above Columbus, the planned road from Montgomery to Mobile would bypass Columbus on its extension from the Gulf of Mexico to Atlanta, where several rail lines converged.[57]

Unfortunately, Mobile and Columbus were slow to raise the money for the project, and in the meantime Montgomery completed a rival line to Pensacola. In 1855 the Montgomery line added a spur to Columbus from Opelika, Alabama. Thereby, Columbus was connected by rail to Montgomery and Pensacola, and soon Montgomery superseded Columbus as the inland marketing center for the cotton of southeastern Alabama.[58]

The railroad clearly affected the course of the Chattahoochee's cotton trade. Columbus receipts fell from 1849 to 1853 as the rails from the east drew closer, and farmers east of town could as easily cart their cotton to the railroad terminus as bring it west to the Chattahoochee. But in 1854, the first full cotton season since the railroad had united Columbus and Savannah, cotton receipts in both Columbus and Savannah rose substantially.[59]

The railroads were not so kind to Apalachicola. Cotton receipts there had moved generally upward along with the valley's increasing output in the 1840s. Figures are unavailable for 1854 (the first railroad season), but in 1855 Apalachicola receipts plunged an alarming 41 percent. Although up slightly the next year, Florida receipts continued their downward trend through the poor cotton season of 1858.[60]

In the last two years before the Civil War, the volume of cotton sent to Apalachicola rose again, but every cotton market was showing improvement. The introduction of the railroad into the interior had encouraged planters to open new fields. There was simply more cotton produced in the late 1850s than ever before. To the unaware it appeared in 1860 that the Apalachicola market had recovered from the railroad's blow, but in fact the increase in cotton receipts represented a marked decrease in Apalachicola's market share. The Chattahoochee Valley's cotton production almost doubled from 1850 to 1860, but Apalachicola's share of the trade had been slashed almost in half, from almost 80 percent in 1850 to just over 43 percent a decade later.[61]

Many Apalachicolans realized early the effect the railroad would have on their city. In 1848 a citizen warned his neighbors that the railroad then moving west toward the Chattahoochee would soon do them in: "It is obvious that this town will soon be well nigh annihilated, unless we take means to avert, as far as lies in our power, impending ruin. I allude to the rail roads of Georgia . . . [T]he circle of trade, that *once* centered at Columbus, Geo., has been circumscribed by the influence of the Macon and Western rail road: increase of production in the circumscribed circle has blinded our eyes to the true state of the case."[62]

However, at the end of the 1850s Apalachicola merchants seem to have been lulled by rising cotton receipts into the mistaken belief that the port's prosperity was returning. In 1860 cotton again crowded the Apalachicola wharf, and some there believed that "the natural course of trade cannot be diverted from a place like ours." This smug logic continued: "The trade and commerce of the Chattahoochee and Flint rivers, are naturally tributary to us, and no matter what amount of business may be diverted from us for a time by artificial channels, in the shape of Railroads, . . . still the trade will find its way back to the old channel as sure as water will seek its own level."[63]

But there was an increasing problem with the Chattahoochee. The rains that fed the river did not come as usual in the 1850s. Paris Tillinghast of Columbus commented in 1855 that there had been "no river here for the last 12 months & very scarce navigation for three years past."[64] As the water level fell, the pace of the river slowed. The slower current meant the river could not hold in suspension as much of the silt that the river naturally carried downstream. As the river dropped its load of sediment, the river (and the harbor at the Gulf) became shallower. Trees on the banks of the river continued to fall in and block navigation. Lawmakers were more fascinated by railroads than by river clearance projects, and the money needed to keep the river clear did not come.[65]

Weaving its way through the cotton lands of Georgia and Alabama, the Chattahoochee River continued to bind the valley's residents together. But the times were changing. Railroads eclipsed the river's predominance, and the brewing Civil War would only make matters worse.

❧

CHAPTER 5

The Civil War Years

HITE SOUTHERNERS WERE ALARMED BY THE presidential election of 1860. Whether they owned slaves or not, they knew that slavery was the key to prosperity in their agrarian world. Republican candidate Abraham Lincoln campaigned to halt the spread of slavery into the western territories. Most southerners (and probably most northerners) believed that if he won the election, it would be merely a matter of time before slavery was outlawed throughout the nation. When southerners believed that a Republican victory could portend economic ruin, they may have been alarmists, but they were not being illogical. For many of them, their only salvation seemed to be secession.

When news came in the spring of 1861 that South Carolina had become the first southern state to secede, many people in Columbus turned out to celebrate with "fireworks, speeches, bonfires, and torch light parades."[1] Within two months, Florida, Alabama, Georgia, Louisiana, and Mississippi also seceded, and representatives from these states formed a new government to be known as the Confederate States of America. A week following the Montgomery convention, a Chattahoochee River planter wrote his brother, echoing the prevailing opinion: "The political skies are cloudy and no one can tell what is in the future but I am hopeful that our Southern Confederacy will be established without blood-shed."[2]

As southerners prayed for peace, they prepared for war. The governor of Florida had given sealed orders to his state troops to seize the United States arsenal on the Apalachicola River (at the lower end of the Chattahoochee) even before Florida officially seceded from the Union.[3] This Chattahoochee, Florida, arsenal was soon used as a base camp for organ-

84   izing state troops and would become an important meeting place for southern troops for the next four years.

Other southern states joined the Confederacy that spring, and a few breathless months passed without violence, but finally, on April 12, 1861, the Confederates fired on Fort Sumter. Living just four miles away from the Chattahoochee arsenal, at Mount Pleasant, Florida, Rabon Scarborough wrote his daughter on April 19 that he could hear the "bellowing of the cannon on the arsenal today as we think pealing forth sounds of rejoicing at the Secession of the Old Dominion though we are not positive that such is the case."[4] He noticed that there seemed to be a "exultation a[t] the success of the first battle and the surrender of Ft. Sumter."[5]

He did not mention the other prevailing sentiment that hung over the river valley that spring like a foul odor: an abiding fear that the enemy would capture Apalachicola, at the mouth of the Chattahoochee River system, and then follow the river through the cotton fields of Georgia and Alabama to the industry of Columbus. In March 1861 an Alabamian had written from the Confederate convention hall in Montgomery to his new secretary of war: "Alabama will suffer more than Florida will if . . . [Apalachicola] should fall into the hands of an enemy."[6]

Apalachicola, like most southern ports, was undefended as the war broke out. While the new Confederate secretary of the navy, Stephen Mallory, was swamped with requests for aid from port cities throughout the Confederacy, the United States capitalized on the Confederates' disorganization. President Lincoln ordered the blockade of all Confederate ports on April 19, 1861.[7] On June 12, Commander T. Durrah Shaw of the USS *Montgomery* officially announced the blockade of Apalachicola. No American coasting vessels were allowed to enter or leave Apalachicola. All foreign vessels had ten days to clear port.[8] Soon the silhouettes of two Union ships appeared off Apalachicola Bay, and residents along the entire length of the river grew anxious.

Yet the Confederacy remained unorganized, and even in the autumn of 1861 Apalachicola's defenses remained uncoordinated and inadequate. Upriver at Mount Pleasant, the local men organized themselves as the "Chattahoochee River True Blues" and moved down to the coast to protect their families still living near the state line.[9] From Camp Retrieve, just west of Apalachicola, Scarborough wrote his wife, "The city is now without any protection save the one gun on the boat [gunboat *Onward*] and our company of muskets and [two others] . . . in all one hundred and seventy-five men with a coast of 7 miles to guard."[10]

Florida governor John Milton was personally interested in holding

Apalachicola, since his plantation was located near Marianna on the Chipola River, a tributary of the Apalachicola River, and his family was there. On October 29 the governor of South Carolina wired Milton that thirty-six steamers had just left Fortress Monroe heading south. Milton feared they were heading for Apalachicola.[11] Although the ships never appeared en masse to attack this or any other Florida port, the event caused Milton to realize how defenseless Apalachicola and its river were. From that day on, Milton began a campaign to have a separate military department with its own commander set up for the river valley. The area was too important to the Confederacy to have its commander preoccupied in Fernandina on the Atlantic coast, or even eighty miles away in Tallahassee. He consulted the governors of Alabama and Georgia, and the three of them petitioned the War Department in early November.[12]

A week later, Milton received word that over eleven Union steamers and schooners were positioned off the passes of Apalachicola Bay.[13] Again he feared the worst, as is evidenced in his urgent note to Secretary of War Judah Benjamin: "An attack threatened at Apalachicola. We need arms and munitions of war. With them we can hold the place. Authorize me [to requisition Confederate cannon, equipment, and arms] . . . and I will defend Apalachicola successfully. Please answer immediately."[14] Rabon Scarborough saw four of these boats from his vantage point at Camp Retrieve: "I could see their maneuverings very plainly. With the glass it was discovered one of them was a transport vessel and had a great many men aboard."[15]

With Secretary of War Benjamin preoccupied with more urgent defenses, a small force of Florida and Confederate troops assembled at Apalachicola and prepared for the enemy. By the end of the first year of the war, the men had thrown up "three miles of breastworks and shallow entrenchments . . . around the land and sea approaches of the city."[16] The Confederates were relieved that the attack never materialized, because Brigadier General R. F. Floyd needed 5,000 soldiers to man the earthworks properly and he had only 612.[17]

As the Confederates scurried to fortify the port, George Emmons of the USS *Hatteras* climbed to the top of the deserted lighthouse on St. George Island where he had a good view of his enemy. He saw a few small fishing boats and occasionally a "small stern wheel steamer near the town."[18] By the steamboats, Rabon Scarborough and his family passed letters and supplies. As the months passed under the blockade, Scarborough's company was unable to procure staples like bacon, lard, salt, soda, tea, and flannel for his family.[19] There was even a shortage of paper, there

86 being "fifteen hundred letters written by the soldiers here every week" and no means of replenishing the supply.[20]

To pass the lonely nights, the men serenaded their officers. Chaplain Simon P. Richardson described such an evening: "The moon was bright. Our headquarters were on the bay. The sound of the many instruments and fine voices swept out over the bay, and all the air seemed alive with music. The old general came to my door and knocked, exclaiming he never heard anything like that. And I never did, before or since."[21]

The romance of these nights was soon to be only a memory. The Florida state troops at Apalachicola were mustered out of service on March 10, 1862, and the Confederate troops were due a furlough at the same time. When Milton failed to find more men in Florida ready to take their places, he appealed to the governors of Georgia and Alabama and the Confederate commander in charge.[22] At the same time, Apalachicola city fathers reminded the governor that fifteen hundred women and children would be left unprotected if their town was abandoned.[23] Upstream at the head of navigation, the city fathers of Columbus urged the War Department to abandon Apalachicola because there was "nothing at Apalachicola to be contended for but the place itself, while a barrier against entrance to the country on the river can be placed some miles above."[24]

Abandoning the coast was exactly what the Confederates decided to do. Without the prospects of more men being dispatched to defend the Florida coast, Florida troops loaded all the cannon, ammunition, and equipment aboard steamers and moved them eight miles upriver. They closed the Apalachicola telegraph office and arrested some river pilots and brought them to Chattahoochee, Florida, as a "measure of prudence, and not because their loyalty was suspected."[25] On the heels of the military evacuation, coastal residents frantically packed up their belongings and fled upriver by whatever conveyances they could find. Only about five hundred remained in town. These were said to consist of "a few white families, a few slaves, and some Spanish fishermen."[26]

Union commander H. S. Stellwagen of the USS *Mercidita* learned of the exodus of the "poor frightened women and children" from some of the black people left behind.[27] They were "taken away at the shortest notice, in a storm, thrown ashore on the low bluffs many miles up the river, with their household goods, furniture, and everything they could snatch up in their flight, and left all night in a deluge of rain, the river rising and threatening to carry them away, with scarcely any shelter for the weak and sick, they most of them laid in the mud, almost perishing with cold, until the latter part of the next day, when they were taken away by rafts and flats over the deluged country."[28]

Most of the refugees went to Columbus on the *Jackson* and other steamers,[29] but others set up camp in the river swamp for the duration of the war. One man built cabins for himself and all his slaves; a fisherman lived with his family in a tent made from a sail.[30] Months later, a traveler found in the Florida upcountry "very few men . . . but plenty of females, who seemed to be suffering for clothing and food."[31]

Stellwagen sent Lieutenant Trevett Abbot into town in March 1862 to ask those remaining to surrender so that no harm would come to them and to urge them to take the oath of allegiance to the United States. Four ardent secessionists who had stayed behind to protect their property stopped Abbot at the city wharf. They told him they had no authority to capitulate and that they knew of no one in the town willing to take an oath of allegiance to the United States, except perhaps "some miserable foreigners."[32] On hearing this, Abbot, who was not prepared for a fight, returned to his ship.

A much larger Union force returned on April 2. This time they took possession of six local boats—one of which, the *Octavia,* had just success-fully eluded the blockaders.[33] Then Commander Stellwagen landed at the city wharf with his forces "ready for action."[34] Almost all the remaining residents—mostly women and children—turned out to hear him. Mentioning the natives' aid to the *Octavia,* the commander said, "We have come here to show you how easily we can retaliate, but that we wish to be merciful; I know there is great distress here."[35] He allowed them to keep their fishing boats and to oyster and fish in the bay so long as they committed no hostile act against the Union ships. The sailors then boarded their vessels and, as they retreated, fired a shot away from the crowd for effect. The Union never did occupy Apalachicola. The troops remained on their boats at the passes and made frequent visits to town.

Everyone upriver believed the Federals would soon make their way up the Apalachicola to Columbus. At Governor Milton's plantation on the Chipola, his children's English governess, Catherine Cooper Hopley, later remembered that they "lived in constant apprehension, after the evacuation of Apalachicola, that the Federal gunboats would ascend the Chattahoochie, and thus cut us off entirely from Northern communication. When the Governor came home now and then for a day or two, his mind was wholly engrossed for the safety of the State: with as much despatch as possible obstructions were to be placed in the river, and defenses to be erected along its banks."[36]

88   Weary of the privations caused by the blockade and anxious for her own safety, Hopley soon decided to return to England. In midsummer 1862 she boarded a northbound steamer near the Chattahoochee arsenal.

> This river steamer was so crowded that . . . I thought we should be obliged to sit up all night, every state-room being occupied. There were, among the passengers refugees from Pensacola and Apalachicola, relatives going to Richmond to visit their wounded brothers and husbands, and several country doctors going to offer their services to the army, who perhaps had never extracted a bullet in their lives, nor dressed a fractured limb.
>
> At last it was arranged for some of the gentlemen to rest in the saloon, so that the ladies should appropriate the berths. . . . [O]n the next morning all the female passengers waited most amiably for the only hand-basin on board to be passed from one room to another, before they could make their toilet. I coaxed the stewardess to bring me a good-sized, broad tin bucket full of river water, and I do not believe any one else was so favoured. This was another effect of war and blockade, for I was told by those who knew the boat, that it had always been famous for the convenience and elegance of its fittings. People were getting accustomed to these things, and made no complaints at all.
>
> Never shall I forget the heat—the burning, scorching heat—of that day, on the Chattahoochie River. . . . Every planter was sending his cotton to the interior. . . . This caused many tedious stoppages at the landings. The banks of this river are uniformly steep, and it was melancholy to see the cotton bales sent tumbling down the rugged precipices, with the casing worn and torn away, and cords broken: the precious staple, for which so many of my countrymen were suffering in penury, floating down the river in large masses, whitening the muddy stream as they wasted away![37]

On her travels northward Hopley left the river at Eufaula, where she noted the general run-down condition of the town. The war had changed Columbus also, but differently. Instead of pulling it downward, the war actually boosted the economy of this manufacturing center to new heights. The Confederacy's need for uniforms and tents meant that Columbus textile mills tripled output immediately. By 1862 William H. Young's Eagle Mill was running around the clock, and every day it produced two thousand yards of gray tweed for uniforms, fifteen hundred yards of cotton duck for tents, and fifteen hundred dollars' worth of other cotton materials and thread. In addition, it produced one thousand yards of India rubber cloth and eighteen hundred pounds of rope every week.[38] Even though the Eagle Mill did not charge full price to the Confederate quartermaster, its profits were huge. (In 1861 it distributed sixty thousand dollars to its shareholders.)[39] Soon others with no previous experience were in the manufacturing business.

Cotton factors and dry goods clerks changed occupations overnight. Broad Street, once the center of commercial activity in Columbus, became a manufacturing center as store owners cleaned out their buildings and set up cutting tables or ropewalks. It seemed the entire business district was consumed in the production of military caps, uniforms, ropes, and shoes. (The largest shoe shop in the South was here.) The Carter factory building, which had remained empty since the 1850s, was converted to manufacture swords, shuttles, and rope. All these enterprises needed labor, of course. Farmers moved to town and found employment. By the second year of the war, the population of Columbus had increased 50 percent to fifteen thousand.[40]

In addition to swords, shoes, and cotton products, Columbus also produced guns, swords, cannon, shot, shells, rifles, and pistols. The Columbus Iron Works was the largest local producer of cannon and ammunition, but it also crafted steam engines and boilers for gunboats. As the war ground on, raw materials became scarce and foundry workers crafted a cannon from the wheel shaft of the steamboat *John C. Calhoun* in 1863.[41]

By the second year of the war, the improvised factories had outgrown their quarters and moved to larger buildings on the edge of town. Broad Street's boarded-up storefronts symbolized the city's full conversion to an army supply center and its wartime prosperity. Because of the economic health of the community, civilian morale remained "higher, longer in this city than in other areas of the South. . . . Jobs remained available, and during the first two years wages rose enough to offset inflation."[42]

Though the business of the war occupied many, all worried about the security of the Chattahoochee. "Could not a bomb-proof battery . . . be constructed . . . at some point commanding the river?" asked the *Columbus Enquirer* in March 1862.[43] The Confederate government sent an engineer to inspect the river and supervise the erection of defenses, but the planters would not spare their slaves during planting time to build the barriers, and the project was not completed. However, by September 1862 representatives from the river counties of Georgia and Alabama had organized themselves. They declared that they were "unanimously of the opinion that the navigation of the River ought to be effectually guarded, and suitable obstructions to accomplish that end, prepared at the earliest practicable moment."[44] They also warned their fellow citizens not to let "local or petty jealousies retard this enterprise. The interests of town and country—of merchants, mechanics, and planters—are all mingled in common stock, and one can not suffer without damage to all."[45] At Fort Gaines, Georgia, gun emplacements were built into the river bluffs.

While local authorities thought in terms of a defensive strategy that would bar the enemy from reaching the river valley, the Confederate officials also had to consider an offensive plan. The officers planned to build gunboats in Columbus capable of breaking the enemy blockade at the coast. Although it was assumed that the boats would be completed before the river was obstructed, both projects proceeded without regard to the other.

The Confederates began shipbuilding in October 1861, when Lieutenant Augustus McLaughlin contracted with David S. Johnston at Saffold, Georgia, in Early County to build a wooden gunboat to be called the *Chattahoochee*.[46] The project was to take only 120 days, but eight months later, in June 1862, McLaughlin reported that the boat was not yet finished: "The department is very much annoyed at the manner in which things have been conducted at that yard. There seems no disposition on the part of the contractor to complete the work, his main view being to construct a permanent arrangement at his place for future operations of a private nature, which is highly detrimental to our cause."[47] Meanwhile, workers at the navy yard at Columbus were busy refitting a schooner, the *Kate Bruce*, with steam power and guns, and building an ironclad steam-powered gunboat known locally as the *Muscogee*.[48]

Since no single person was in charge of river defense, all the military projects remained fragmented. To cure this, the governors of Alabama, Georgia, and Florida assaulted the War Department with petitions to create a separate military department for the river valley.[49] Meanwhile, leaders of Columbus and Eufaula reminded their neighbors that the low water level that prevented enemy gunboat navigation on their river during the summer of 1862 would soon end, and they must be ready to defend themselves.[50]

Finally, in November 1862, six months after the evacuation of Apalachicola, the War Department created the long-awaited military district composed of the valley of the Chattahoochee, Flint, Chipola, and Apalachicola Rivers, with General Howell Cobb in command.[51] Cobb was well known to Chattahoochee residents. He had served as a Georgia congressman, Speaker of the U.S. House of Representatives, and governor of Georgia from 1851 to 1853.[52] His eminence instilled confidence locally that the river valley would be protected.

With Cobb's appointment, the many defense projects along the river finally were coordinated. He dispatched an engineer to survey the Chattahoochee River system to select the best site for obstructing the river and building batteries to defend those impediments. The primary site selected was at the Narrows, a point in the Apalachicola River near the confluence of the Chipola River where the river became so narrow that it was easy to blockade.

Cobb also tried to raise an army large enough to effectively man the batteries and the roads leading to the river. He estimated he would need five thousand, but again the Confederates could not spare men from the front.[53] According to historian Horace Montgomery, "there were never more than four hundred men on duty along the river system."[54]

As the obstructions were being placed in the river, shipbuilders were putting the finishing touches on the imposing *Chattahoochee,* a three-masted schooner about 130 feet long from bowsprit to stern and 30 feet across the beam. Its black hull had a draft of five feet fore and eight aft. Six cannon of varying size adorned its decks. In addition to its square sails, it was propelled by two engines at speeds of up to twelve knots.[55]

The gunboat's commander, Catesby Jones, had been transferred from the CSS *Virginia* (formerly the USS *Merrimack*). Many of the 120 crew members of the *Chattahoochee* had also served on the *Virginia* when it battled the USS *Monitor* in the first duel ever between ironclads. Duty on the *Chattahoochee* would not be so illustrious. Cobb's first priority was defending the river. He decided he could not wait for the ship to be finished before he ordered the chains to be drawn across the waters. Instead, he asked for the *Chattahoochee,* "now effectually stopped from going to sea," to be ordered to guard the new obstruction at the Narrows until the land battery could be completed there.[56] Instead of the exhilaration of battle on the high seas, the tedium of life aboard a ship that could not reach the ocean awaited the crew of the *Chattahoochee.* On January 2, 1863, Cobb wrote to Jones, "I am gratified to know that I shall have your cooperation in the defense of the river, whilst I regret on your account that you can not have a larger and more congenial field of operation."[57]

Still, the crew of the *Chattahoochee* had hopes of reaching the Gulf. High water broke the obstructions, and the gunboat was ordered down to guard the Narrows until it could be fortified. With luck, the gunboat could still get out to sea.

But good luck never rode with the *Chattahoochee*. On its maiden voyage, the engine failed and the ship struck a rock, tearing a hole in the hull. Lieutenant George Gift wrote a friend afterward: "So you see we are in splendid condition for service. I wish the confounded vessel in Jericho. We are neither the one thing nor another."[58] Another crew member complained: "So the fate of the *Chattahoochee* has been decided on and the officers and crew will share the same ignominious fate. Laying here in the river to be prostrated by chills and fever in the Spring and Summer."[59]

The crew devoted the early months of 1863 to repairing the hull and engines and holding drills and target practice. Gift wrote in early February 1863: "Our organization is growing rapidly towards perfection which makes every one the more eager to face the enemy and try conclusions at the muzzles of our guns." Gift and Jones also worked to make good sailors out of the raw recruits. In one instance Gift punished one of the steerage officers for swearing by " 'tricing' him up by the wrists to a hammock hook for four hours." He threatened others who committed the same offense with two weeks' quarantine onboard ship. On another occasion, Captain Jones "blacklisted" several of the crew for being untidy. Gift admonished them to "buy soap and scrubbing brushes. Some of them however are incorrigible and I will punish them to the full extent of the law."[60]

By far the most engrossing daily activity involved daydreaming about the eligible young ladies who lived on nearby Georgia plantations. "Either the Young ladies of Early County or their books will cause much delay in the progress of the outfitting of the good steamer 'Chattahoochee,' " Gift wrote, "and absolutely prove an impediment to the advance of her Midshipman in the study of the Science of Navigation."[61] Members of the crew were often invited to call at the homes of local residents. This is where Gift met Ellen Shackleford of "The Pines" plantation near Saffold. He instantly fell in love with her, and his frequent letters to her comprise a valuable diary of events on board the *Chattahoochee*.

Gift was not the only smitten crew member. Charles Mallory, his aide and friend, was another. He visited a plantation on the nearby Flint River and returned to the boat with praise for three meals a day, sleeping late, and "the finest young lady in Florida or Georgia." Yet another was the assistant surgeon, Marcellus Ford. Gift wrote of him: "Dr. Ford has been writing and re-writing a letter to his dulcinea since breakfast; it is now 8 o'clock and he is getting ready for a new beginning. . . . I sincerely pity 'Miss Susan,' for the Doctor makes the most horrible scratches and calls them words and letters."[62]

Occasionally the ladies would pay a visit to the gunboat. Gift noted that a party of "nice innocent country girls" was on board when General Cobb and his chief of artillery came to witness a gunnery exercise. The artillerist had particularly wanted to see the target practice, but lost all interest when he became engrossed in the ladies.[63]

The women of Columbus contributed so many of their brass candle holders and andirons that a cannon known as the "Ladies Defender" was cast in their name. They also volunteered endless hours at seven different Confederate hospitals located there. Laura Beecher Comer of Columbus explained their devotion when she wrote in her diary that at the beginning of the war she had "felt Atlas-like; as if the weight of the Confederacy was on *my shoulders!* How earnest and sincere I was—but what folly for *one woman* to have been so completely absorbed!"[64]

While the servicemen of the *Chattahoochee* appreciated the women's patriotic gifts, they also were grateful for a chance to socialize. Women were a welcome diversion from their uncomfortable and unhealthful station. Several men died during the first months, apparently from swamp fevers. Twice in eight days Gift noted burial ceremonies: "The burial of these men forcibly reminded me of the singular life poor sailors lead. Amongst the *seamen* of this ship, there is not one in ten, who has a relative in the Confederacy; their shipmates of today are their only friends If one dies, we put him away according to military form; some sinner like myself reading the burial service; a head board marks his resting place for a few years, and then all is oblivion."[65]

As the days dragged on, the number on board the *Chattahoochee* diminished from deaths and desertions. The captain himself was soon ordered to Texas. "What is to become of the 'Chatt' and her crew?" Gift wondered. "We are certainly to leave the river."[66] But even as he wrote this, the engineer in charge of the river obstructions was rebuilding the fixture that would wall off the gunboat from the sea. After sinking a raft floated down from Columbus and tying off a chain to either bank that would trap floating debris to create a dam, Captain Theodore Moreno needed a second chain to complete the obstruction. None could be found in Columbus, but he heard of a long, heavy chain that was lying on the wharf at Apalachicola. With fifteen soldiers he rowed down to the port under cover of night. This was a dangerous mission, since the Union navy patrolled these waters. Moreno later wrote that he would "never forget

94   the terrible clank it gave as it dropped on board."[67] His men feared for their lives, but the enemy did not hear them. Moreno and his men returned upriver and fastened the purloined chain to opposite banks. The obstruction was completed when high water piled on more driftwood. In this way, the gunboat *Chattahoochee* was shut off from the sea.

A new captain swaggered aboard the *Chattahoochee* in late February 1863 to replace Jones. John Julius Guthrie had recently been George Gift's senior officer on the floating battery *New Orleans* at Island Number 10 in the Mississippi River.[68] Gift did not write of his prior working relationship with Guthrie, but his later references to him were not flattering. From this day forward, Gift's letters are full of dissatisfaction with the new executive officer and discontent at being stuck in the backwaters of history.

Given their differences in personality, Gift and Guthrie were bound to clash. Gift loved action; Guthrie was more timid. On April 7, Gift complained to Ellen Shackleford, "He is absolutely afraid to get the ship underway for fear of an accident! We have been at anchor in the middle of the river for a week waiting and procrastinating: My patience is threadbare worse than my coat."[69]

A few days later Gift related the story of the gunboat's trial trip down to the obstructions; he was irritated by the timidity of the captain and the pilot, who were "both in a state of continual alarm for fear of an accident." To make matters worse, the captain ordered gunnery practice at no particular target, an exercise which in Gift's opinion wasted ammunition without instructing the men.

Downstream, "our peacock Captain" called on "a cross eyed 2nd Lieutenant" commanding the land batteries that protected the obstructions. There Guthrie ordered another gunnery practice, and Gift was indignant at his "absolute ignorance in regard to the most commonplace matter in the art of gunnery, and the use of shells. . . . And to cap the climax he spoke of the Efficiency of *his* crew—made so by Jones' precepts and my hard work—confound him!"[70]

Gift was restless. He wrote Ellen on May 4: "It has been uncommonly dull . . . nothing has occurred to disturb our weary monotony. The long days drag their length along bringing no change or excitement to startle the blood or arouse the energy. If we are to pass the summer in this hum drum manner I shall certainly die of ennui."[71] Gift occupied his imagination by devising daring plots to write himself into the history books.

The Confederates were not the only ones in the vicinity chafing from inactivity. At the mouth of the river was the Union blockading fleet. Lieutenant Commander George H. Morris of the USS *Port Royal* learned at the end of May 1863 that a Confederate blockade-runner was being loaded with cotton above Apalachicola (and below the obstructions at the Narrows). Fearing that the sloop would elude the Union blockading vessels if allowed to pass out of the river, Morris sent up three of his tenders to seize her. On May 26 the expedition surprised the *Fashion* and towed the prize back to the *Port Royal*.[72]

Upstream at Chattahoochee, Florida, Guthrie heard rumor of the attack and determined to go to the *Fashion*'s rescue. Ironically, Gift was not on board when Guthrie finally shook his lethargy. He was in Quincy, Florida, discussing one of his schemes for glory with General Cobb.[73]

The *Chattahoochee* got no farther than the sandbar at Blountstown, Florida, which now carried only seven and a half feet of water. Guthrie needed eight feet. While waiting for the river to rise, he anchored the *Chattahoochee* and took a launch down to the next river battery. There he learned the fate of the *Fashion*. Since he could do nothing to aid the Confederate sloop, he went back to his boat and prepared to return to Chattahoochee.[74]

A violent storm was brewing as Guthrie ordered up steam the following morning. Edward Conn of Apalachicola, Enoch Lanpher of Columbus, Joseph Hicks of Georgia, and Billy Moore (a landsman whom Gift referred to as "his boy") commenced stoking the fire, and Guthrie returned to his cabin. After about two hours the engine room was congested with men, among them pilot William Bilbro, who had run the river for thirty years.[75] Bilbro and the engineers then began discussing how much water was in the boiler. Senior engineer Henry Fagan was lying in his bunk, sick with a chill, and overheard the discussion in the engine room.

Alarmed "at the length of time since the fires had been started," he jumped up from his bunk and hurried to the ladder that led into the engine room. At that moment someone, probably Bilbro, started the donkey engine to fill the boiler with water, and instantaneously it exploded.[76] Moore was blown up the hatch and onto the deck, where he lay writhing in pain for several hours before he died. Gift's friend Charles K. Mallory, sick and lying on a cot in steerage at the time, was scalded severely by the sudden escape of steam. Bilbro and Fagan were killed instantly. The survivors panicked as water began filling the bottom of the boat. Some feared the magazine would explode. The cracked deck of the *Chattahoochee* was covered with the blood and skin of the scalded men as

96 survivors jumped overboard. Three or four men drowned trying to reach shore. In the raging storm the uninjured dragged the dying men ashore, where they remained until the next afternoon. During the panic, the ship's captain was rarely seen except in administering baptismal rites to the dying.[77]

A courier reached an army outpost upstream at sunset, and Captain Moreno ran down at once in the *William H. Young*. The next morning, when the storm subsided, Gift finally caught up with the *Young* as it traveled upstream with the dead and wounded.[78] The dead were buried at Chattahoochee. On the following day the *Young* started for the Soldier's Hospital at Columbus with the injured. Not until five days after the accident were the wounded seen by a competent doctor. Assistant Surgeon Ford, whom Gift had earlier found to be practically illiterate, was not up to the task. He had neither the expertise nor the materials to dress the burns, so he had waited.

Lieutenant McLaughlin, who had been responsible for the construction of the *Chattahoochee* and had remained close to her crew, sadly relayed the news to Catesby Jones, then at Selma, Alabama. Probably his hardest task was relating the death of Charles K. Mallory, who had served under Jones on the *Virginia* and was said to have been the first Confederate aboard the USS *Congress* when it was surrendered at Hampton Roads.[79] McLaughlin wrote:

> Poor Mallory! I shall never forget his appearance, I would not have known him had he not spoken. His face, hands, and feet were scalded in the most terrible manner; he plead piteously to have his wounds attended to. I urged the doctor, who, by the way, was almost used up himself, to pay Mallory some attention. He then told me that he would have to wait for some assistance. He then said that Mallory could not live. You would have thought differently had you seen him. I could not make up my mind that he would die. When they first commenced to remove the cloths he was talking cheerfully, but the nervous system could not stand the shock. He commenced sinking and was a corpse before they had gotten half through.[80]

Gift also took Mallory's death hard: "Had he fallen fighting the foe, I would not have minded it half so much."[81]

At Columbus the women who had doted on the crew of the *Chattahoochee* flocked in to nurse them. According to McLaughlin, "The Home was literally besieged with ladies, and for one week the street in front of the Home was blocked up with vehicles of all descriptions. . . . The four worst cases were placed together in the room upstairs," he continued. "It was with the utmost difficulty that I could remain in the room sufficiently long to ascertain what was required and to see what service I could render, the atmosphere was so unpleasant, yet the ladies did not seem to notice it and remained at their post till the last."[82]

All told, nineteen men died from the explosion. The survivors were soon scattered over the Confederacy. Thirteen deserted (two of whom went directly to the USS *Port Royal* and joined the enemy),[83] and most of the others were quickly reassigned to the CSS *Savannah*, which was just being commissioned on the Georgia coast. McLaughlin wrote Jones, "The men were all nicely dressed when they left here, and on their arrival at Savannah, being all straight and in good condition, were the cause of many remarks. It was certainly reflecting great credit to those who had organized and disciplined the crew. I felt proud of them." Then he added, "They would have been willing to have gone anywhere to have gotten rid of the vessel."[84]

Guthrie went to North Carolina, where he served briefly on a boat commissioned by that state. He soon returned to Eufaula with his family. The navy had already reassigned Gift to Mobile before the accident took place, but he did not receive the orders until he arrived in Columbus with the wounded.[85] Guthrie and Gift fired parting salvos at each other. Guthrie reported Gift to the Office of Order and Details for using navy funds to buy whiskey "for the relief of the sufferers of" the *Chattahoochee*.[86] Gift "considered it [his] imperative duty to report Lieut. Com'g. John J. Guthrie to the Secretary of the Navy, for gross neglect of duty in allowing the 'Chattahoochee' to sink and three of her crew to drown."[87]

Gift had a point. What caused the vessel to sink was the "breaking of a pipe connecting with the boiler and the bottom of the ship under water." Gift believed the vessel "could have been kept free by bailing her with buckets until the powder and shells could have been removed."[88] It took forty hours for the ship to sink. Lieutenant McLaughlin at the Columbus Navy Yard was later in charge of restoring the gunboat, and he wrote Catesby Jones after examining the wreck: "It has been to me still more a matter of surprise why that vessel should have been allowed to sink. A pine plug driven into the feed pipe, which had been blown off, would have been all that was necessary [to save it]."[89]

Gift and McLaughlin both felt that Guthrie was in a state of shock after the crisis, McLaughlin stating that Guthrie "appeared to be laboring under some bodily infirmity while in Columbus." Gift was more

98   direct: "The facts of this case were simply that the Captain has not recovered his fright yet."[90]

The "poor Chat" (as Gift often referred to it) did not reach Columbus for repairs for several months. David Johnston, who had built it, was
authorized to raise the hulk. But after Johnston raised the vessel he left
it in the "charge of his negroes," who "stripped off everything that could
be converted into money."[91] It was not until December 1863 that
McLaughlin started restoring it.

Eventually the *Chattahoochee* was towed to the Columbus Navy Yard
for repairs. There she joined the ironclad gunboat *Jackson*, known locally
as the *Muscogee*, which was still under construction. Because of a lack of
supplies, though, the Confederate boat builders made little progress on
the two.

During the last months of the war, both the Confederates and the
Union concentrated on defending their position because both lacked
the men and materials to launch an offensive. The Union blockaders on
the coast still had no vessels of light draft to ascend the river and take
Columbus. They could only send out small search parties in the ships'
tenders below the Narrows to capture and destroy Confederate stashes
of corn, ammunition, and cotton and occasionally to take prisoners and
"contrabands," or slaves.[92] Upon hearing rumors that the *Chattahoochee*
and *Muscogee* were completed and that the Confederates were preparing
to raise the blockade, the Union sailors requested more boats of lighter
draft and heavy batteries so that they could enter St. George Sound,
thereby reducing the chances of a Confederate ship getting past them.[93]

The Union fears were actually unfounded, because the *Chattahoochee*
never returned to action, and the *Muscogee* (or *Jackson*), although successfully launched in December 1864,[94] "was never fully plated."[95] Governor
Joe Brown of Georgia purchased the Confederate steamer *William H.
Young* with the intention of running the blockade at Apalachicola,
but Florida governor Milton and the Confederate general commanding
Florida refused to help him clear an obstruction in a tributary so that
the *Young* could bypass the Narrows. Because they knew there were in-
sufficient numbers of men at the river fortifications to fight off a Union
counterattack, and because they had overestimated the strength of the
enemy in the bay, the two Floridians believed that such a maneuver
would be inviting trouble.[96] In reality, the trouble they invited came from
Governor Brown, who was furious with Milton for not cooperating. But
Milton had given up. Before he received Brown's last letter of protest, he
killed himself.

In the final months of the war, virtually everyone along the river was ready for the war's conclusion. In January 1865 a man living on the Florida end of the river system wrote that if Confederate leaders were to allow a vote on it, "there would be instant peace."[97] During the summer of 1864, William Tecumseh Sherman's army had crossed the Chattahoochee River near Atlanta and, after burning the city, had marched across Georgia to Savannah, destroying everything of worth to the Confederacy as it went. Although the river below West Point was ignored by Sherman, the Columbus area soon felt the privations of the war.

In the wake of Sherman's march, Confederate casualties and civilians deserted Atlanta for Columbus. Food and supplies became scarce. Inflation was out of control. One woman said she did not see a decent dress in Columbus that cost less than $250.[98] Chickens cost four to five dollars each, and butter was five to six dollars per pound.[99] Unemployment was also a problem.

Ironically, when the enemy finally arrived, he came overland from the west instead of northward by way of the river. On April 2, 1865, the day Richmond fell, Union cavalry led by General James H. Wilson moved into Selma, Alabama, bent on destroying everything of use to the Confederates as they moved toward Georgia. After destroying military stores and industry, the Union soldiers marched eastward to capture Montgomery. From here, Wilson divided his raiders into two wings. One drove toward West Point, where they intended to cut the railroad lines and destroy supplies. The other, larger force headed for Columbus, which Wilson called the "key to Georgia."[100]

On April 16, eight days after Robert E. Lee surrendered to Ulysses S. Grant, Brevet Brigadier General E. F. Winslow's cavalry galloped toward Columbus while Colonel Oscar H. LaGrange led his brigade toward West Point. At the latter place, the local defenders—consisting of young boys, convalescents, and a few soldiers on furlough—were no match for the larger, well-supplied, and seasoned Union foe. LaGrange's men burned both river bridges and destroyed nineteen locomotives, "340 railroad cars loaded with quartermaster's and commissary stores, machinery from factories, leather, osnaburgs, etc."[101] Eighteen defenders died.

At Columbus, factory workers, young boys, and old men waited nervously for the enemy on the Alabama side of the river, but in the darkness of that Easter Sunday night, the Federals slipped past them. The next day the invading forces destroyed every industrial facility except the three gristmills. They torched all the textile mills, the sword factory, the paper mill, the navy yard, the ironworks, and other foundries. They

100 set the cotton warehouses on fire, and 50,000 to 100,000 bales went up in smoke.[102]

The two gunboats built at Columbus never fired a shot in defense of the city. With Union forces bearing down on the city, the Confederates torched the *Chattahoochee* and set it adrift. It came to rest a few miles below the city at the bottom of the murky river that shared its name. The next day the Federals set fire to the ironclad *Muscogee,* only two weeks away from completion. When it was released from its moorings, the ship drifted twenty-five miles downstream before the river claimed it.

Three days after the Union forces knifed into Columbus, other Federal troops arrived in Eufaula. U.S. Brevet Major Benjamin Grierson surveyed the town and found it to be filled with Confederate wounded. While there, he learned officially that the war was over and left Eufaula unharmed. In the ensuing weeks, as Confederate soldiers drifted back home, they found Federal soldiers waiting to inspect their parole papers at the covered bridge over the Chattahoochee.[103]

The United States officially took possession of Apalachicola and its one thousand bales of cotton on June 4, 1865. Two days later, a U.S. officer wrote, "People are returning to Apalachicola from rebeldom as well as from the North, anxious to resume their former vocations."[104] But Apalachicola's preeminence as a commercial port belonged to the past.

At the head of the river, Columbus now emerged as the rising symbol of the "New South" with its emphasis on manufacturing and railroads. The war had been both a catalyst for the growth of Columbus's industry and a cause for the decline of Apalachicola's cotton-based economy. And what had become of the river that connected them? Silted up and choked with wreckage, the river had suffered as much as the people during this war. But as the people rebounded, so would the waterway. While the river was never again as central to the valley as it had been before the railroads came, the next era would be its last hurrah. The golden days of steamboating still lay ahead.

CHAPTER 6

2

Moonlight and Magnolias

FTER THE CIVIL WAR, THE FIRST STEAMBOATS TO
run the Chattahoochee brought up goods not seen in months
or years: salt, whiskey, oysters, and oranges, among other things.
The captains looked for cotton to load for the return trip to the Gulf.
Bales materialized on the riverbank, and river commerce quickly revived.

Two years after the war closed, a Columbus journalist rode the
steamer *Barnett* to the bay and back. His description of the valley, augmented by others of the period, portrays a region that had not yet recovered from the late war, yet which retained its former respectability. He
wrote of Eufaula, "No place has more polish, or more lovely women."[1] A
female college had been built there, and a new hall was nearly completed.
The *Eufaula News* was again in business. However, just as before the war,
in the off-season, things were dull: "Old Monotony Pasha has registered
there and unpacked his things for the summer. Fat men swelter and fume
around, and sweat, and swear and broil and fry in their own grease under
the burning rays of a red hot sun, while the lean ones damn their bank
anatomy as the sunbeams shoot right on through them, simmering the
marrow in their bones."[2]

In the spring of 1879, a decade and a half after the war ended, another
reporter packed nothing but an extra collar and boarded the *T. H. Moore*
to update his readers on the valley's recovery. At Chattahoochee, Florida,
he found that a common wharf for both the railroad and steamboats was
under construction. The railroad pier was to be built at the end of a dou-
ble-track road that ended immediately above the water. A steam elevator
was planned to facilitate loading from one conveyance to another. There
was an elegant little hotel and passenger depot there by this time, but the

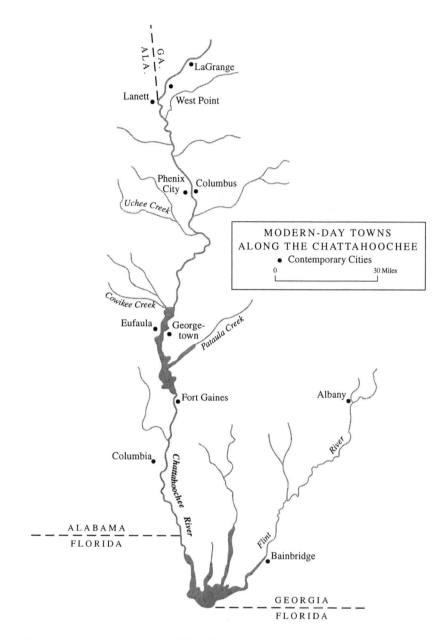

Modern-day towns along the Chattahoochee

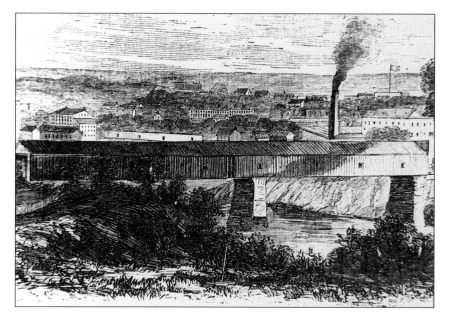

This 1868 view of the Dillingham Street Bridge at Columbus, which was built and rebuilt by Horace King, appeared in *Harper's Weekly* on September 19, 1868. *Courtesy of Columbus College Archives.*

An 1886 perspective map of Columbus. *Courtesy of the Columbus Museum.*

104 outdoors seemed to beckon more passengers than any other place. As the boats paused to load and unload, hunters rambled through the woods in pursuit of game, while couples strolled around picking wildflowers.

Blending with the fresh country air was the acrid odor of fertilizer which accompanied every springtime river passage.[3] Guano, the accumulated excrement of seabirds used as fertilizer in the cotton fields, was the most prevalent cargo of the early months of the year. Originally, workmen shoveled it from offshore platforms into bags that were hauled to waiting farmers. In time, the natural fertilizer was mixed with other nutrients such as phosphate by such firms as W. C. Bradley of Columbus and the LaGrange Fertilizer Factory, whose brand-name was "Chattahoochee Guano."

The 1879 Columbus reporter was surprised to find how much the once-proud port of Apalachicola had declined since the war. He wrote, "The stranger who first approaches Apalachicola . . . is rather unfavorably impressed. A feeling of desolation and decaying quiet seems to pervade the very atmosphere. The crumbling ruins of former solid warehouses, the shackly looking wharf, an unfinished tug-boat left to moulder away, . . . a few listless and unoccupied men loitering along the shore, remind us alike of the former commercial importance of a seaport town and its present insignificance."[4]

Apalachicola's population had shrunk by almost one-half, to sixteen hundred, from its prewar heyday. Economic diversity had replaced the prewar cotton obsession. Most inhabitants now made their living in fishing, while a few raised stock or oranges. The non-native population was predominantly Irish and German, and the residents enjoyed a quiet life in a healthy climate where living was "cheap and good." A sponge industry had taken hold there, and a trade in lumber was budding. The seafood industry was in its infancy, as well. Ten thousand barrels of oysters had been exported in the previous season.[5]

Abbeville, Alabama, the county seat of Henry County, also bore the marks of a postwar economic slump. The reporter noted that the old, dignified dwellings could have used a hammer and a paintbrush, and "The store-houses look as though old man Noah might have been the architect."[6]

War had also taken its toll on Fort Gaines, Georgia. Though once "one of the most enterprising and thrifty little towns in the state," since the war it had suffered "a set back which the citizens are slow to overcome." The stores were run-down, and the courthouse was "better suited for the home of goats and bats than for the hall of justice." Practically the only thing this traveler liked about Fort Gaines was the people. And the only place in town he considered beautiful was the new cemetery, situated on the riverbank. The journalist believed that if the residents had taken "as much interest in fixing up their homes for the living as they do for the dead, Fort Gaines would be one of the most attractive little towns in the country."[7]

Years later, in 1901, another newspaper reporter noted some improvement, at least at the seaport. Apalachicola was now the center of a large logging industry. Lumberjacks felled trees in the river swamp for miles upriver of the port, then awaited high water for the opportunity to ride the logs down to the mills. At the coast, the lumbermen boarded the river steamers which returned them upriver to repeat the process.

In spite of two devastating fires that destroyed the downtown area in the 1890s, the town of Apalachicola was looking prosperous by the turn of the century. Remains of the many brick warehouses still guarded the waterfront. Large business houses had replaced small wooden shanties. The town finally had a bank, as well as an electric light plant and pretty electric streetlamps. A new telegraph cable strung across the bay to Carabelle connected Apalachicola with Western Union.[8]

The postwar steamboat period displayed more sophistication than the antebellum period had. New, opulent thoroughbreds replaced the more practical workhorses of the antebellum period. Lines of boats replaced the single-operated vessels. Innovations in service made river travel more reliable, and technological breakthroughs made the ride safer.

An example of the vessels that graced the new era was the *Pactolus*, which steamed into Columbus for the first time in 1886. The boat had twenty-eight staterooms in the cabin and eight in the "texas," a small cabin on top. It drew only two feet of water, was said to be a fast boat, and could carry eight hundred bales of cotton in addition to the passengers.[9] The boat's name was inspired by the story of Midas, who, when starving because everything he touched turned to gold, asked for help from a god who ordered him to bathe in the river Pactolus. Midas did as instructed; his golden touch lost its power when it came to those things essential to life; and, in the process, the sands of the river turned into gold.[10] The steamboat's owners hoped the river Chattahoochee would have the same fate.

One of the most elegant boats on the river during the postwar years was the *Rebecca Everingham*. This boat, launched in 1880, was state-of-the-art. She had two high-pressure engines and a stern wheel thirteen feet in diameter that made twenty-eight revolutions per minute. She was clocked at seven miles an hour. Twenty-four staterooms, all "elegantly furnished and carpeted," had the latest cork life preservers (while crew and deck passengers got wooden ones). The hall that ran between the two rows of staterooms was lined with Brussels carpet and graced with four chandeliers. The oak walls of the cabin were so well finished that they felt like "highly polished marble."[11] When farmers came aboard, the captain had them remove their dirty boots and replace them with gold velvet slippers.[12]

The *Rebecca Everingham* was one of the first boats on the river to have electric lighting. In fact, this vessel had two different types. One, a "Brush Light" (the same as was used in one of the Eagle and Phenix mills), lit up the surroundings with a bright but mellow glow. It was said to burn as bright as daylight, and next to it gas light "fade[d] into nothingness." The Brush Light replaced the lighted pine knot torch which until then had been used for lighting. The flaming "light wood" (or "light'erd") was extremely dangerous because it often burst into sparks that landed on the highly flammable cotton bales.[13] In addition to the Brush Light, there was also a searchlight purchased from the United States Electric Light Company. This was the same "bull's eye" that train locomotives were using in those days. These concentrated lenses projected light for hundreds of yards during nocturnal navigation.[14]

The *Chattahoochee,* another plush steamer of the early 1880s, had a steel hull and was 155 feet long. Its staterooms accommodated up to fifty white passengers, and rooms in the texas could sleep up to eighteen black passengers. The spacious staterooms were paneled in bird's-eye maple and mahogany. The walls of the saloon were "finished in black walnut and bird's eye maple, with embossed papier-mache panels."[15] Crimson velvet covered furniture, and revolving chairs and steam heaters adorned the saloon, which was adjoined by bathrooms and a barbershop. The galley was situated above the dining room, and meals were passed down on a dumbwaiter.

Traveling on one of these moving palaces was a memorable experience for J. Truman Holland, who, as a lad in the 1890s, boarded the glistening *Naiad* at Eufaula with his mother. The *Naiad* was probably the best-known steamer that ever plied the river, since it held the record for the longest continuous service on the Chattahoochee. It was named for the water nymphs of ancient lore who lived in and gave life to bodies of water.[16] Holland remembered that he was clad in a white sailor suit and standing at the top of the steps leading to the Eufaula landing when the

The *Naiad,* a well-known Chattahoochee steamer. *Courtesy of the Florida State Archives Photographic Collection.*

Naiad came into view: "The echo of the whistle, the ripples chasing one another across the river as the prow divided the water, the passengers waving on the upper deck, the joyful crewmen shouting their greetings, and the soft music of the bell, all recorded on memory's tape, have never lost their charm."[17]

The *Naiad's* dining room was set on the upper deck. The room was brilliantly lighted, the tables gleaming with white cloths and polished silverware. "Dress was formal. The men wore dinner jackets and black ties. The ladies were in the intriguing style of the gay nineties, low cut necklines, leg-of-mutton sleeves, small tightly bound waists and long billowing skirts. Some of the ladies had ostrich plumes in their hair and around their shoulders scarves of fluted Irish lace."

Waiters moved noiselessly among the tables in their "spotless white uniforms," while dinner conversations were quiet but convivial. Holland recalled that having a meal aboard the *Naiad* "was one of the rare moments of life when trouble and worry did not dare intrude."[18] Boat cooks were renowned for the flavor and abundance of their fare. On the down

108   trips there were "plenty of hot biscuits, hot cakes, meats, vegetables, pastries and the like."[19] Returning from Apalachicola, plates brimmed with fresh shrimp, oysters, and fish.

Lemon slices floating in finger bowls of warm water signified that the meal was over. The stewards cleared the tables, and some men gathered in a corner to play poker. Other passengers walked outside to sit and watch the scenery. From the back decks, visitors watched as the water spray was flung into the air by the stern wheel. To a youngster, it looked "like thousands of diamonds in the sunlight." As the sun sank behind the trees on the western bank and "twilight and shadows of night crept in from the east," the tranquillity was "broken only by the low swishing sound of the boat plowing through the water." Birds flew to their roosts and whippoorwills called to each other as "bright acetylene lamps were turned on all over the boat, around which thousands of candle flies circled in huge glowing balls. . . . Then as if coming from some enchanted realm, the Negro crewmen, sitting upon bales of cotton below, began to sing. The steep banks, topped by the walls of the woodland, made a perfect sounding box, blending the voices of the singers into perfect harmony." Lulled by the music, the fresh air, and the night sounds, the passengers were soon soundly sleeping in their staterooms.[20]

Yet not all first-class passengers experienced the same accommodations or service during these days of Jim Crow segregation. An unnamed African-American sailor boarded the steamer *George W. Wylly* in 1876 after paying first-class fare, but instead of being assigned a first-class stateroom he was shown to the quarters reserved for "servants." At dinner he sat down with his two white companions at a first-class table. The steward asked him to leave and "wait his turn" to eat, but he refused, saying that since he had paid full fare he meant to have it. The ship's clerk came in at this moment with a knife, caught the man by the ear, and led him away.[21]

Although the color line that ran down the decks was indelible, all passengers could enjoy the scenery and the slow pace of river travel. To pass the time, some entertained themselves by playing cards or the piano. Some read. Children played with the boat's mascot. "Q.C." was a game rooster who perched himself on the top of the *Queen City*'s boiler after the sun went down, but during the day it promenaded the boat, looking for a handout. Other sojourners kept travel logs. Many used the time away from their workplace to rest. The refreshing breezes, the lush scenery, and the drone of the engine hypnotized them into slumber. As one

Women posing on the *Queen City* at rest at a river landing. *Courtesy of the Columbus Museum.*

traveler put it, "Oh! the splendid rest, how welcome to the weary one! Reading became burdensome, it seemed much best to do simply nothing."[22]

But just as some passengers were nodding off in their deck chairs, there came the crack and boom of rifle shot. The ruckus was caused by men shooting at alligators from the guard railing. Shooting *at* them was considered quite a sport, although few were actually killed. In answer to most attempts by the marksmen, the gator "slyly wink[ed] the other eye, and dropp[ed] quietly out of sight." One fellow admitted that he had wasted two boxes of cartridges before finally bagging one on the return trip.[23]

Another traveler wrote that he was enjoying the peaceful beauty of the scenery from the pilothouse, "fairly drinking in the entrancing spectacle" as the band below struck up a sweet song, "when bang! bang! the illusion was roughly dispelled by the well aimed shot of one of our vigilant sportsmen, and as we looked in the direction of the shot, a huge alligator reeled over into his watery grave." While people hurrahed from

110   the lower deck, this man's "sweet contemplations" came to an end as other hunters rushed over to join in the sport.[24]

There was other excitement aboard. Certain stretches in the river were dangerous to pass through, and notice of this fact was given the passengers by the pilot's ringing of bells in order to signal directions to the engineer. Down on the lower river was the spot where the river had been obstructed by the Confederates in order to keep the Union gunboats from coming upstream. The obstruction had forced the water to cut a new channel and made navigation particularly treacherous. The current ran as swiftly here as in a mill race. Turns were very short.[25]

> It was a continual jong-a-long (stop her), jing-a-long (back her), jong-a-long (stop backing), jing-a-long, jing-a-long (come back on her slow), jong-a-long (stop her), jong-a-long, jing-a-ling (come ahead slow), jing-a-ling (increase to usual speed) and jong-a-long, jing-a-ling (stop and back for the next position). This is kept up all the time while going . . . a distance of about three miles through the narrows. . . . In making this distance a minimum of 88 bells must be rung and answered by the engineer, and in many cases twice that number is obliged to be rung.[26]

Passing upstream through the Narrows, the crew used lines to pull the boat against the rushing water. Running this at night was an unforgettable experience. One man recalled: "At certain points, lines are put out and then the snorting of engines, voices of command, negroes with lights crashing through the cane thickets, strange weird shadows cast across the rushing, narrow stream, and the roaring of a strong wind through the dense forest—all create a wild scene of fantastic attraction."[27]

At times, there was plenty of drama on even the calmer stretches of the river. For instance, in 1897 a lady gave birth while the steamboat was aground. The baby girl was named Florence Naiad—Naiad for the steamer and Florence for the nearest landing.[28]

Though today's passengers would consider any stop to be lost time, yesterday's travelers enjoyed the diversion of calling on the many landings along the way. So did those on shore. As a child, Meddye Tipton Willis took her first trip on a Chattahoochee steamer in 1911. Stopping at steamboat landings was her favorite part of the trip. Waiting on the banks were always a dozen or more wagons. Women cooked over big fires while children ran to watch the stevedores load and unload the freight. Everyone enjoyed listening to their songs. People laughed and children played. According to Willis, each stop required a couple of hours. "And all through the night that happened, and I can remember . . . just sitting on the deck, wrapped in a quilt at past midnight, and . . . at every plantation down the river that was the procedure, regardless of the time of night, the family was there having a picnic, . . . and it was a family affair."[29]

Even the more urban landings had similar goings-on. In towns like Columbia in the southeastern corner of Alabama, a camping ground was set aside near one of the landings so that people had a place to pull up their wagons and livestock. Some people slept overnight in their covered wagons so as not to miss the boat.[30]

At river towns, the residents dropped whatever they were doing when they heard the steamer's whistle. Housewives were particularly expectant of the boats' arrival as the Christmas season neared. November was fruit-cake month. Young girls went down to the landing to claim their orders of nutmeg, cinnamon, and candied fruit.[31] Spices were only one of the deliveries made at Christmastime. During the holidays of 1885, for instance, the freight list of the *Rebecca Everingham* included 930 "jugs."[32]

The country landings were usually distinguished from each other by some unique geographical feature. One of the landings at Columbia was marked by a huge brown rock that everyone called "the chocolate layer cake."[33] The picturesque Ochesee Landing on the lower river was marked by two enormous live oaks. Each tree measured twenty-three feet in circumference at the base of its trunk. The canopy formed by their spreading branches covered more than an acre and invited a stroll or a picnic.[34]

Neal's Landing, just one mile south of the Alabama line on the lower river, was one of the most important landings for south Alabama and north Florida. It boasted a two-story hotel, livery stables, two large store-rooms, a post office, a two-story ginhouse, a cotton press, and a cotton storage shed. A warehouse situated directly on the water's edge measured forty by eighty feet. Its second floor was above the high-water mark, and an elevator made it easy to hoist freight up to it.[35]

The river's busiest wharf was always inadequate. At the end of the Civil War, the Columbus landing was so pitted with gullies that it was impossible for the drays to get up the hill. "Such approaches are known only to a one horse town," complained a citizen in 1865.[36] Fifteen years later, the wharf was still in a state of disrepair. In high water, there was no dock at all. Rain transformed the banks into a "mess of slush, through which mules and men toil painfully."[37] In 1895 the wharf was described as "an eye-sore, as well as a discomfort, to the public."[38]

People were still complaining about the landing in 1900: "The mud at the wharf is disgraceful. It is so deep and sticky that the teams can hardly pull through it. Every bale of river cotton that is handled here gets a liberal coating. Springs have developed in the middle of the roadway there, and the constant use that it is put to has caused the roadway in some places to be two feet deep in a nasty, slimy, yellow mud. . . . All the boatmen . . . are complaining."[39]

Construction of a stone retaining wall was begun in 1899 and completed the following year, but the landing between this wall and the bank needed to be filled in and paved. The city also needed a dockmaster to oversee landings and departures. Steamers pulled up to the dock in the order they arrived. Smaller boats and barges tied up wherever they could. Departing boats had to load across idle vessels standing between the wharf and the outgoing steamer.[40]

Even as late as World War I, the wharf was in need of improvement. At that date, it was described as a wooden deck supported by a rubble retaining wall on the waterside and resting on the riverbank on the back side. Day laborers loaded and unloaded freight by hand because the wharf was too rough and uneven for them to use hand trucks. There was no public waterside warehouse or convenient railroad connection.[41]

Eufaula had better facilities. In 1916 the Alabama wharf was located under the tall bluff leading into town. It consisted of a rock wall filled in behind with dirt and cinders. This dock was owned by the Eufaula Grocery Company (which was associated with the Merchants and Planters Steamboat Company), and it had an adjoining warehouse.[42]

Approximately thirty miles downriver, at Fort Gaines, there was a simple natural landing at the foot of a high bluff. A warehouse stood halfway up the bluff, and an inclined track led from the landing at the water's edge to the warehouse. Laborers winched freight up the tracks with a capstan and slid freight to be loaded through a chute. Further downstream at Columbia, a natural landing with a warehouse owned by the Chattahoochee Grocery Company connected to a side track of the Central of Georgia Railroad. The Atlantic Coast Line Railroad owned a small warehouse near Alaga, Alabama.[43]

Thanks to the invention of labor-saving devices, life was becoming a little easier in this new industrial age. Urban people found they had a few hours of free time to enjoy themselves, and "excursions," or day trips, became popular. Riverboat men promoted these outings to encourage water travel at a time when the railroads were stealing many of their passengers. As early as 1867 the captain of the steamer *White Rose* tried to promote such an excursion. Captain Mills advertised that if a troupe of up to one hundred passengers could be collected, he would transport them from Columbus to Apalachicola and back for only half price, or twenty-five dollars each. He even offered to take along an orchestra for free. This captain's idea was, however, ahead of the times. The trip did not take place, and it would be over a decade before excursions became popular on the Chattahoochee.

The first account of a postwar-era river excursion was published in 1878. The Young America Fire Company No. 5 sponsored a day's outing on the *George W. Wylly* for a picnic at Wright's Landing. The boat left the Columbus wharf early in the morning, and as soon as they arrived at their destination the men hurriedly hammered together a dance platform. After dinner on the grounds, the dancing commenced and continued until the whistle of the steamer summoned everyone aboard. On the upriver run, the excursionists danced and sang their way home. The crowd was small on this first outing, but the fire company cleared expenses, and everyone had so much fun that it inspired others to raise funds in this way.[44]

Party barge excursion on the Chattahoochee. Note the musicians on right. *Courtesy of T. W. Tillman and the Columbus Museum.*

Only one week later, the Sunny South Brass Band copied the fire company's motif by selling round-trip tickets to Wright's Landing for only seventy-five cents. This time there was a boatload. Three hundred people packed aboard the *Jordan* as it departed the Columbus wharf early one spring morning, leaving behind one tardy passenger who stumbled headlong into his picnic baskets. As the unfortunate one wiped meringue from his broad face, the boatmen cast off, and the Sunny South Band began a recital on the hurricane deck. Simultaneously, down below an African-American string band played "beautiful waltzes and cotillions, to which nimble feet tripped to measure."[45] The May air was filled with the sounds of birds chirping and music playing.

At the picnic site, the excursionists danced on the now-canopied dance platform for four hours. The band sold ice cream, cake, and lemonade and offered ice water to the thirsty. In the afternoon as they returned upriver, a father-and-son duo sang operatic selections upstairs, while downstairs the deckhands performed a stag dance. Everyone had a grand time, and the band members made enough money to purchase a new set of instruments.[46]

The following spring brought more excursions. The City Light Guards of Columbus sponsored a day on the river aboard the *Mary Elizabeth*. Like the others, this outing also boasted dancing and ice cream. But the militia added to the festivities a shooting match for the ladies. To the men's surprise, there were quite a few good marksmen among the "gentler sex," and the scribe of the occasion felt obliged to give them their credit: "Man . . . ignores her as being fit only to contribute to his tastes, to give joy to his griefs, to add comfort to his trouble and be an ornament to his home. That she is successful in all the acquirements none will deny. . . . That she can do more than these if the necessity requires it, the contest of to-day demonstrates."[47] This day of frolic closed with a "hop" at the Villa Reich, a place of recreation on the riverbank at Columbus.[48]

Other excursions toured all the way to the bay and back. One troupe, consisting of a few young women "under the command of a staid matron" as chaperon and young men "under command of a gallant Captain," whiled away the time on the down voyage playing games, reading books, and making music.[49] At the coast, the ladies stayed on St. James Island with Oliver H. Kelly (founder of the Grange, or Patrons of Husbandry, a national farmers organization) while the men found quarters in a boardinghouse owned by a black man named William Fuller, who was renowned for his mouth-watering meals of fresh oysters and fish.

These adventurers chartered a schooner for three days, each spent on the islands protecting Apalachicola Bay from the Gulf of Mexico. There they walked the beach, collecting seashells. One night they missed the boat's return to town and spent the night on St. Vincent Island in a vacated dwelling. They found a haunch of venison to feast on, then walked down to the beach and spent hours singing sea songs and dancing the Virginia reel under a bright moon.

The rest of the night did not go as well. Imagine seven ladies sharing one mattress in a hot, stuffy room swarming with hungry mosquitoes. The party kept their spirits high, though. One young lady remarked at daybreak, "I thought I should be dead, but I feel real nice." The men caught perch in the lake for breakfast, and eventually their schooner reclaimed them.[50]

Men often formed fishing excursions to the bay or to the Dead Lakes, a body of black water off the Apalachicola River where stood thousands of dead or dying cypress trees. In witnessing the Columbus departure of the "Red Snappers" on their annual pilgrimage to the coast, one would have thought these men were leaving for war. Tears streaked the faces of the loved ones left behind, and "even some gentlemen ran the back of their hands over their eyes to rub away the glistening tear."[51] The crusty captain noted, however, that part of the waterworks might be attributed to the ladies' standing in a patch of wild onions.

Since the boat was chartered, it stopped only to take on wood, or when aground. (In the latter case, the passengers got out and pushed it over the shoal.) There was no music on this trip—only the crack of rifle shot as the men took turns firing at birds, alligators, or anything else that moved in the surrounding wilderness. Once near the coast, they stopped often to fish. Nights were spent in telling ghost stories—like the one about the ghost who lived at Smith's Bend.

There, in the days before the Civil War, an old black man lived in a hut. Recent hunters had discovered his body, lying in a heap with his five pet alligators and a dog, all of them dead. Some months afterward, "just as the roosters were crowing for midnight," a witness saw the old man "sitting stiff and motionless in his bateau, which was being drawn to the river by the shadowy forms of five alligators, yoked two abreast, and in the lead crouched on the neck of the leading reptile was the form of a dog" with phosphorescent insects lighting his eye sockets. The entourage glided into the water, then eventually veered back to the old man's hut, a fish tail protruding from each gator's mouth. Henry Moore, captain of the *Jordan*, claimed to have seen the "Black Ghost of Smith's Bend" more than once.[52]

Other excursions were planned strictly with romance in mind. One such outing was a moonlight trip aboard the *Mary Elizabeth* in 1879. As the craft glided downstream in the river breeze, an orchestra serenaded everyone "on deck and below deck, from the capstan to the aftpart, . . . in the saloon and on the hurricane deck, and even in the pilot house, where two is company, and three considered an immense crowd." Some danced, others chatted. When just five miles from town, the captain tied up the boat to a tree. Fireflies danced in the darkness. The group listened to a harpist and waited for the moon to rise. At last the silver orb broke through the cypress trees, bathing the couples in a flood of blue light. With this romantic ambience, it is no wonder the excursion was pronounced a "strict social success."[53]

A similar soiree was held in the early 1880s when a group of prominent young bachelors planned a "voyage de luxe" with an orchestra for dancing and hampers of baked goods, turkeys, and hams for a midnight champagne dinner. Cupid's arrow was right on target this evening. Three couples soon announced their engagements. Later imitations of this cruise towed a barge for dancing, with seats around the inside rails for the spectators and chaperons.[54]

One did not have to board a standard steamboat to find entertainment on the Chattahoochee. In 1891 a Professor Moore painted his "Ark and Floating Theatre" red outside and blue inside and refurbished the stage for another tour down the river with his "Fat Woman, Snake Charmer, rope walkers, and other wonders."[55]

Those who were lucky enough to ride a steamboat in the late nineteenth century never forgot their experience, for few lived in such opulence or were favored with such pampering as those travelers. Of course, the life of the officers and crew of the steamers appeared to the passengers to be quite idyllic. The officers in their starched white uniforms treated the women like queens and the men like gentlemen, rising in an emergency to the level of heroes. Even the lowly stevedores were celebrities. Their amazing dexterity always drew a crowd as they loaded a vessel, and their work songs were legendary. Steamboat employees appeared to be having the times of their life. But what was it really like to work on a steamboat?

CHAPTER 7

Workin' the River

H OW A PERSON REGARDED THE CHATTAHOOCHEE River depended on one's perspective. Passengers dallying on the upper decks saw the river as an enchanted highway. But to a boatman, the river was a beautiful tyrant. It charmed you into submission, but it could just as easily take your life. Working on the river was physically demanding. It required long hours with little sleep, days away from loved ones, backbreaking labor, and even the threat of death.

The master of the steamboat earned the respect of passengers honestly. The safety of passengers and crew depended on how well he knew the river and his boat. The job description required him to be "a master mechanic, a first rate plumber, a better-than-average carpenter and something of a naval architect."[1] He had to understand physics well enough to comprehend the principles of steam power, the performance of certain metals under extreme pressure, and the construction and mechanics of extremely complicated and dangerous machinery.

Passengers glimpsed him commanding the wheel or charming them in the dining hall in his starched white trousers, but these were only a small part of his job description. When the passengers did not see him, he was often below decks, reading pressure gauges and watching for mechanical malfunctions or boiler leaks. The steam engine was a dangerous beast. Constant vigilance was required to keep it from exploding like a bomb. Even though an engineer tended it, the threat of explosion was too great to merely delegate the responsibility to others.

In addition to having a knowledge of the mechanics of his boat, the captain also had to know the river. A steamboat captain was also a river pilot. A steamboat ran night and day, regardless of the weather. The pilot

Columbus Sun Print.

Table of Distances on Apalachicola, Chattahoochee and Flint Rivers: Presented by Steamer Shamrock.

Apalachicola River.

* Apalachicola,		Fla.
Iola,	75	"
Porter's,		"
Riccoes' Bluff,		"
Estiffanulga,	23 98	"
Jackson Wood's		"
Sim Baker's		"
C. R. Gregory		"
J. I. Griffin		"
West Wynnton		"
Blountstown		"
† Bristol	22 120	"
Rock Bluff		"
Ochesee		"
Coe		"
‡ Aspalaga	22 142	"
‡ Cedar Bluff		"
† Chattahoochee	8 150	"

Chattahoochee River.

Hawley's		Fla.
Hare's		Ga.
Geo. Robinson's		Fla.
Birds		Ga.
Trawick's		"
Raines'		Fla.
‡ Port Jackson	13 163	"
Painter's		"
‡ Bellvue	5 168	"
† New Bartow		"
Drury Rambo		Ga.
Mc Hunter's		Fla.
John P. Dickerson		Ga.
Dickerson, St'm. Mills		"
† Neil's Landing	12 180	Fla
Crawford's		Ga.
Allen's		"
Ely's		Fla.
Mrs. Gibson's		Ga.
Donaldson's		"
Perry's		Ala.
Shewmake's		Ga.
Saffold's		Ala.
Johnson's		Ga.
Aleck Hays		"
† Gordon	14 194	Ala.
Amelia		Ga.
Porter's Ferry		Ga.
Durham's		Ala.

Shackleford's		Ga.
Wilson's		Ala.
Speights		Ga.
A. C. Fullmore's		Ala.
Dr. Corbin's		Ga.
† Columbia	15 209	Ala
Broom's		Ga.
McDonald's		"
Alford's		Ala.
Purcell		"
Hardwick's		"
Price		"
T. T. Smith's		"
‡ Howards	14 223	Ga.
Wingate's		Ala.
Chambers		Ala.
‡ Gilbert's		Ga.
Stamper's		"
Mrs. Chitty's		Ala.
M. E. Barnett's		"
Mrs. Bennett's		Ala.
Martin Bennett's		Ga.
Bennett's		Ala.
Mrs. Colby's		Ga.
Clarke's		Ala.
Jeff. Farmer's		"
† Fort Gaines	13 241	Ga.
† Franklin	1 242	Ala.
Mrs. Spanu's		"
Mandeville		Ga.
Rick's Lower		"
Mrs. McCoy's		Ala.
Starke's Clay Place		Ga.
Berry's		"
† Otho	10 252	Ala.
Matthews		"
Willcox		"
Castlebury		Ga.
Alexander's		"
Williams'		Ala.
Rick's Home Place		Ga.
Zeke Alexander's		Ala.
McTyer's		"
Shorter's		Ga.
Dowdey		Ala.
Doctor Thornton's		"
James Flewellen's		Ga.
* Eufaula	25 277	Ala.
† Georgetown		Ga.
McGhee		Ala.
Flournoy's		"
Starke's Shep'd Place		Ga.

Wiley's		Ala.
Starke's Home Place		Ga.
Dr. Hill's		Ala.
Rankin's		Ga.
Rood's		"
Dawson's Lower		Ala.
Roanoke		Ga.
Gabe Toombs		"
Williams'		Ala.
Turner's		Ga.
† Florence, Up'r & Lw'r	25 302	"
Shepperd's		"
‡ Jernigan	5 307	Ala
Fontaine's Lower		Ga.
Fitzgerald's		"
Hurt's		Ala.
Fontaine's Middle	10 317	Ga.
Towns'		Ala.
Fontaine's Upper	3 320	Ga.
Boykin's		Ala.
Chesnut L'dg		Ga.
Cottonton		Ala.
Flewellen's		Ga.
Dawson's Upper		Ala.
G. Y. Banks' Lower	12 332	Ga.
Fitzsimmons'		Ala.
Wright's Lower	5 337	"
Magruder's		Ga.
D. C. Cody's		"
Wright's Upper		Ala.
Chambers'		"
W. F. Alexander's		Ga.
Benton's		Ala.
Fort Mitchell		"
* Columbus	30 367	Ga.

Flint River.

Chattahoochee to			
Gaulding's	4		Ga.
Widow White's			"
Wiley's Ld'g			"
Fort Scott			"
Early White's			"
‡ Hutchinson	16	20	"
Lundy's			"
Patterson's			"
Munnerlyn's	13	33	"
Cloud's			"
Arnett's			"
‡ Whitaker's			"
* Bainbridge	12	45	"

* Cities.   † Towns.   ‡ Warehouses.

List of Chattahoochee landings for the steamboat *Shamrock* and a table of distances. *Courtesy of Frank Schnell.*

had to know the river's idiosyncracies. Every bend and shoal, each dangerous rock and snag had to be avoided, even when visibility was im-
peded by fog or night. He had to be aware of the depth of water, whether
it was rising or falling, and at what rate, so that he would not get stranded
on a sandbar or crunched under a bridge.

To become certified as a pilot, a man had to apprentice for three
years, then gather the signatures of three older, licensed pilots under
whom he had learned his trade. Every five years he had to renew his
license by standing for a written examination given by the United States
Board of Steamboat Inspectors.[2]

The job was a hazardous one. In 1887, Captain T. A. "Bose" Marcrum,
standing on the gangway of his boat loading flour at Bainbridge, got
caught between the vessel and a runaway hand truck. The blow hurled
him twenty feet, and he fell unconscious. Following the work ethic required of boat masters, he went back to work as soon as he revived. A
year later this same officer found himself again in harm's way. When the
engine died on the *Amos Hays,* the boat pounded into the Pensacola and
Alabama Railroad bridge, which was not high enough for his boat to pass
under. Marcrum leapt down from the pilothouse just as it tore away, "sustaining severe bruises and flesh wounds."[3]

Whenever a ship sank or caught fire, the officers were expected
to keep cool heads and to save the passengers and the ship, if possible.
When Hezikiah Wingate's new boat *Alice* struck a snag near Rico's Bend

The *Queen City* at Fort Gaines. *Courtesy of the Columbus Museum.*

120   on the lower river, the captain tried his best to save her. He rushed below and squeezed quilts and mattresses into the gaping hole, but the freight shifted and trapped him below. He went down with the ship.[4]

Late one foggy night as Captain O. M. Sparks was steering the *W. D. Chipley* near Fort Gaines, he was blinded by the light that someone was waving from ashore. Just then the vessel struck a pointed boulder in the bank of the river with such force that it made a gash more than twelve feet long. Water rushed in. Captain Sparks called for the electric lights, and with them he could see everyone in "immense confusion." People jumped overboard. As the boat listed to starboard, cotton tumbled over into the river. Swimmers caught hold of the floating bales, and the swift current carried them downstream. So many tried to jump into the lifeboat that the pilot brandished a piece of firewood to prevent them from sinking it. The officers and crew eventually got the steamer tied up near shore, and Sparks believed that if the passengers had stayed aboard as ordered and not panicked, the ten who perished would not have drowned.[5]

One of the worst steamboat disasters ever was the wreck of the *George W. Wylly* in 1883. The water was high and the current treacherous as the *Wylly* steamed downstream. At the covered bridge at Fort Gaines the river itself was running ten miles an hour. As the vessel went under the bridge, it was caught in a boil of water which slammed the *Wylly* against the bridge piling so hard that the boat broke in two and sank instantly. Passengers and crew alike were thrown into the mad river. They grabbed planking, barrels, or anything else floating and rode them for miles in the midnight darkness until the river spit them out in the swamp downstream.

The officers and crew of the *Wylly* risked their lives to save the passengers and their belongings. The purser, a clerk, and eight deckhands perished. Only three passengers died. Herndon Palmer, the purser, had gone back to save the ship's papers, and was never seen again until his body was found floating in the water ten miles below Columbia. The steamer *Thronateeska* picked it up and brought it to the Columbus wharf, where hundreds of people waited in silence to escort the coffin to the cemetery.

Besides the dangers that the river posed, the passengers themselves occasionally threatened the safety of the crew. Southern society in the post–Civil War "Gilded Age" was a violent one. Guns and other weapons were ever-present, and boatmen often needed to defend themselves or others. When a well-dressed African-American took first-class passage on board the steamer *Apalachee* no one dreamed he would turn out to be a dangerous man, but when the porter went up to his stateroom to collect his fare, the man refused to pay. When the porter went back later to demand it, the passenger pulled out a pistol and shot him in the chest. Officers rushed upstairs to find the man standing over the porter's body clutching a smoking revolver. The captain knocked the weapon out of the man's hand, and others helped lock the assailant in a room with iron bars securing the windows. Fortunately, the bullet hit a button on the porter's uniform, and he lived.

The black man was sent ashore to jail and was charged with attempted murder, but a justice of the peace turned him loose. The river men had no intention of letting him off. They sent telegrams up and down the river describing him and urging his arrest. The man was eventually captured and taken aboard the *Fannie Fearn* to Apalachicola, where he was held until the grand jury could meet. There is no record of his fate beyond the Apalachicola jail.[6]

Sometimes passengers came aboard in the midst of a feud and fights broke out on deck. When "a Dago named Scott" who was standing on the lower deck got into an argument with a man on the riverbank, "they abused each other terribly" until the man standing on the shore grabbed a couple of bricks and heaved them at the other. The missiles struck him on the cheek and killed him. There was no ceremony about disposing of this corpse. The crew stopped at the next landing, unloaded his body onto the riverbank, and shoved off again.[7]

The river men were not always innocent bystanders in angry altercations. Occasionally, rival captains came to blows themselves. On Christmas Eve 1888, Frank Lapham of the *William D. Ellis* and his competitor Charlie Wingate of the steamer *Fannie Fearn* were both drinking when their quarrel turned into a brawl. Lapham threw a chair at Wingate's head, smashing the chair to pieces, then lunged at him with a knife and cut his face. At that point others broke up the fight, and the two were hauled down to the police headquarters. However, Lapham got into another fracas three months later as his steamer lay at the Columbus wharf. By the time the police got there, though, Lapham was sleeping soundly below in "the arms of Morpheus."[8]

In return for the long hours and perilous work, the officers of a steamboat received certain perquisites. The best of these was probably the food. The proof of the abundance and quality of the food aboard boats such as the *Glide* was the "rotund and healthful appearance of the officers and crew."[9] Besides the generous grub, the men enjoyed the respect of their patrons. The officers were celebrities whose arrival in town brought them notice in the local newspaper. As soon as their boats landed, the wharf was crowded with important people who wanted to learn the latest news from the other end of the river. Women admired their crisp white uniforms and their exotic life. Some officers met their shy future brides on the job. One such was Captain Poley McDaniel, who spied a pretty young girl at one of the landings. It was love at first sight. Soon they were married, and she was helping out in the galley and even occasionally steering the boat.[10]

As for officers' pay, it was adequate in good economic times, but whenever a panic hit (and there were big ones in the 1870s, 1880s, and 1890s) the men suffered substantial wage cuts. Their labor union, the Marine Officers' Federation, pushed for restoration of wage rates during good times. In 1901 the members received a 20 percent raise, which actually only served to restore their wages to the rates given in the pre-recession era.[11]

Under the officers' authority were a host of other workers. Stevedores, or "roustabouts," handled the freight. (In Eufaula these jobs were separate. "Rolladores" rolled cotton bales down long wooden chutes from the top of the bluff; stevedores stowed the cotton on board.)[12] Firemen fed wood into the roaring boilers in the engine room. Pursers acted as clerks. The engineers operated the steam engines according to the pilots' commands. Chambermaids tidied the staterooms. Cooks prepared the sumptuous meals in the steamy galley while stewards served the guests. Some of these, no doubt, pulled double duty.

The lower deck of the boat, where the dangerous boiler transformed water into steam power, was the domain of the African-American deckhands. A dozen of them were usually required per trip. While the boat was under way, stevedores enjoyed a break from work. As the firemen stoked the fires which turned the great paddle wheel, the deckhands sat around on the cotton bales and barrels, talking, napping, or playing cards. In the evenings, passengers came downstairs to listen to them sing.

Their songs were simple, usually consisting of only a few lines, but grandly elaborated by each troubadour in turn. As in the tradition of the African-American church, there was usually a shouter who jumped into the midst of the melodious circle, swinging his arms and echoing the words of the rest of the choir. To the rhythm of the lively songs, the stevedores clapped their hands and stomped their feet as their faces reflected the red glow of the furnace. A reporter for the *Columbus Enquirer-Sun* in 1894 noted that religious songs were accompanied by "demure and serious countenances." But at the conclusion of each song, "however short, and no matter what kind, everybody must have a drink to clear up the voice." They passed the spirits around from one to another "in an alligator-brand, oyster can."[13]

Here is one of the songs they sang on a moonlit Chattahoochee night in 1894:

WHOA, MULE WHOA!

De moon and de stars,
De stars in de heaben are shin' as bright,
That's what Uncle Gabriel's preachin about
Down in de church house,
On his knees.

Dere's no use talkin' bout de moon and stars,
It's whoa, mule, whoa!
Doan you hear him holler,
Tie a knot in his tail, and he'll jump through his collar.
Why doan you put him on de track,
Every time he turn around,
It's whoa, mule, whoa!

Didn't dat mule go wash, go wash,
Give him a little more hay
Dere stans de old ship by de ocean deep
Dey tell me dat, she reel and she rock,
From de bottom to de top,
By de ocean deep.
     Ti ty i ty um tum,
     Ty ty i oh—
     Ty ty i ty um tum,
     Ty ty i ty oh—
     May God bless you all.[14]

Sometimes the deckhands painted their faces with black grease and came up to the upper deck before footlights where they put on an exceptional show for the mostly white passengers, blowing "gullspat juba," jumping "Jim Crow," and cutting the "double shuffle." They were always a hit.[15]

During the day, or whenever the boat stopped to take on freight, the

The *W. S. Holt* at the Columbus wharf. *Courtesy of the Columbus Museum.*

The *Hard Times* unloading Chattahoochee cotton downriver. *Courtesy of the Florida State Archives Photographic Collection.*

The *Three States* loading freight on the Chattahoochee. *Courtesy of the Fred Wickham Collection.*

The *Queen City* being loaded with cotton in the early twentieth century. *Courtesy of the Florida State Archives Photographic Collection.*

The *City of Eufaula* loading with cotton near Eufaula, Alabama. *Courtesy of the Florida State Archives Photographic Collection.*

Loading cotton at the Columbus dock. *Courtesy of the Eagle and Phenix Collection, Columbus College Archives.*

stevedores entertained onlookers with another talent: their amazing dexterity. "I could sit all day and watch the deck hands come down the bank with barrels of spirits and rosin with the greatest ease," wrote a sojourner at the turn of the century. With the barrels spinning before them, the stevedores ran down the steep hills to the boat. They moved so fast that they appeared to be running out of control, but they knew how to put a spin on the barrel so that it curved or stopped abruptly "as though it knew his wishes."[16] Sometimes it took two of them to restrain a barrel as it rolled down a bank. Heavy cotton bales were permitted to tumble down of their own will while men at both ends of the incline used hooks to guide them. "By the time it hit the gangplanks it was bouncing like a ball."[17] On deck, two roustabouts caught it, still bouncing, and stacked the bales two or three high. To keep in rhythm with each other, the workers chanted something like the following, which was heard on the steamboat *South Carolina* in the 1850s:

> We're up the Chattahoochee
> On the good ole South Ca' lina
> Goin' to see my true love.
> How are you my darlin'?
> Now the work is over.
> We're all comin' home![18]

This was dangerous work. Roustabouts often got their hands caught between a barrel and the edge of the wharf, smashing hands or severing fingers. The force of a tumbling four-hundred-pound cotton bale could easily knock a man out. Furthermore, since their work stationed them on the boiler deck, the stevedores and firemen were the first ones injured when the machinery exploded. Many also drowned after falling overboard.

In 1876, two workers were lost in a single night on a boat plying the Flint River. A steward noiselessly fell overboard from the roundhouse and the stern wheel hammered into him. The engineer heard the wheel thumping against something. Thinking he had hit a log, he stopped the engines but found nothing and proceeded. Only later when the officers needed the steward's services in giving a passenger a room did they realize what had happened. That same night, a deckhand, apparently blinded by the light of the torches, stepped overboard and was never seen again. At Christmastime in 1900, in two separate incidents, a fireman and a deckhand fell overboard.[19]

128   Fatigue caused many accidents. The hands were on call twenty-four hours a day when the boat was moving. Even though they rested between stops, they sprang to work at every landing, rain or shine, stowing and unloading freight. Since a round trip to the bay took six days, the roustabouts went a week before getting a full night's sleep. Nelson Hortman was napping on deck of the *W. C. Bradley* when he and the others were roused to prepare for the next landing. Groggily he walked over to the guardrail and stretched. He lost his balance and fell into the river. The captain immediately stopped the boat to search for him, but he never found Hortman's body.[20]

The roustabouts were the most vulnerable when an accident occurred, especially if the accident involved a boiler explosion, since they were quartered around this ticking time bomb. When the boiler of the little steamer *Chipola* exploded in 1867, four of the six deaths and three of the four wounded were black crew members.[21] When the *George W.*

Chattahoochee stevedores. *Courtesy of the Columbus Museum.*

Stevedore at the Columbus dock in the early twentieth century. *Courtesy of the Columbus Museum.*

Wylly went down after striking the bridge at Fort Gaines late one night in 1883, eight of the thirteen who drowned were deckhands.

As the deckhands lay asleep on their quilts around the boiler of the *Julia St. Clair* in 1873, it exploded, blowing one overboard to his death and burning two others to death instantly. Ten others were so badly scalded that they screamed for God to take them. Their wails of agony echoed out over the water and drifted back from every direction to the horrified passengers. None of the passengers were injured, as was often the case. Most of them simply gathered their belongings and walked to Eufaula, where they took a train home.[22]

Fire was a constant danger to crew members. Cotton was highly flammable. All it took was one spark to set the cargo ablaze. This is how the *Rebecca Everingham* went down in 1884. The wind was howling when the cotton caught fire, and the flames raced throughout the ship. Panicked passengers in their nightclothes leapt into the river. Before the vessel could be turned into the shore, flames were "leaping far above the roof and meeting over the pilot house."[23] Of the eight persons who perished in the flames, six were black crew members: a chambermaid, a pantry man, a fireman, two deckhands, and a stevedore.

Sam "Hog" Stafford was a deckhand on the *J. W. Hires* the night it caught fire. In the shouting and confusion as men ran to save themselves, Hog ran back to the boat to rescue his pet rooster. He was "just about off the doomed boat" when the flapping rooster flew out of his hands and back into the flames. The rooster perished, and Hog was the last person to get off the boat before she went under.[24]

Besides falling victim to an accident, virtually every black deckhand was verbally or physically abused by his superiors. Chattahoochee deckhands were subjected to a spew of profanity by the officers who shouted directions to them from the roof. The language was so offensive that ladies avoided sitting out on the boiler deck.[25] Standard forms of discipline on all American steamers called for workers to be "beaten, knocked down, and clubbed," and it was not unusual for them to also be "stabbed, shot, or thrown overboard."[26] The rationalization for such treatment was that mutinies were fairly common, and the roustabouts outnumbered all the other employees combined.

In 1865, Captain C. A. Klink found himself at the mercy of his deckhands when the *Uchee* struck a snag and began to sink. He ordered his hands to man the pumps, but they abandoned them and began to fight among themselves. Klink got out his gun and ordered them again to return to work. All did except one, who came at him with a stick of fire-

130   wood. The captain shot him; the others returned to work. At the trial, which exonerated the captain of murder, the black men present were warned "against mutiny and strikes."[27]

Soon after the steamer *Three States* had left the Columbus wharf, Captain Long discovered that his hands were gambling. He ordered them to put away their cards, dice, and money, but they refused. Long said he was going to make an example of a couple of them by throwing them off the boat. The stevedores replied that if one went, they all would. One of them brandished a pistol. The captain waved his empty Winchester rifle at them. Now fifteen miles from town, Long decided to turn the boat around for Columbus. As he did, two hands jumped ship. With a pistol borrowed from a passenger, the other five hands were driven into the boat's hold and eventually turned over to the sheriff. The captain hired another crew of roustabouts and resumed his voyage. In court, the workers were found guilty of gambling and sentenced to twelve months on the chain gang or a fine of one hundred dollars. Undoubtedly, none was able to make bail.[28]

One never knew when or why a fight would break out. Engineer T. B. Rivers of the *J. W. Hires* and his deckhand, Theo Jackson, were both known as "quiet and peaceful" men, but something kept setting Rivers off. Just as the boat was docking in Columbus, Jackson accidentally brushed against the officer as he was securing the stern line. Words passed between them and the two drew knives. The argument was broken up, but the next day when the vessel was again under way, Jackson again brushed up against the engineer as he threw off a line. He apologized, but Rivers cursed him and followed him into the engine room, where he struck him in the head with a piece of iron, making an ugly gash. Then he pulled out his pistol and shot at the black man again and again as he lay on the floor. The officer was standing at the guardrail, behind a pile of sacked guano, reloading his gun when the roustabout grabbed a nearby rifle and returned fire. The force of the shot pushed Rivers overboard. His body washed up a month later about thirty miles downstream. The roustabout lived and was charged with murder.

Sometimes the freight itself was dangerous. Around the turn of the century, there was a healthy business in making tupelo honey. Beekeepers placed hives in the river swamp. In the springtime, as the tupelo came into bloom, they hired the steamers to move their hives to wherever the bloom season was. Sometimes the bees buzzed out of the hive as they were being loaded on the boat. One can just imagine the chaos that ensued.[29]

The combination of backbreaking work, low pay, and demeaning treatment eventually compelled the workers to strike for better conditions. At the turn of the century, the crew of the *W. C. Bradley*, exasperated when the mud on the banks at the Columbus wharf was "up to their eyes" and the heavy sacks of fertilizer mired them further, demanded more pay and went home until they got it. The captain had no choice but to concede.[30]

The *Three States* had similar labor problems later that same year at the Columbus wharf. After the hands had unloaded the boat, they called for their pay. When the captain tried to delay them, they began to demonstrate. With that, Captain Lapham had the ringleaders arrested. The policemen took them directly into police court, where they were sentenced to five dollars or twenty days. All but two spent the next three weeks in jail.[31]

Even with the authorities' stand of solidarity against them, the black stevedores continued to stand up to the boat companies. The following year, as the weather turned bitter, the local newspaper commented that the "steamboat men are finding great difficulty in hiring men. They have to go out short-handed right along."[32] The busy fertilizer season was upon them, and the boats needed more than ever "a strong supply of negroes to carry the two hundred pound sacks around." However, demonstrators were still being arrested, for the columnist cryptically reported that "the police will not allow negroes to loaf around the wharf."[33] Yet within two weeks the hands had triumphed, and the newspaper reported that the "labor famine" was over. The hands got a raise to twenty dollars per month plus meals and lodging.[34]

As the above illustrates, life on the river was not always as pleasant as travel logs portrayed. The occupation of a river boatman required long hours, little sleep, backbreaking labor, exposure to danger, and days at a time spent away from loved ones. It was outdoors work in the sweltering sun of summer and the frosty bitterness of winter. In return for it all, the riverboat men earned the respect of patrons and riverbank gawkers alike. And every day the crew members had the good fortune to travel along the enchanting Chattahoochee, a privilege others were happy to pay for.

❦

CHAPTER 8

The Business of Steamboating

THE RIVER ITSELF WAS THE BIGGEST CHALLENGE boatmen faced after the Civil War. In 1871 and 1872 the U.S. Army Corps of Engineers conducted surveys of the river system to assess how badly it was in need of improvement.[1] These surveys found the river to be in particularly bad shape on the Apalachicola end. The channel in Apalachicola harbor had gradually filled in so that seagoing vessels could get no closer to town than several miles. Thirty miles upriver at the Narrows, the Confederates had so thoroughly obstructed the river that the current had found a new access to the Gulf through Moccasin Slough.[2] The new channel was even more narrow and crooked than the original one, and the current was so swift that navigation to the Gulf was precarious at best.

Farther upriver were other problems. Between Columbus and Eufaula, several shoals obstructed the Chattahoochee to the point that it became impassable at low water. Below the latter place, "thirty-four shoals, bars, and rock fingers" were hazardous to navigation. All along the river system, overhanging trees, logs, and snags choked the channel.[3]

The Corps of Engineers proposed to cut a channel one hundred feet wide and four feet deep at low water from Columbus down to the Chattahoochee's juncture with the Flint River, which was also to be improved to Bainbridge. A separate project for the Apalachicola proposed a six-foot channel from the bay up through Moccasin Slough to the confluence of the Chattahoochee and Flint Rivers. Congress approved these projects in 1873 and 1874, respectively.[4] In the 1890s the Corps conceived a project to open the river above Columbus by constructing locks and dams to create a minimum depth of three feet at low water between Franklin and

The *Queen City* loaded with turpentine barrels. *Courtesy of the Fred Wickham Collection.*

West Point, a distance of forty miles. However, funding was never suffici-ent to achieve anything more than clearing overhanging trees and snags, and the project was discontinued in 1899.[5]

In the problem areas just south of Columbus, the engineers proposed using "wing dams" to deepen the river. The idea was to dam a portion of the river, forcing the current to cut a deeper channel in the remaining width. It was believed that this arrangement would scour the bottom of the river, thereby easing navigation and permanently solving the Chatta-hoochee's shortcomings.[6]

As the engineers began to improve navigation, the steamboat owners set business goals. Before the war, the river men had not thought in terms of owning more than one boat, but in the new age of commercialization of the 1870s, Chattahoochee boat owners came to see the advantage of operating several. By basing vessels on different stretches of the river, the same entrepreneur could offer patrons frequent and coordinated service on the entire waterway. The first steamer line on the Chattahoochee was the Barnett Line. Aaron Barnett of New York and Captain C. D. Fry had associated their two boats during the last year of the Civil War, transporting men and supplies for the Confederacy. Though this "line" may have been informal in the beginning, it was not long before others pooled their assets to form riverboat companies.[7]

The free market of the early industrial age has earned a reputation for being cutthroat. The postwar steamboat companies found competition deadly. The new technology available in the Gilded Age meant owners had to constantly upgrade their equipment and services to remain competitive. The stringing of telegraph lines down the valley in 1867 heralded these new technological conditions. With instant communication now possible between Columbus and Apalachicola and points in between, the whereabouts of the steamboats could be ascertained so that patrons had a better idea of when to expect their ride or their freight.[8]

While the advent of the railroad had worried antebellum entrepreneurs because they were not sure how it would affect their trade channels, by 1868 the river men had learned that the iron horse actually had increased river usage. At least, this would be the case for the next three decades. When the Atlantic and Gulf Railroad was completed from Savannah, Georgia, on the Atlantic coast to Bainbridge on the lower Flint River, the languishing steamboat business of the Chattahoochee was actually revived. The railroad built a wharf in Bainbridge by which, a *Macon Telegraph* reporter wrote, "they can unload cotton from the steamboats without it ever touching the earth."[9] The pioneer steamboat company, the Barnett Line, joined with the railroad company to provide an all-purpose transportation service. Like all good ideas, this combination of steamboat and railroad service was soon imitated by competitors. The Central of Georgia Railroad, which connected with the Chattahoochee River at Columbus and Eufaula, bought a fleet of steamboats. This further opened options to travelers and shippers.[10]

This Central Line and the Barnett Line together ran eight steamboats between Columbus, Bainbridge, and Apalachicola in 1868, and the next year a new entry, the Independent Line of Steamboats, challenged the others by promising to keep to a schedule. With this innovation, it was predicted that "the arrival and departure of these boats can be [as] surely told as the arrival and departure of railroad trains."[11] This dependability was also a great relief to travelers, though the owners meant by this promise to announce the day—not hour—of their vessels' departure and arrival. Not to be outdone, the Central Line quickly adopted the practice as well, and before long it bought out the Independent Line.

This left the Barnett and Central lines to fight among themselves

The *Rebecca Everingham* draped with bunting to mourn the death of Central Line president Colonel William M. Wadley in 1882. *Courtesy of the Fred Wickham Collection.*

over control of the river trade. The Barnett Line looked into another railroad connection, this one to join the river system at Chattahoochee, Florida (soon to be called River Junction), where a railroad line was being completed between there and Jacksonville, Florida. This new connection gave upriver residents another outlet to the Atlantic Ocean. As in Bainbridge, a combination wharf was eventually built at River Junction that connected the river dock to the railroad depot.

To keep the game interesting, the two lines challenged each other to a race to the bay and back in December 1870.[12] The outcome was not, however, an indicator of future success. Although the Barnett Line won the battle, they lost the war. By 1872 the original steamboat line had gone out of business.[13]

The Central Line added the Barnett's Atlantic and Gulf Railroad connection at Bainbridge to its Eufaula and Columbus railroad juncture and enjoyed a monopoly on the river for the next six years. The other railroad line from the Atlantic to cross the Chattahoochee, Henry Plant's Savannah, Florida, and Western Railroad Company, eventually combined its stockholders with investors from the Columbus business community to produce the People's Line of Steamers, incorporated in 1879. To attract

The *J. W. Hires*, the Mobile and Girard Railroad, and the Dillingham Street Bridge circa 1890. *Courtesy of the Fred Wickham Collection.*

business, it offered the first excursion to venture all the way to Apalachicola on the steamer *G. Gunby Jordan.*[14] After only seven months in business, the People's Line had already earned over $11,000 in profit.

Both the Central and People's lines were challenged by the arrival of a single boat in late 1878. The *Mary Elizabeth*, affectionately known as the *Long Lizzie*, threw the river trade on its ear. While the line boats had trouble negotiating the upper river in low water, the *Mary Elizabeth* came to the rescue of the Columbus businessmen by bringing up a partial load of freight. This was not cost-effective, but it was a surefire way to win the allegiance of the Columbus business community, who were stranded from their downstream customers by the low stage of water. While commending the new boat, a local newspaper article called the line boats "unpatriotic."

Miffed by the aggressive entrance into the Chattahoochee river trade of the *Mary Elizabeth*, the two lines fell into league against the independent boat. They formed a pool that divided the river trade among themselves without making room for the new boat. The *Mary Elizabeth* began to make short trips instead of competing head-on with the line boats, which ran the entire river. The lines countered by threatening "to put a boat behind and before the 'Long Lizzie,' if she did not quit making the short trips."[15]

With the river trade out of kilter from the introduction of a competitor, it was not long before the two incorporated steamboat lines turned on each other. John D. Rockefeller referred to pools as "ropes of sand." They were gentlemen's agreements that worked to stabilize competition during fair times, but when the going got tough, the tough usually went back on their word. Even though the two had made an agreement as to what rates they would charge, the Central Line broke it by slashing its freight rates from fifty cents to only ten cents per bale of cotton without consulting the People's Line.

Neither company could afford to run at a loss for long, and the People's Line decided to fight back by appealing to the intelligence of its patrons. Warning consumers of the dangerous monopoly that would ensue if one line was driven out of business, they argued that rates would remain low only if there was competition to drive down prices. The People's Line guaranteed that its freight rates would not go above fifty cents per bale for the next three years. The owners asked patrons to divide their freight between the two lines to ensure that both could remain in business. The local newspaper editor supported this argument, saying, "We hope we will never again see [the river trade] under the control of any one company or combination."[16]

In response, the Central Line backed away from its suicidal ten cent rate and announced that it, too, would guarantee that its freight rates would remain at fifty cents per bale for the next three years.[17] Meanwhile, the *Mary Elizabeth* found a route of its own on the Flint River, and nearly a thousand people turned out in 1879 to witness the arrival of the first steamer to make it up the length of the Flint to Albany in many years.[18]

Though they feuded with each other, the steamboat owners combined forces to ride the Corps of Engineers into completing the planned improvements to the Chattahoochee. In 1876 the engineers reported that the Chattahoochee had been made "tolerably navigable," but their work continued.[19] By 1881 the boatmen were exasperated with the government's engineer. Not only had navigation not improved, but according to the river pilots, the Corps had actually made matters worse. By changing the natural course of the channel, sandbars developed upstream of each wing dam. Furthermore, where the channel had been widened the river actually was made shallower than it had been before the "improvements" were made. The two steamboat lines operating in the upper river petitioned

138 the government to cease work on the river until the matter could be investigated.[20] After getting no satisfaction from the officer in charge of the project, the two lines jointly hired an attorney to represent them in Washington. The attorney appealed directly to the chief of engineers and explained that "the complaint made was one of an honest difference existing between an educated engineer and graduate of West Point, and plain and practical men who claimed to understand the navigation and knowledge of the rivers better than he did."[21]

The plain and practical men were overruled, and the Corps continued its project. Although the riverboat men disagreed, the Corps claimed in 1883 that, after the expenditure of $123,582, the Chattahoochee had a "fair navigable channel the whole year."[22] At the Gulf of Mexico the engineers worked on opening the harbor, but the appropriations were never sufficient to completely cut through the bar that blocked ocean-going ships from reaching the port. Whenever dredging stopped, the channel filled again. By 1891, silting in the channel was occurring faster than progress was being made. The local project manager recommended an expenditure of $60,000 (more than half of what had been spent on the harbor in the previous fifteen years) just to prevent the stoppage of traffic by even the shallowest-draft tugs and lighters.

Upstream, the jetties built on the Chattahoochee required constant repair, and the government did not keep pace in its appropriations. During periods of low water, the steamboat lines incurred extra expenses in carrying only a partial cargo and in repairing those boats and barges injured while attempting to run between Eufaula and Columbus. Government appropriations for river improvement became as shallow as the river, and the companies bore the entire expense of keeping the river open in 1895.[23] Several times, local river men or city fathers traveled all the way to Washington to plead for more attention to their river.

In one instance, a Chattahoochee skipper who was testifying before the congressional commission on navigation went overboard in stating his case. In stressing the importance of the river to southern commerce, he mentioned that the Chattahoochee was four hundred miles in length.

" 'How's that?' interrupted one of the congressmen, closely examining a map that was spread out before him. . . . 'The map gives it as two hundred miles?' "

" 'Yes,' replied Captain Moore, blandly, 'but you see, gentlemen, we work both sides of it.' "[24]

Although the captain may have exaggerated the length of the waterway, the Chattahoochee was indeed the South's longest and most important river east of the Mississippi. Yet no matter what means were used to convince the lawmakers, the country was in the midst of a depression, and the boatmen were always told that appropriations on all river improvements were being cut. Bars and shoals continued to plague navigation. In the 1897 season the *Columbus Enquirer-Sun* lamented the sorry state of the river: "Every year when the busy season sets in there is some ugly old place down the river that bobs up and 'interrupts the game.' Last year 'Old Head' and 'Francis Bend' got in their work; year before and for many years preceding 'The Mound' and 'Woolfolk's Bar' furnished their share of trouble and now 'Gun-Boat Shoals' seldom before heard of in the history of 'hang-ups,' comes boldly to the front and what she has furnished for the given time, would make 'Shell Creek' or any other bad place ashamed of itself."[25]

"The river is lower than it has ever been in the history of the city," wailed the same pessimistic newspaperman a few weeks later, "and it is probable that it will be as low each succeeding year, and it may be even lower."[26]

Who was responsible for the shrinking of the river? Atlanta! The Columbus journalist claimed that Columbus was suffering because Atlanta was wastefully siphoning off seven million gallons of water a day. "The boats cannot come within many miles of Columbus . . . the cotton mills of Columbus are not able to run on full time. . . . These facts are sufficient to convince every one that Columbus is in danger."[27]

Water levels fell to their lowest in the summer months, and Columbus businessmen fretted when the line boats halted service north of Eufaula. Even in this railroad age the river was still their sole north-south commercial artery, and commerce was left high and dry when the line boats did not serve Columbus. In August 1881 the resolute merchants proposed to build and operate a boat of their own that could reach Columbus during low water with as little as two hundred bales of cotton. "We don't intend or wish to conflict with any other lines," they stressed, "we don't want to cut rates or do anything of a like character, we were perfectly satisfied at their rates; we simply want to protect ourselves."[28] They named their new enterprise the Columbus Steamboat Company and began shopping for a boat.

Even though this newest company reiterated that it was not antagonistic to any other line and that it simply wished to have freight moved in and out of the city "when the water is too low for the other boats to run," the Central Line used a heavy-handed approach to squelch the new company—blackmail. It announced it would raise its rates to one dollar

140   per bale (twice the current rate) for all cotton coming into Columbus, even though the company still had one year to go on its three-year rate guarantee. The local newspaper editor voiced his disapproval of this action: "There is not a merchant in our city that is not interested in the river trade, for it is the best trade we have. This company has no war to make on any one, but simply desires to get a boat that will come to our city at all times. . . . If the river is the property of any individual or set of individuals the sooner we know it the better."[29]

The Central Line backed down, and the Columbus Steamboat Company went ahead with its purchase of a light-draft steamer. After such a hard-won victory, the eventual appearance of the *Caddo Belle* was a decided disappointment. On its maiden voyage up the river, it went aground at Abercrombie's bar just south of the city. The following day when it finally reached the city wharf, the usually boosterish newspaper editor admitted the steamer was "not very attractive" but hoped she could do the job she was purchased for.[30] Apparently she did not, for two months later the People's Line purchased the *Caddo Belle*.[31]

Though nothing further became of the Columbus Steamboat Company, another company, which had two of the same directors as the former company, was organized in 1883.[32] It was known as the Merchants' and Planters' Line.[33] With this addition to the river fleet, three lines served the river valley between 1884 and 1887. However, breaking into the Chattahoochee trade was never easy. The Central and People's lines formed a pool in the hopes of destroying their common enemy. These two now announced in the same advertisement that each would charge only twenty-five cents per bale, or half the going rate.[34]

Somehow the upstart Merchants' and Planters' Line held on, and within a couple of years the older lines allowed it to join them. In October 1886 the three lines, though belonging to "separate corporations," were then "on the most harmonious terms." Their passenger and freight charges were identical, and the trio had divided up the business so that "each line ha[d] a particular day for leaving."[35]

In the 1880s, profits were large enough for all three lines to generate not only a period of cooperation but also an era of innovation. The first important change to come to the Chattahoochee boats in some time was the addition of improved lighting. Ironically, this modernization came to the steamboats via the rails. The *William S. Holt* was the first steamer to have spotlights for navigation purposes. In 1878 the *Holt* replaced its torches of "light wood" for headlights "like those used on locomotives."[36]

Three years later, electric lights came to the river, and because of their brilliance someone predicted that "chickens along the river will come down from the roost."[37] A representative of the United States Electric Lighting Company fitted the People's Line steamer *G. Gunby Jordan* with electric lights for illuminating the cabin, as well as with running lights. "The approach of the steamer," a writer noted in the summer of 1881, "was a beautiful sight, three powerful lights piercing the darkness and showing the angry threatening clouds which obscured the entire sky. . . . The result is all that could be wished for."[38] The People's Line planned to install electric lighting on their new boat being built in Pittsburgh, and also added them to their *T. H. Moore.* Unfortunately for this progressive company, it lost both the *Jordan* and the *Moore* to accidents within weeks of each other that same year. The one thing they salvaged from the latter for reuse was the electric generator.[39]

The People's Line was also the first company to institute running on "schedule time." In 1886, for the first time ever on the Chattahoochee, the steamer *William D. Ellis* kept to a schedule that included the hour as well as the day of arrival and departure from seven river ports.[40] This bold undertaking duly impressed valley residents. The *Ellis* was already making the fastest round-trip of all riverboats, and now she was also keeping to her "schedule time." People marveled at the idea of knowing "exactly when to listen for the whistle." One pronounced the achievement "in the nature of a revolution in the steamboat travel."[41]

The *Ellis* improved its speed in running the full length of the river by instituting the "Cannon Ball Route" that same spring. With this new route, the *Ellis* made an amazing two round-trips per week. Such a schedule had never been undertaken before, and consumers worried about the hazard involved in traveling at that speed. What they did not immediately understand was that the steamboat was not moving any faster, but was merely cutting out most of its stops. Simply by eliminating a stop at Bainbridge on the lower Flint River, the *Ellis* saved twelve hours; and by concentrating on passenger service instead of freight, the boat was able to avoid many other stops.[42]

As the 1880s came to a close, all the steamboat lines were compelled to deal with the nagging problem of low water. One visionary redesigned the hull of his steamer to resemble a shallow-draft barge that ran under its own steam. The "steam barge" *Aid,* built by Columbus merchants, began serving the river valley as an independent boat in December 1885 and continued until its end came in 1888. The new hull design did not impress many. The local newspaper editor encouraged patronage of the *Aid* by stating, "She is a small boat, but is perfectly safe."[43]

Although most innovations were quickly adopted by all, it would be a decade before other companies followed this design trend. For the time being, some built unmotorized barges which drew very little water. In low water these could be towed by the steamboats, whose loads were lightened to diminish their draft. In the high-water season following the spring rains, the riverboat men used the barges to host waterborne dances.

Eventually, in 1898 the water level reached an unusually low stage, and the idea of resurrecting the forgotten steam barge was tossed about the Columbus business community as though it were an original idea. By June it was announced that four steam barges were nearing completion and would be on the river by fall. They were built to operate on the upper stretches of the river below Columbus only, connecting with the heavier boats at Eufaula.[44] The local editor reflected the hopes of many businessmen in the valley when he proclaimed that the new steam barges would "no doubt revolutionize the river business. The vessels were light-draughted, and as they carried no passengers, they will not have to carry expensive officers and crew required by law of steamers carrying passengers. For this reason, the cost of running the barges will be small compared with the cost of operating a steamer. Merchants and businessmen are keenly interested in the result of the experiment with the steam barges. They hope for a still lower rate of freight."[45]

As the decade of the 1880s, which had been characterized by cooperation and innovation, came to a close, the rivalry among the various steamboat lines intensified again. In 1887 the Columbus and Gulf Navigation Company joined the People's Line, the Central Line, and the Merchants' and Planters' Line in providing water transportation for the Chattahoochee Valley residents. In that year the four lines entered into a pool agreement, and each line operated one boat. However, by 1889 the agreement was scrapped by the People's Line because the Central Line refused to haul freight to Bainbridge, where the Central's rival railroad line met the river. Additionally, the People's Line accused the Central of taking one of its sailing days from Columbus. With the breakup of the cartel, it was said that "every tub will stand on its own bottom, and it is thought that the war will be a long and bitter one."[46] The People's Line started off the bidding for patronage by returning to it called its "half rate charges" of fifty-five cents per cotton bale.

In 1899, adding further to the river business confusion, the steamer *William D. Ellis*, formerly of the People's Line, was sold to George Lapham, who operated it independently of the other boats. It was probably for that reason that a rumor circulated that the *Ellis* took only black passengers. That the "only independent steamer on our river should be so foully accused" offended Lapham's friends, who declared that he "carries his share of the best white passengers."[47]

It is not known how long the 1889 feud continued, but it probably did not take long for the owners to settle down and realize that their best interests were met by collusion with the enemy. Even the independent *Ellis* joined the pool for a while. Pool agreements were limited to only one year's time, so periodic rate wars were as common as catfish.

The decade of the 1880s was also the era when businessmen above Columbus caught steamboat fever. The ambitious Lanier family of West Point used their own money to have the rocky shoals of the river dynamited to clear a channel from West Point to Franklin in Heard County, Georgia. Before the project was completed, the Laniers had a steamboat built. The local newspaper editor congratulated the family for their "go-aheadativeness in pushing through an undertaking attended with so many uncertainties."[48] Their steamboat, the *Franklin,* was launched in the autumn of 1884 before fifteen hundred excited citizens.[49] The local newspaper applauded the "Messrs. Lanier [who] . . . have thrown their great hearts and big, level heads together, with their plethoric purses, into this grand work."[50]

Though much was expected of the new river steamer, the *Franklin* apparently made only one trip to the town of Franklin. Even with the excavation done in the river channel, the current was so swift in one spot that a pole had to be planted into the bank upstream. A rope was threaded around the pole, and the boat was winched through by hand. But on its initial voyage, there was trouble. A deckhand drowned. The steamboat returned to West Point to await further channel improvements that never materialized. Another steamboat eventually was built in West Point, but it burned as it was tied up at the city landing, probably in the 1890s. A local old-timer who wrote down the facts he had heard about West Point as a young man recorded that both boats motored up the streets of the town during the flood of 1886.[51]

Below the fall line, as the cotton season opened in 1891, all Columbus river interests met to divide the spoils of the river trade. Two boat owners did not like the percentages they received and left the meeting to run independently. The remaining three lines (the Central, the People's, and the Merchants' and Planters') formed a syndicate to compete against the other two (the independent *Ellis* and the Columbus and Gulf Navigation Company's *Fannie Fearn*).

To punish these two, the syndicate boats marked down their rates on cotton from fifty cents to only fifteen. The only thing the *Ellis* and the *Fannie Fearn* could do was to reduce their charges as well. As it happened, the *Ellis* was the first boat to leave Columbus after the word spread of the rate cuts. Merchants, ecstatic at their good fortune, sent down freight to the wharf by the ton, and the *Ellis* loaded the largest freight that any boat had received that season. The captain blew his whistle for joy as he pulled away from the city wharf and headed downstream. "There will now be some fun," predicted the local newspaper man.[52]

Order soon returned to the riverboat business, but another river war raged in 1896 when the syndicate was challenged by a new corporation, the Queen and Crescent City Navigation Company. This firm was made up of "grocery men, mill men, and cotton men."[53] Everyone knew this would mean another rate war, and consumers welcomed it. Though past independent lines had not been able to survive the competition of the pool, many hoped it would be different with the Queen and Crescent City.

This newcomer had more than competition to overcome. It lost both of its boats to the river in its second year in operation. Refusing to capitulate, though, it promptly bought two more vessels and continued to resist the syndicate through 1898.[54] In that year it reorganized itself as the Independent Navigation Company and persevered in its war against the four pool members (People's, Central, Merchants' and Planters', and Columbus and Gulf) through the 1898–99 commercial season.[55] In 1899 it reorganized again, this time as the Georgia and Florida Steamboat Line.

As the curtain fell on the nineteenth century, the observant saw that the future of steamboating on the Chattahoochee was not rosy. After twenty years of operation on the river, the People's Line closed its doors in June 1899. Perhaps it was fitting that only one day after the death of its president, Henry Plant, the last remaining steamer of the People's Line, the *Apalachee*, snagged an obstruction in the Chipola River Cut-Off and sank.[56] During the previous two years, seven other steamers had also sunk or burned on the Chattahoochee, and within a few months the oldest steamboat line on the river, the Central Line, after thirty years of business, would also sell off its assets and close its doors. Likewise, the Columbus and Gulf Navigation Company would soon close.[57]

In 1900 only three companies were still in operation: the Georgia and Florida, the Merchants' and Planters', and a newcomer known as the Merchants and Naval Stores Transportation Company. The first two companies entered into a pool agreement and called themselves the Columbus Steamboat Association.[58] As usual, the new corporation on the river entered into business as an independent boat and intended to remain so. But, as history had proven, the *M. W. Kelly* found it impossible to remain outside the pool for long. Its general manager adamantly denied rumors to the contrary in January 1901, but by April it had capitulated.[59]

The announcement stressed the public-service nature of the business as the primary reason for the merger, but it also admitted that none of the lines had made any money when the independent boat competed with the syndicate.[60] The newly organized Columbus Steamboat Association named the manager of the former independent line as its general manager. The association opened an office in Columbus to attend to the members' mutual interests. The influence of this merger on freight rates was predictable. The fare for cotton bounced back up to fifty cents.

Though occasionally over the next four years capitalists on the lower reaches of the river sponsored a few boats, the Columbus Steamboat Association continued to hold a monopoly on service to Columbus through 1905 with its five boats: the *M. W. Kelly*, the *Queen City*, the *W. C. Bradley*, the *Three States*, and the *J. W. Hires*.

After 1900 the nature of river service changed noticeably. Gone were the days such as just after the Civil War when the steamers stopped at more than 260 landings between Columbus and Apalachicola.[61] Instead of calling on every homestead or business along the river, by 1906 boats stopped at only twenty-eight major communities or railroad junctions from Columbus to the bay.[62] And sixteen years later, the steamers made only five stops.[63]

The river's natural character of drying up to a rivulet in the region north of Eufaula during periods of low rainfall was exacerbated by settlement of the lands along its banks. As farmers and developers loosened the red clay by forest clearing and plowing, wind and rain swept the dirt into the riverbed. Silt filled the channel, and dredging operations were never thorough enough to remedy the situation. After 1900 the river trade shifted to the lower river, where navigation was not so difficult. John W. Callahan of Bainbridge, who had made a fortune in the naval stores and timber industries, opened the Callahan Line of steamboats in 1906. He ordered the construction of the 153-foot *John W. Callahan* the following year, and it became the centerpiece of his service between Bainbridge, River Junction, and Apalachicola.[64]

As water transportation became less reliable, its competition im-

146   proved. Steel rails bored deeper and deeper into the river's terrain in the twentieth century. By 1916 the rail lines crossed over the Chattahoochee and Apalachicola Rivers in eight places below Columbus. At Columbus five different rail lines radiated from the city, and three railroads crossed the upper river between Columbus and Atlanta. To make matters worse for the future of river travel, rails now ran in the same direction as the river instead of perpendicularly. The Georgia, Florida, and Alabama Railroad paralleled the Chattahoochee by running down the Chattahoochee Valley while keeping a distance of twenty miles from the river. This rail line joined the Apalachicola Northern at River Junction, and the Florida line shadowed the Apalachicola River to the coast.[65] When railroads competed directly with the river, their more dependable and direct routes won.

    In addition to the railroad, the river had to compete with improved roads. By World War I the automobile had become affordable to most Americans. New car owners pushed for better roads. Paved roads encouraged a nascent trucking industry, which also challenged river travel. For all these reasons, river commerce died a slow death. From 1901 to 1914 commerce on the Chattahoochee declined by over 25 percent.[66]

    The character of the freight carried by boat also had changed by the turn of the century. Cotton no longer predominated in river freight. Although farmers still cultivated cotton to the virtual exclusion of other commodities, the railroads carried over 90 percent of the crop to market.[67] In the place of cotton bales, general merchandise and naval stores such as resin and turpentine filled the steamers' holds now. Beekeepers collected honey from tupelo gum trees on the riverbanks and shipped barrel after barrel via steamboats to market. Tons of cypress shingles and other cut lumber were shipped downstream. Hundreds of Chattahoochee catfish were caught daily near several fish camps along the river and shipped by steamer to Apalachicola, where they were cleaned and shipped by rail to the West.[68]

    Navigational hazards continued to plague the riverboats. By World War I the Columbus Power Company had contributed to the navigation problems by damming the river at Goat Rock. The utility company stored water every weekday evening and all weekend. This storage created a series of waves and troughs below the dam. Boats caught in the troughs had less water than normal in which to navigate, and during low-water seasons many a boat was left high and dry. The Corps of Engineers was perturbed with the power company and wanted the government to forbid it from storing water during low-water seasons, but the reality was that without the dam, Columbus industry would be injured. In the competition between a growing industrial complex and a dwindling river commerce, the future held more promise than the past.

By 1916 commercial boat traffic had so dwindled that W. C. Bradley's Merchants' and Planters' Line ran only one boat on a regular basis, keeping one other boat in reserve for especially busy times. Captain D. Ray ran a small boat twice a week over the least navigable stretch of the entire river, between Columbus and the next landing nine miles downstream. The *Callahan* ran from Bainbridge south.[69] These four were all that remained of the once-proud Chattahoochee fleet.

In 1916 the Corps's district engineer recommended that no further improvements be made on the Chattahoochee. The next year, the value of river freight was one-third what it had been only six years earlier.[70] What had happened in the Chattahoochee Valley was happening to all but the largest of rivers in the twentieth century, and no amount of government funds or engineering projects could alter that. Rail lines con-

Sister boats *Queen City* and *W. C. Bradley* at the Columbus dock. The *M. W. Kelly* is being used as a wharf boat in foreground. A snag boat is in the distance. *Courtesy of the Eagle and Phenix Collection, Columbus College Archives.*

148 nected the river valley to the rest of the world now. Traveling by river was too limited. The river's major usefulness was as a backup to rail travel and, in so doing, in keeping railroad rates lower.

W. C. Bradley's son-in-law D. Abbott Turner, who managed the Merchants' and Planters' Line after 1918, was fed up with the aggravation of keeping boats on schedule in a river full of snags and bars. He suggested to Bradley that he give away his steamboats to the Columbus Chamber of Commerce. While the city appreciated the gesture, it did little good. When rains swelled the river in 1923 and swept debris from upstream into the boats moored at the Columbus wharf, the lines could not hold the added weight. Fearing the worst, Turner walked down to the dock just in time to see the three remaining Bradley boats snap loose from their moorings. The boats drifted downriver, hit snags, and sank.[71]

In 1921 John Callahan decided to throw in the towel. He signed over his assets to a Columbus management company called the Tri-State Navigation Company.[72] It was the sole and final steamboat line on the Chattahoochee River. The 1922 closing of the United States Steamboat

The *John W. Callahan*, built in 1907, was one of the last steamers to service the Chattahoochee. *Courtesy of the Florida State Archives Photographic Collection.*

Inspection Service in Apalachicola was another sign of the times. This government agency had worked to keep steamboat travel safe during its heyday, but there was no longer enough work to warrant its remaining in operation.[73]

In 1923 the *John W. Callahan*, the last of the old-time paddle-wheelers, struck a snag and sank in the Chipola River Cut-Off near Wewahitchka, Florida. Only one more passenger steamboat would ever paddle up and down the Chattahoochee. In 1939 Thurston Crawford bought the *George W. Miller*, an old ferryboat, at Vicksburg, Mississippi, and brought it to the Chattahoochee for running excursions. During the World War II expansion of Fort Benning, business was good. The *Miller* was sold after the war, and its hull was turned into a barge.[74] The last two steamboats on the river were workboats of the Corps of Engineers—the *Guthrie* and the *Montgomery*—which continued service into the 1970s.

Gone are the days of the glorious paddle wheel, throwing off a rooster tail of silver spray as it disappeared around a bend; of captain's caps tipped to bustle-armored ladies; of belching wood smoke, clanging bells, and chest-rattling steam whistles; of country landings where tumbling cotton bales and chanting stevedores overlooked many a tearful embrace; of deck flirtations and poker games played out against the backdrop of an ever changing, ever green panorama.

The public would never again know the Chattahoochee as intimately as it did during the age of the steamboat. Yet the river was far from forgotten when the old packet liners disappeared. In the ensuing era, reliance on the river would actually increase as people came to depend on hydroelectric power to light both the cities and the countryside, and to turn the wheels of industry.

🍃

River Power

HE AMERICAN CIVIL WAR MAY HAVE PRESERVED THE
nation as a political entity, but it destroyed the South's economy.
Georgia and Alabama, which had formerly ranked eighth and
sixteenth nationally in per capita wealth, plummeted to fortieth and
forty-fourth, respectively, after the war.[1] The thriving industrial complex
at Columbus lay in ashes after General James H. Wilson's raid in the
spring of 1865. But no mere army could destroy the thundering Chattahoochee.

The river beckoned the industrialists back to its falls to begin again.
In spite of their losses, factory owners started over with optimism and
energy. The welfare of hundreds of their employees now thrown out of
work added a sense of urgency to their plans to rebuild. Within a month
of Wilson's raid, the city foundry was operational. In four months the
furnaces of the Columbus Iron Works burned brighter than ever. Within
five years, eight foundries were forging Columbus into a city of the "New
South."[2]

However, the centerpiece of postwar industrial activity was not iron,
but textiles. The old Clapp's Factory resumed operations by December
1865. Downstream at the Eagle Mill, the optimistic company directors
looked at the charred remains of their plant and saw a phoenix rising
from it. Early in 1866 when they reorganized, they formally added the
mythical bird's name to their company title. William H. Young, who still
controlled the company, quickly set his workers to cleaning the burned
bricks. The company still controlled three-quarters' interest in the old
Water Lot Company. This antebellum concern had engineered a dam
to divert river water into a canal capable of turning waterwheels at the

Clapp's Factory at the future site of Oliver Dam circa 1890. *Courtesy of Columbus College Archives.*

riverside "water lots." By 1868 the ten thousand spindles in the recently opened five-story Eagle and Phenix Mill were spinning, and a second mill stood on the old Howard Factory site. In 1869 the company built a new dam to more effectively divert water into its canal.[3] At the edge of the canal, the mill's waterwheel turned a shaft that drove all the other wheels and pulleys in the mill, turning the equipment.[4] Business must have been booming, because in 1873 the company decided to double its output by building a third mill on the site of the recently burned out Palace Mills. Upon its completion, the Eagle and Phenix became the South's largest textile plant and Columbus's primary employer. Housing for the textile workers was erected on the Alabama side of the river, a site that became known as Phenix City.

The only other factory to be located at the old water lots was Muscogee Manufacturing Company, successor to the antebellum Coweta Falls Factory. George Parker Swift founded this mill in 1867. By 1880 it had doubled its output by the addition of a second mill, and a third was added in 1886.[5] Except for the site of the Muscogee Manufacturing Company, the rest of the river-powered factory sites in downtown Columbus were

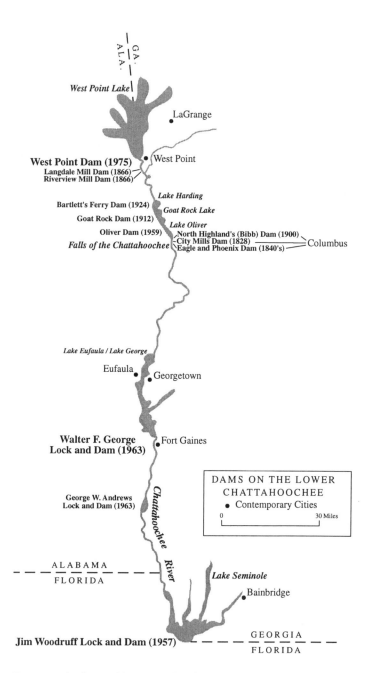

Dams on the lower Chattahoochee River

Eagle and Phenix Dam and powerhouse circa 1900. *Courtesy of the Columbus College Archives.*

Aerial view of the Eagle and Phenix Mills with dam and powerhouse in the foreground. This is the site of the first major industrial water power plant on the Chattahoochee River. *Courtesy of Georgia Power Company.*

154   eventually controlled by the Eagle and Phenix. This monopoly on hydro-mechanical power prevented any later industries from building down-town. Smaller industries, such as the Clegg Factory and Steam Cotton Mill of the 1870s or the Swift and Paragon Mills of the 1880s, located within a few blocks of the river but relied on steam power instead. Up-stream of the water lots, the smaller Clapp's Factory and City Mills (a gristmill) had their own dams. Since others were denied access to the river at Columbus, future large-scale textile mills were forced to build their own dams upstream, and Columbus fell behind Augusta, Georgia, in textile development by the 1880s.[6]

Upstream, postwar economic development began in 1866 when planters and merchants in the West Point area built two small textile mills at Langdale and River View. The latter was known as the Alabama-Georgia Manufacturing Company of River View. The former was con-ceived as the Chattahoochee Manufacturing Company of Langdale. It moved into the site of the three-story antebellum Trammel Grist Mill where Elisha Trammel, when traveling to a Baptist association meeting, had first noticed how swift the river ran at this place.

In 1880 the Langdale cotton mill was reorganized as the West Point Manufacturing Company.[7] Eventually the River View mill became a division of West Point Manufacturing. One of its founders, LaFayette

Aerial view of Langdale Mill of West Point Manufacturing Company with hydro-electric and steam plants. *Courtesy of Georgia Power Company.*

Lanier, married the daughter of the River View mill's owner. Lanier was president of West Point Manufacturing from 1896 until 1910. His son, George, took over management of the enterprise as his father's health failed him. In 1908 the company improved its dam at Langdale to produce hydroelectric power for its plants in Langdale and Shawmut. By this time the business also included the Lanett Cotton Mill, Lanett Bleachery and Dye Works, and the Chattahoochee Valley Railway.[8] By the 1930s, West Point Manufacturing Company included five mills located in Lanett, Shawmut, Langdale, Fairfax, and River View and constituted one of the six largest textile-manufacturing centers in the United States.[9]

Because George Lanier had inherited both the business and a patriarchal interest in it from his father, the son established a health program for the mill workers, with visiting nurses to attend not only the injured employees but also sick family members. He instituted night school for employees wishing to complete their education, a kindergarten, an intramural sports program, and Boy and Girl Scout clubs. He also paid to enlarge existing educational and religious facilities and supplement teachers' pay.[10] Industrialists like Lanier also fostered the development of industrial technology from reliance on hydromechanical power to hydroelectrical. Instead of turning pulleys and belts, the new phase converted the rush of river power into electricity.

One evening in 1882, hundreds of Columbus residents gathered on Broad Street to witness the lighting of the first electric bulb.[11] The Brush Electric Light and Power Company used the waterwheel in George Swift's Muscogee Manufacturing mill to turn their twenty-light dynamo after the mill closed for the night. This generator soon powered the lighting of several nearby stores. From this modest beginning the Brush Company continued to expand so that within five years "all major thoroughfares, hotels, mills, and steamers were lit by Brush arc lamps powered by the river."[12] Lamplighters soon went the way of steamboats.

John Flournoy built the city's first hydroelectric central station in 1895 at the dam at City Mills.[13] His major purpose was to power his trolley line, but he rented two turbines to the Brush Company and eventually acquired the lighting company. Even though the river powered an increasing number of Columbus businesses, most of the power generated in the city still originated from independent coal-burning steam plants.[14] In 1899 a consortium controlled by Bibb Manufacturing Company constructed the North Highlands Dam about two and a half miles north of the dam at City Mills. This project was the "first large-scale dam . . . built in the South."[15]

Looking southward from Lover's Leap at City Mills and Muscogee Mills circa 1900. *Courtesy of Georgia Power Company.*

The Columbus Railroad Company powerhouse at City Mills Dam was the site of the first commercial central hydroelectric power plant in Columbus. *Courtesy of Georgia Power Company.*

The site had been known for generations as Lover's Leap because of 157 the rocky heights that guarded the river there. The terrain had been too steep to build a factory directly on-site, so its potential could not be used until engineers learned how to transmit electricity over distance. Bibb built two powerhouses at North Highlands; one produced mechanical power for its new textile plant via a rope drive to the mill; the second generated electricity for the Columbus Power Company, a subsidiary of the textile plant.[16] With expansion in the 1920s, Bibb Mill became the largest southern textile operation housed under one roof. Its capacity to generate electricity encouraged four new textile mills to germinate.[17]

At this point, self-admitted amateurs at power generation controlled the two sources of river-driven electricity in Columbus (at City Mills and Bibb Mill). However, just as the North Highlands Dam was rising out of the river, an expert in the new field of electrical generation came to Columbus to find "the best method of turning this (Chattahoochee water) power into money."[18] By 1906, George Baldwin and his associated Stone

A 1912 Columbus Chamber of Commerce promotional piece. *Courtesy of the Columbus College Archives.*

158   and Webster Company of Boston merged all electrical power interests
into one company known as the Columbus Power Company. After 1930
this entity became a part of the Georgia Power Company.

The power company held a monopoly on power generation and also
owned riparian rights to 44 percent of the succession of waterfalls that
cascaded southward from West Point to Columbus. This portion was the
most valuable section of river for power generation because within this
fifteen-mile stretch the river dropped almost three hundred feet. (In contrast, the river dropped only about a foot per mile between Columbus and
Eufaula, and even less farther downstream.)[19] However, without competition to inspire it to further development, the power company sat on its
potential, playing "dog in the manger."[20]

As the power needs of Columbus grew and the company did nothing
to meet the new demands, Columbus businessmen and city fathers ran-
kled under the power company's self-imposed growth restrictions. Seasonal low-water periods crippled power generation and restrained economic development further. Finally, in 1909, B. H. Hardaway, who had
built the dams at both City Mills and North Highlands, organized the
Chattahoochee Power Company to develop the falls north of the Columbus Power Company properties.

Once the power monopoly was threatened, a deal was made. Hardaway's company agreed to withdraw from the electrical generation business if Columbus Power Company would build a dam at Goat Rock
(thirteen miles north of Columbus) and use Hardaway as the contractor.[21] While Columbus Power Company felt it had little option but to
make this deal if it wanted to retain its monopoly, building a new and
powerful dam put the company in the predicament of flooding its own
market with an overabundance of electricity. In order to have sufficient
customers to make the building of Goat Rock Dam financially feasible,
the company had to look elsewhere for new customers. The company
managers investigated linking their new dam via power lines to West
Point and LaGrange, Georgia. There, Columbus Power Company could
"feed into municipally-owned lighting circuits" and perhaps convince
the cotton mills that lined the riverbanks to connect to a central power
source.[22] Eventually, its power lines would extend all the way to Atlanta's
Georgia Railway and Power Company.[23]

Hardaway Construction Company began erection of the Goat Rock
Dam in 1910. On December 19, 1912, special trains brought over one
thousand Columbus residents to witness the dedication of the new power
plant. Before throwing the switch that sent electricity surging down the

power lines that stretched out from Goat Rock Dam, Columbus mayor L. H. Chappell anointed Chattahoochee River water over the head of a goat said to have descended from the original herd that had once grazed at the dam site.[24]

The construction of Goat Rock Dam and the concomitant advent of long-distance electrical transmission forever changed the way industrialists viewed both the river and the city of Columbus. The Chattahoochee had once served only those towns located along its banks, but now the river provided power and lighting to people who could not even see the Chattahoochee from their homes. Before this new development, Columbus's proximity to the falls of the Chattahoochee had ensured its preferential status as an industrial center. But now that river power could feed factories far from the waterfalls, Columbus no longer held a strategic advantage. New mills in West Point, Newnan, and LaGrange took advantage of the power produced by hydroelectric dams. While the river was more important than ever to the valley's economic development, Columbus could no longer claim exclusive use of it.

The power company added to its generating capacity in 1924 when it built the largest dam yet in the Columbus area. The Bartlett's Ferry Dam was the northernmost dam in the rapids of the Chattahoochee. Built four miles upstream from Goat Rock, its storage reservoir, known as Lake Harding, covered almost six thousand acres. The reservoir ensured that all the downstream dams had a constant flow of water for power generation and added eighty thousand kilowatts to the power company's transmission system.

As the primary function of the river changed from transportation artery to electrical power generator, Chattahoochee River neighbors were more likely to chat about dams and power plants than riverboats and roustabouts. The golden age of steamboating had passed. The navigability of the river had declined due to natural forces, but certainly the power companies added to the degradation of navigation. With waters dammed upstream of shipping operations, steamboat captains were left high and dry during the arid summer months. By World War I the steel bands of the railroad lines wrapped tightly around the river valley.

However, the brewing world war caused some civic leaders to reconsider the value of river transportation. In 1910 the U.S. Army Corps of Engineers had urged the construction of an intercoastal waterway system to connect all Gulf of Mexico streams by a protected saltwater channel. With his usual air of urgency, President Woodrow Wilson supported this project, saying, "The value of important waterways and the commerce

Goat Rock Dam under construction in 1911. *Courtesy of Hardaway Construction Company and Thomas L. French, Jr.*

Goat Rock Dam in the 1920s. *Courtesy of Georgia Power Company.*

development of the country cannot be exaggerated, and the necessity that
the federal government should adopt a definite and fixed policy that will
provide for their speedy improvement must be evident to every one who
considers the matter at all."[25] Since there was brief talk of erecting a wartime nitrate plant at West Point, the Chattahoochee's navigational importance was highlighted.

Just as America braced itself to enter the war, the chief of engineers
of the U.S. Army authorized a survey of the Chattahoochee to consider
improving the channel all the way to Atlanta by a series of locks and
dams. The eventual report by the district engineer recommended that no
improvement be made unless all existing dams were abandoned and a
new dam built north of Columbus that would back up water to Atlanta.
This suggestion was not a part of the intent of the survey and was ignored by Washington.[26]

However, civic leaders along the Chattahoochee took up the mantle
of river improvement and labored for several decades to lure progress into
the valley. Their motives were varied. Businessmen wanted to reintroduce
competition to transportation. The railroad companies had enjoyed their

Construction of the first concrete bridge at Dillingham Street in Columbus circa 1910.
This replaced the Horace King covered wooden bridge. *Courtesy of the Hardaway Construction Company.*

Construction of Bartlett's Ferry Dam in the 1920s. *Courtesy of Hardaway Construction Company and Thomas L. French, Jr.*

Bartlett's Ferry powerhouse and dam. *Courtesy of Georgia Power Company.*

advantage as the primary shipping agents, and rates were profitable. Naturally, railroad lines did not wish to jeopardize this situation, but many businessmen believed their future economic success depended upon cheap freight rates. Even Atlantans hoped for a water canal to link it to the Gulf of Mexico and loosen the grip of their railroad monopoly.

Other river residents hoped that river improvement would address flood control. In 1886 the river slithered into West Point like a stealthy red serpent. As the waters covered downtown streets, the steamer *Charlie Jones* circled the block. Businesses near the river, such as African-American Lit Harper's blacksmith shop, were soon covered to the roof. The next day, Harper's building floated downstream, leaving "the old man destitute."[27] The covered bridge that spanned the river met the same fate. Someone said, "It rolled down the river like a log!"[28]

William H. Scott recalled that his grandfather hurried downtown to help when he heard the waters were flooding businesses, leaving Scott's grandmother to cope with the rising waters alone. As the river lapped at the house's foundation, she pulled up the carpets and led the cow onto the back steps. Soon the waters swirled inside. As dawn broke, she heard a neighbor at the top of the hill hammering away. She called to him to save her, and he promised he would when he finished building a boat. Eventually, he rowed over and into the parlor where the family was standing on the furniture. When the floodwaters finally receded, she told her husband, "If you go back to that house, you'll have to go alone." They moved to the top of the hill.[29]

Other floods followed in 1901, 1912, 1915, 1916, and 1918.[30] The people of West Point learned to coexist with the river's quirky nature. They raised their wooden sidewalks to five feet above street level so that they were less inconvenienced during the periodic inundations. But the worst flood of them all tumbled down the valley in 1919. When it finally crested, the river stood at ten and a half feet above flood stage.[31] The *Atlanta Journal* disclosed the extent of the destruction:

> The town of West Point is all but bankrupt. Until last Tuesday night there was no fairer or more prosperous community in Georgia. Clustered in the lap of the Chattahoochee river . . . it was rich in possessions and rich in resources. Its mills were humming, its merchants were preparing for a record Christmas season, its farmers were holding their cotton for higher prices, its homes were as cheerful as any you could find in Dixie, its 5,000 people were happy.

The 1919 flood in West Point. *Courtesy of the Cobb Memorial Archives.*

The West Point flood of 1929. *Courtesy of the Troup County Historical Archives.*

Then the yellow Chattahoochee, swollen with the heaviest rainfall in its history, burst from its banks, swept through the streets of the city, rose above the high sidewalks, rose above the high foundations of the buildings, rose above the stocks of goods on the shelves, rose above the pianos and sideboards and beds, rose until West Point was only one vast lake of mud and water.[32]

The waters claimed the newest bridge across the Chattahoochee. Carolyn Danforth remembered hearing it snap loose soon after she looked out her door to see her "neighbor's hatbox floating down the street, ribbons and straw hats bobbing in the water."[33] The flood closed George Lanier's mill and left half of the five thousand residents destitute. The mayor and the Laniers telegrammed the governor and the mayors of nearby towns for aid. An American Red Cross relief train and the neighboring towns of LaGrange, Opelika, LaFayette, and Newnan offered some relief. (LaGrange reportedly raised $20,000.) The Atlanta Chamber of Commerce called a meeting to raise $25,000. George Lanier, whose business *was* West Point, pledged $10,000.[34] When the Atlanta newspaper published an appeal for donations, Atlantans displayed a preoccupation with channelizing the river, as well as concern for the flood victims: "The relationships between us and our sister city have been ever of a most cordial nature. We have admired her enterprise and growth, and have looked forward to a larger province of mutual interests in the coming development of the Chattahoochee and its commerce."[35]

Although West Point residents were the hardest hit, downstream residents were not spared. In Columbus the deluge was referred to as "the Pershing Flood" because it coincided with the visit of General "Black Jack" Pershing to Fort Benning. Since the regular traffic bridge from the post to Columbus was buried under twenty feet of Upatoi Creek, the general's car was driven across a railroad bridge. When he visited the post again in 1922, another deluge was dubbed "the Second Pershing Flood."[36] Commenting on the frequency of the Chattahoochee floods, the general said, "I thought all along Columbus would make a good Army post, but I'm beginning to think it could also be used by the Navy."[37]

While most blamed the tragedy of the Pershing Flood on Mother Nature, a minority believed the responsibility lay with progress. Poet F. W. Nash wrote the following lament of the land-clearance practices of the day.

THE RIVER'S VINDICATION

It's true I've gone on the war path
I've smitten your cities and homes
I've cracked the walls of your stately halls,
I've threatened your spires and domes.

I've spoiled your gardens and orchards,
I've carried your bridges away.
The loss is told in millions of gold;
The indemnity you must pay.

But had I not cause for anger?
Was it not time to rebel?
Go, ask of the springs that feed me;
Their rock ribbed heights can tell.

Go to my mountain cradle,
Go to my home and see,
Look on my ruined forests
And note what ye did to me.

These were my silven bowers,
My beds of bracken and fern,
The spots where I lie and rest me
E'er to your valley I turn.

These you have plundered and wasted,
You've chopped and burned and scarred,
Till my home is left of verdure bereft,
Bare and lifeless and charred.

So I have gone on the war path;
I've harried your lands with glee.
Restore with care my woodlands fair
And I'll peacefully flow to the sea.

West Point telephone company owner Smith Lanier believed the cure for the periodic deluges was not less, but more, development. In the wake of the 1919 flood, he employed hydraulic engineers to design a series

Fort Benning soldiers practicing construction of a pontoon bridge across the Chattahoochee between the world wars. *Courtesy of Columbus College Archives.*

of dams and lakes that would "reduce the flood hazard and facilitate further industrial development."[38] Lanier's dream of controlling water levels by dams did not come true until 1975. In the meantime, the U.S. War Department tried stopgap measures. In 1935 it spent almost $600,000 on "stream clearance, drainage, levee construction and bridge work," using labor from the depression-era relief rolls of Troup and Chambers Counties.[39] Yet floods of at least four feet above flood stage covered West Point again in 1936 and 1948, and in 1961 the waters crested at six feet higher than flood stage.

Coping with the river's extremes was part of the way of life in West Point. A siren was installed to warn folks that the river had left its banks. A river gauge was placed under a floodlight at Smith Lanier's telephone building on the riverbank. It became custom for men to keep vigil there when high water threatened, as if by their will alone they could hold the waters back.

Even though little was accomplished in the early twentieth century toward the dual goals of flood control and navigation enhancement, it was the latter that received the most energy. In the early 1920s, U.S. Senator William J. Harris of Georgia worked to get the Apalachicola and

168   Chattahoochee Rivers added to the intercoastal waterway project so that
the Chattahoochee would be deepened for barge traffic. A 1926 hearing on the feasibility of doing so resulted in the Columbus Chamber of
Commerce's forming the Inland Waterways Committee, whose charge
was gaining congressional approval of connection of the Chattahoochee
system with the Mississippi via the intercoastal waterway. In 1927 the Inland Waterways Committee hired a private firm to make an independent
economic survey of the valley to prove the feasibility of such an expensive
project. Cities along the stream—including Columbus, Eufaula, and Fort
Gaines, as well as Columbia, Alabama, and Blountstown and River Junction, Florida—promised that if the Chattahoochee canal was built, they
would finance the construction of local water terminals to service the
barge business that was sure to flower.[40]

      In 1928 regional business interests formed the Chattahoochee Valley
and Gulf Association for the purpose of promoting all forms of transportation—rail, water, and air—in order to develop the regional economy.[41]
The following year this association resolved to pressure Washington lawmakers to authorize a survey of the Chattahoochee from Columbus
to Atlanta for the purpose of opening the upper reaches of the river to
self-propelled barges that would connect with the intercoastal waterway
system at the Gulf of Mexico.[42]

      This resolution was passed, however, in the wake of the stock market
crash of 1929. The early 1930s, which represented the worst years of the
Great Depression, proceeded with little action by either Georgia cities or
Washington. In 1935 a third organization was formed to promote the economic interests of the Chattahoochee region. This Chattahoochee Valley
Chamber of Commerce was organized by a man who would continue to
work for river development for many years, James W. Woodruff, Sr.

      In 1936 the Corps of Engineers surveyed the river again. This time
they endorsed a nine-foot channel to Columbus but doubted that
extending the canal all the way to Atlanta would ever pay for itself.[43] The
next step in river development was to gain congressional approval and
funding. In 1938 and 1939, Congress seemed to be more receptive to the
chain of letters and personal contacts between Woodruff and friends and
the legislators. But Adolf Hitler grabbed the spotlight about that time,
and war preparations received priority in the federal budget.

      When World War II ended in 1945, James Woodruff headed for
Washington again, and this time he got what he wanted. The Rivers and
Harbors Act of 1946, together with a resolution adopted in 1953, author-
ized the Apalachicola-Chattahoochee-Flint Project, which envisioned

the construction of four dams on the Chattahoochee to address flood control, hydroelectric power generation, and navigation. It also called for dredging the Apalachicola River and cutting a channel through St. George Island to allow watercraft a more direct connection between Apalachicola Bay and the Gulf of Mexico. By this project, the Chattahoochee would be joined to the national intercoastal waterway system that extended westward to the Mexican border.

The four dams to be constructed were scattered along the river beginning with the southernmost one, the Jim Woodruff Dam, at Chattahoochee, Florida. Here the waters of the Chattahoochee and Flint Rivers converged. This undertaking would include a dam for electrical power generation and a lock to allow boaters to pass upstream. Water dammed behind this structure would be known as Lake Seminole. When completed, the lake would provide recreation for thousands living near the Georgia-Alabama-Florida boundary. Fifty miles north of the Jim Woodruff Dam, a second lock and dam was planned at Columbia, Alabama. The reservoir behind this George W. Andrews Dam would not widen so much as deepen the Chattahoochee so that a nine-foot navigational depth could be maintained for the next twenty-six miles.[44]

The Walter F. George Lock and Dam was planned for the area near Fort Gaines, Georgia, and Eufaula, Alabama (about eighty miles north of the Jim Woodruff Dam). This structure would constitute the largest producer of electricity on the entire river, and its 45,200-acre reservoir would soon become a fishing mecca. At the opposite end of the Chattahoochee, approximately 350 miles from the Jim Woodruff Dam and fifty miles north of Atlanta, the Buford Dam was designed to regulate the streamflow of the entire system so that a controlling depth of nine feet could be maintained from the Gulf to Columbus. The lake behind the dam would be called Lake Sidney Lanier, after the renowned poet of the Victorian era who wrote "The Song of the Chattahoochee."[45] The estimated completion date for the entire project was 1962.[46]

The development of the Chattahoochee River represented only one cog in a gargantuan wheel of river development in the Southeast. Following World War II, the Corps of Engineers planned a peacetime project large enough to keep them employed for years. Their ambitious plan was to create "a national inland navigation network of dams and hydro-electric plants intended to encourage a new era of prosperity everywhere."[47] To receive congressional approval for so expensive a project, the Corps needed regional backing as well.

In 1951, General Lewis Pick, chief of engineers for the Corps, visited

170   Columbus to promote local support for the Chattahoochee portion. The officer likened the fight to open the river to a real war with victors and vanquished. A newspaper editor reported that Pick "discard[ed] his prepared text . . . and gave the assembled group valuable and exciting advice which, if heeded, could lead to a revolutionary industrialization of this section or, if ignored, could result in complete stagnation of business and industry." The general told the crowd that the Chattahoochee Valley was "one of the industrial frontiers of the nation," but if they slept on their interests, coastal cities like Mobile and Jacksonville would win out over inland towns like Columbus. Apparently, Pick got the response he had hoped for. The newspaper editor took up the call to action, writing, "We have the leadership; we have the desire to grow industrially. Do we have the determination and are we willing to put forth the effort?"[48]

Woodruff and the other members of the Chattahoochee Valley Chamber of Commerce had already rallied to the cause. In 1950 they had reorganized and enlarged their lobbying association to include members from the seventy-two counties that bordered the Chattahoochee and Apalachicola Rivers. They renamed the organization the Three Rivers Development Association.[49]

Through the combined efforts of congressmen, commercial interests, and the U.S. Army, the Chattahoochee development project became a reality. Both the Jim Woodruff Dam and the Buford Dam, framing both ends of the river, were completed in 1957. Construction began on the Walter F. George Dam in 1955 and the George W. Andrews Dam in 1959. These intermediary dams were both completed in 1963.[50]

Georgia Power Company also joined in the development. In 1957 it began construction of its most modern hydroelectric generating station, Oliver Dam, located within the Columbus city limits. With the completion of Oliver Dam in 1959, Georgia Power owned four power-generating dams at the Falls of the Chattahoochee. They were, beginning with the southernmost and moving north, North Highlands, Oliver, Goat Rock, and Bartlett's Ferry. The three older dams were upgraded with new generators as Oliver Dam was being planned and erected. None of the four dams had locks that would enable boats to reach Atlanta, but the Oliver Dam engineers made provisions for the "future installation of navigation locks on the Alabama side of the dam at the option of the federal government. This is in keeping with the Company's policy of providing full cooperation in the event the government should decide to develop the Chattahoochee River as a waterway between Columbus and Atlanta."[51]

Beyond the Georgia Power dams at Columbus and the rocks and

white water that forbade navigation between Columbus and West Point, Georgia's capital city refused to be excluded from the high-stakes game of post–World War II prosperity. Quoting E. L. Hart of the Atlanta Freight Bureau, in 1951 the *Atlanta Journal-Constitution* urged its citizens to get moving: "There is an inescapable necessity to develop navigation on the Chattahoochee to complete an adequate transportation system. . . . Longer delay . . . would imperil our entire commercial and industrial structure. The new day absolutely demands the facilities of water for transportation of heavy goods which must be [at] a low cost." The article then editorialized, "Atlantans generally regard their river as something jaundiced looking and full of rocks, mainly suitable for the production of catfish. It is not an impressive sight, but an impressive amount of water flows down its channel, plenty for the production of power and the operation of the necessary locks."[52]

As the Jim Woodruff Dam opened, making Bainbridge, Georgia, the state's first inland port, Atlantans devised their plan of attack. The first step was the promotion of a dam just north of the West Point area that would back the Chattahoochee's waters to the Atlanta city limits. They could worry later about the Georgia Power obstructions below. Residents of the West Point area jumped at the chance to combine forces with the might of the capital city in promoting a dam that would save them from another devastating flood.

When Georgia Power publicly announced in 1956 that they had no intention of using the permit they had held since the 1930s to build a dam on the Chattahoochee above West Point, citizens of West Point and Atlanta pressured their congressmen to authorize a feasibility study of a multipurpose dam to be built by the Corps of Engineers. The marriage of the interests of West Pointers and Atlantans gave each arguing power the two did not possess individually. "The Valley's greatest selling point in plugging for a dam at West Point is . . . Atlanta," advised a West Point–area editor in March 1957. "Flood control is not our major selling point because the U.S. Army Engineers stand ready to come down here and re-dredge the river to the south if we are faced with that necessity. The need for hydroelectric power, while it may develop, has not materialized. . . . Navigation, then, seems to be our most effective argument. . . . So we must become close associates of our friends in Atlanta."[53]

Congress responded to the regional pressure for a West Point dam by approving a feasibility study in 1958. The news heartened everyone in the river valley, from the Gulf of Mexico to Atlanta. As a token of faith in the completion of the channel to Atlanta, "Apalachicola Mayor Jimmie

172 Nichols presented Atlanta Mayor William B. Hartsfield with a two-ton anchor that had been dredged up from the Gulf."[54]

The following year, interested parties organized themselves into the Middle Chattahoochee River Development Association, patterned after the Three Rivers Development Association that had successfully promoted improvement of the lower river. Shaefer Heard of West Point was named president. As a boy, he had been trapped on the second floor of his family's house for four days during the 1919 flood. He never forgot how his family suffered with little food and boiled river water as their only source of drinking water.[55] Heard was joined in urging the West Point Dam by Atlanta's Mayor Hartsfield, who informally explained what the Middle Chattahoochee River Development Association wanted: "All we ask is a few million measly dollars here to get the full benefit out of this great Chattahoochee."[56]

Mother Nature added her voice to the persuasive powers of influential businessmen and politicians. Early in 1961, 5.67 inches of rain fell on Atlanta in a twenty-four-hour period. As the waters rushed downstream they washed out eight bridges in Troup County alone. Twenty others were damaged. Columbus, West Point, and neighboring towns were declared disaster areas.

Newspaper headlines showed that the dam's promoters took advantage of the disaster: "Flood Proves Case for Dam" and "Flood Evidence Rushed to Promote Dam Study," proclaimed the *Atlanta Journal* and *LaGrange Daily News*.[57] Both West Point and Atlanta sent resolutions to the U.S. Congress requesting the immediate funding of the West Point Dam, and local state legislators urged the Georgia legislators to use their influence in Washington to get the dam approved. A portion of their memorial read:

> . . . both Georgians and Alabamians alike who have wallowed and waded through life, saturated with fear, and burdened with the constancy of imminent danger, and Whereas, a flood of public indignation has at last been unleashed with a power and a purpose to match the river itself at the highest crest; and Whereas, the General Assembly of Georgia and every agency of Government would rise in arms at the slightest attempt of a foreign power or any lawless body to harm a single citizen, to deprive him of his rights, or to subject him to suffering, property loss, . . . and death . . . and, Whereas, the answer and solution to these periodic catastrophes is neither mysterious nor unknown . . . [58]

West Point in the flood of 1961. *Courtesy of the Cobb Memorial Archives.*

The arguments were compelling. Congress finally authorized construction of the West Point Dam by the 1962 Flood Control Act. Four years later, valley residents celebrated the long-anticipated dam. Five sticks of dynamite "ushered in a 'new era' in the mid-Chattahoochee River Valley." The ceremony took place on the anniversary of the Civil War's Battle of West Point. "Maybe the Yankees are paying us back for all they tore up that day," said a spectator.[59]

The West Point Dam was not completed until 1975. In the meantime, people began to say their farewells to their home places that soon would be inundated. The Indian town of Burnt Village was hastily excavated. Archaeologists dug up, cataloged, and saved skeletons, pottery, buckles, and musket balls. A Burnt Village Park was planned near the new dam. Families prepared to move from the lands of their ancestors and also to move their dead to higher ground. One curious headstone soon to be covered by the Chattahoochee was inscribed: "R. M. Young's arm." Eighty-eight years before, a boy had lost his arm in a new steam thresher. The first thing his father did was to have the child carve out a stone memorial to his amputated arm.[60] This grave and those of pets and people forgotten to their descendants soon were covered by the river that had attracted them to live there in the first place.

174   In spite of the fact that many lost their family lands to the new reservoir, the people of West Point were happy that they would never again have to worry about a flood destroying all they had worked for. Atlantans had hoped that the dam's completion would be only the first step in connecting them by water to the Gulf of Mexico. But times were changing. The immense cost of the Vietnam War, which ended in 1972, as well as an international fuel crisis, fed a virulent strain of inflation throughout the 1970s. That condition, coupled with a postwar recession, sucked the vibrancy out of the American economy. No longer would discretionary funds necessary to alter the physical landscape be invested merely for the sake of conforming it to man's economic ambition.

By the 1970s, environmentalists were attacking the Corps of Engineers for its destruction of the natural order. Americans began to read about the dangers of water pollution to wildlife and humans. While most people appreciated the benefits derived from damming the Chattahoochee and other rivers, they also began to feel guilty for their cavalier disregard of nature. The coming years would require tough decisions about water rights and environmental protection that would haunt those who simultaneously enjoyed the river's "improvements."

❧

CHAPTER 10

Troubled Waters

THROUGHOUT TIME, THE CHATTAHOOCHEE RIVER HAS served man in four ways: as a means of transportation, a power source, a drinking water reserve, and a repository for sewage.[1] Pollution has been a problem ever since the first white men entered the valley. Just twenty years after white settlement began and the clearing of land for cotton had encouraged soil erosion, driving rain cut deep gulleys into the earth and carried the loose dirt into the river. In the river towns, rain turned the unpaved streets into muddy quagmires whose filth flowed down to the river. One early resident noted that the river was at times so "stifled by the mud" that it killed the fish.[2]

A half century later, the city of Columbus was already having difficulties providing its citizens with safe drinking water. In 1882, the private corporation known as the Columbus Water Works piped in water to the city "from Holland's Creek in southern Lee County, Ala. Within a decade, both the quantity and quality were suspect."[3] When civic leaders commissioned an independent study in 1894, the report sparked a two-decade-long debate on whether or not to use the Chattahoochee as the source of Columbus's drinking water. This study recommended pumping water from the river, and a later report confirmed that this would be the cheapest way to supply water.

However, opponents of the plan pointed out that even the pro-river report acknowledged there were some health risks involved in drinking river water: "The knowledge that a large amount of filth running from the sewers of Atlanta is pouring into the river in a ceaseless stream makes the thought of river water, for drinking, anything but pleasant." The writer of this report added that Atlanta's sewage would be so diluted by

176   the time it reached Columbus that he *thought* "the water could be safely adopted as a city supply."[4] Sides were drawn over the issue, and local politics flooded over with the controversy of choosing a water source for Columbus. Finally, in 1912, the "river plan" was adopted, and the resultant waterworks pumped five million gallons of river water a day into Columbus homes and businesses.

Though people drank from the river, they did not necessarily eat the fish they caught from it because of fears of pollution. An old-timer from the West Point area of the river above Columbus recollected that in his childhood prior to the 1920s, "I can't recall any people I knew buying cat fish caught in waters around West Point and Lanett because of the open sewers that fed them."[5]

In 1890 a sanitary engineer hired by the city of Atlanta reasoned that since no one lived on the banks of the river immediately south of the metropolis, he saw "no reason why the sewage of Atlanta should not be turned into [the creeks that were tributary to the Chattahoochee] . . . for some time to come."[6] In 1908 one-third of Atlanta's sewage flowed directly into Peachtree Creek, one of these tributaries. The creek was so fouled that persons unaccustomed to the stench "found it difficult to breathe."[7]

Atlanta, West Point, Columbus, Phenix City, Eufaula, Fort Gaines, Dothan, and Columbia all ran their sewage directly into the river until the 1960s. When Columbus first began treating waste before turning it into the river in 1964, its method of treatment amounted to simply holding sewage in a pond long enough for pollutants to settle out before returning the water to the river. Another decade passed before a secondary treatment was added.

Although municipalities were guilty of pouring the largest amounts of effluent into the Chattahoochee, industry was causing at least as much damage. Textile mills, paper manufacturers, and other industries that had been drawn to the river in order to exploit its hydroelectric power dumped all their chemical wastes directly into it. While their discharge may have been smaller than that of a city like Columbus, the toxicity of their waste was many times more threatening to all who drank from, bathed in, or ate fish from the Chattahoochee River.

As towns and factories polluted the stream, the Corps of Engineers dammed the Chattahoochee. With the natural flow of the waterway halted, the river's ability to flush itself was stymied and pollutants infected the backwaters. As the last of the government dams was completed in 1963, it was becoming obvious that Chattahoochee neighbors no longer had the luxury of passing on their problems downstream.

By the mid-1960s the river had become a cesspool. Though the *Columbus Ledger-Enquirer* made light of the river pollution in 1964, commenting that there had "seldom been a fish kill" and, in the last dozen years, "no known outbreaks of illness traced to river water,"[8] a 1966 U.S. Department of the Interior report stated that "the Chattahoochee is grossly polluted for about 100 miles below Atlanta from sewage and industrial wastes. . . . Also, bacterial contamination from sewage in certain reaches below West Point and Columbus is of a serious nature, a public health hazard." This study, conducted between 1961 and 1965, found that fifty-one industries dumped untreated or inadequately treated industrial wastes directly into the river. Twenty-two municipalities were guilty of direct river pollution.[9] "Like a Gulliver set upon by countless Lilliputians," the Chattahoochee was bound by those who had once worshiped her.[10] Even the Corps of Engineers acknowledged many years later that "in the early 1960s" the river "was polluted to a great degree."[11]

The Chattahoochee's pollution problem was distinct from most other American rivers, for rarely were cities the size of Atlanta placed near the head of a river system. Most major American cities were located near the coast at the bottom of a waterway, and from there they could do little damage to a river. But the Chattahoochee had to swallow the filth of Atlanta and carry it inside its belly for hundreds of miles to the ocean.

To make matters worse, the metropolis of Atlanta did not develop uniformly from its center. Instead, several communities and counties grew at variance to each other under separate governance. The pell-mell growth following World War II had no central planning board to oversee and coordinate such problems as the dumping of sewage and the intake of drinking water. In 1963, Fulton County pumped 1.15 million gallons of raw sewage directly into the river only two thousand feet upstream from the water intake for Cobb County.[12]

In 1970 the Environmental Protection Department of Georgia reported that the Chattahoochee's water quality was uneven but alarming nonetheless. From the confluence of Yellow Jacket Creek downstream to West Point's water intake, the river was "moderately polluted." "Below Columbus, urban runoff and lack of adequate wastewater treatment resulted in high fecal coliform densities . . . [which were] observed as far downstream as the headwaters of Walter F. George Lake." The lack of flow in the lake allowed the contaminants to settle out so that waters there were classified as safe for "recreational use." Farther downstream, the Great Northern Paper Corporation at Cedar Springs, Alabama, south of Andrews Lake, was singled out as a major polluter. Its emission "reduced the visibility in the water to about six inches" and killed aquatic plants.[13]

With time, the state of America's rivers became so noxious that the federal government became an active agent in cleaning them up. In 1970 the U.S. Environmental Protection Agency (EPA) was created to act as the public's advocate for a livable environment. The government required the Corps of Engineers to study the "environmental impact" of their new and ongoing projects. In doing so in 1979, the Corps found that "even though Columbus, Phenix City, Eufaula, and other communities along the river provide treatment adequate to remove total solids [from their sewage before releasing it into the river,] . . . a large quantity of nitrogen and phosphorous compounds are still released with the treated effluent." Those two nutrients entering the Chattahoochee River were found to be "far in excess of the amounts which phytoplankton can assimilate in this particular aquatic habitat."[14] The Corps also admitted in 1979 that their dams contributed to a low dissolved oxygen content in the impounded lakes, resulting in two fish kills in Andrews Lake in the hot months of 1964 and another in 1972. Two near kills occurred in 1965 and 1969.[15]

The U.S. Congress mandated an end to the dumping of chemical and sewage wastes directly into the river in 1972 by the Clean Water Act. The bill set three national goals on water quality: first, "zero discharge" of pollutants into the nation's navigable waters by 1985; second, that the nation's waters be "fishable and swimmable" by July 1, 1983; and third, that "no more toxics" be allowed into the rivers.[16] In order to conform to the Clean Water Act, Columbus added a "secondary" treatment of its wastes. Pollutants that did not settle out of the holding pond were consumed by bacteria. Workers then added chlorine before returning the water to the river.[17] Other cities also converted to a two- or three-step water treatment system.

The new systems worked effectively except after a rainstorm. Both Columbus and Atlanta (and eleven hundred other American cities) had patched together a new sewer system around an antiquated one. When a downpour filled up Atlanta's new storm-water ducts, the old sewer lines discharged raw sewage and rainwater directly into the river, instead of circuitously through a treatment plant. While this "combined sewers overflow" problem was not unique to Atlanta, it was still considered one of the "worst in the country."[18] One inch of rain sent "220 million gallons

of raw sewage" coursing into tributaries that fed the Chattahoochee.[19]
(Imagine enough sewage to fill 220 Olympic-size swimming pools.)

Bacteria that grew in the water because of the runoffs made the river unsafe for swimming below Atlanta. The EPA ordered Atlanta and other Georgia cities to clean up its "combined sewers" in 1989.[20] However, in 1992 the city of Atlanta was paying daily fines to the state of Georgia of up to $8,000 for "plopping the equivalent of three or four 32,000 ton dump-truck loads of raw sewage sludge into the Chattahoochee each week." (The tab for these penalties had reached $1.6 million by June 1994, and was still rising.)

Eleven years after the target date for cleaning up the nation's rivers called for by the Clean Water Act, the Chattahoochee still failed the "fishable and swimmable" test.[21] In 1989 the EPA found "dangerous levels" of cancer-causing PCBs and chlordane in both the Chattahoochee River and West Point Lake. Phosphate levels in West Point Lake were so high that it caused the growth of algae which sapped the lake of oxygen the fish needed.

In response, the Georgia Assembly passed legislation to allow local governments to ban the sale of detergents containing phosphates. Quickly, Fulton, Gwinnett, and DeKalb Counties adopted the ban, and Columbus city councilor Stephen Hyles urged his city to join the counties of Troup, Cobb, and Douglas, which also were considering it.[22] However, other chemicals, such as chlordane, lay in suspension in the Chattahoochee, and no legislation addressed a remedy for them. The Georgia Department of Natural Resources advised that the public "use their own discretion in deciding whether to eat carp" caught between Atlanta and West Point Lake.[23]

In 1992 the city of Columbus hired Karen Plant to serve as the city's first "Riverkeeper," one of only ten in the country at that time. Her assignment was to monitor an eighty-mile stretch of the river from West Point Lake to Fort Gaines and to educate the public on the importance of the river to their own well-being.[24] Yet public consciousness was not raised overnight. In 1992, Georgia industries "dumped 95 tons of toxic chemicals into the watershed."[25]

While the river was declared by a state official in 1993 to be "better, much better, than a number of years ago," the Chattahoochee on the south side of metropolitan Atlanta was still unsafe for swimming or eating bottom-feeding fish because of the high levels of fecal coliform bacteria.[26] In fact, cities for sixty-five miles downstream from Atlanta could not use the river for drinking water, and for fifty miles downstream could

180 not eat fish caught from it. Dangerous levels of mercury were found in West Point Lake, the main source of drinking water for LaGrange. It was considered inadvisable to eat channel catfish from Lake Oliver, a source of drinking water for Columbus. In 1994 environmentalists declared the Chattahoochee one of the country's "most threatened" rivers, and the EPA identified the Chattahoochee south of Atlanta as "one of the nation's five worst in terms of 14 toxic chemicals found at dangerous levels in fish tissue, including PCBs, dioxins, trichlorobenzene and banned pesticides such as DDT and chlordane."[27]

This revelation jolted some to action. The Turner Foundation, established in 1990 to fund grassroots environmental groups, appointed a riverkeeper to act as "citizen advocate" for the protection of the upper river around Atlanta. A month after this second riverkeeper was hired for the Chattahoochee, a headline in the *Atlanta Journal-Constitution* read: "If We Clean the Hooch, We Won't Have to Shoot It." The accompanying article announced a second annual River Awareness Day. Activities included testing river water, trash pickups, and labeling storm drains to warn people not to dump pollutants there that would flow directly into the river.[28]

But assaults on the waterway continued upriver, and this time from so-called friends. When a federal water expert and his wife, a college professor, took their annual hike to the headwaters of the Chattahoochee to show students "how a river begins," they were shocked to find "how it ends." "Where thick forest once grew, they found a gaping clearcut the size of a football field within a few feet of the water." The U.S. Forest Service had committed the crime in order to make room for restrooms and campsites. "It looks like something out of Vietnam," Marshall said. "They've gone and ruined the birthplace of this river."[29]

Georgia's Environmental Protection Department did not come to the rescue either. In 1990 the legislature ordered the department to draw up guidelines that stated the upper limits of how much pollution could be poured into the river without hazard to life. This information was needed before policy makers could legislate dumping restrictions. Four years later, the state was still waiting for the standards.

In the meantime, Georgia regulators had to rely on industries to be forthright in reporting the amount of pollutants they were dumping into the river. Even if they were honest, punishment for those who "exceeded the limits specified in their discharge permits" was unlikely. Of the 554 violations made between 1991 and 1994, "only six resulted in fines, typically less than $10,000."[30] Part of the problem was a lack of manpower.

Georgia's Environmental Protection Department had only "20 employees
working on clean water compliance and enforcement, while Alabama
ha[d] about 100 . . . and Florida about 185."[31]

The U.S. Congress has abandoned the Chattahoochee, as well. The
last time it amended the Clean Water Act was in 1987. Since then, the
act (which includes grants to states for wastewater treatment plants) has
expired. In 1995 the House and Senate committees charged with author-
ing a comprehensive reauthorization bill could not reconcile their differences, so they both abandoned efforts to reauthorize the Clean Water
Act during the 103rd Congress.[32] Unless the government can rally to
make some tough decisions, it appears the Lilliputians will win.

❧

CHAPTER 11

Will the Water Last?

WHEN THE LAST OF THE FOUR DAMS ON THE CHAT-tahoochee was dedicated in 1963, Alabamians and Georgians celebrated the reopening of commerce on the Chattahoochee. "We opened the gates and the water came over the spillway, and the band was playing, and the artillery was shooting. We had a sense of great achievement, great pride," said Dan Raymond, district chief of the Army Corps of Engineers.[1] The Corps had promised a nine-foot channel from Columbus down to the Gulf of Mexico that would be open 95 percent of the time. However, by 1971, members of the Tri-Rivers Development Association who represented the barging interests of the lower Chatta-hoochee were complaining. "The fact of the matter is," they stated for-mally to their representatives in Washington, "that there is not a nine foot channel over the length of this river system. . . . [T]he absence of this channel is seriously affecting this area's ability to progress."[2]

The low-water hazard was actually below the Jim Woodruff Dam in the Apalachicola River, at the Florida end of the Chattahoochee. In the southern end of the river system there was a nine-foot channel for only 83 percent of the year. Several years of low rainfall exacerbated the prob-lem. Prospective industries attracted to the banks of the Chattahoochee needed to be able to rely on the river for cheap transportation year-round. After various business interests in Georgia and Alabama complained for several years that the river's unreliability was hindering economic growth, the Corps of Engineers began to consider a dam on the Apalachicola River at Blountstown, Florida, to remedy the problem. But when Floridi-ans got wind of these plans, they howled.

The Chattahoochee River system empties into Apalachicola Bay, one

of the largest nurseries in the nation for oysters and other seafood. Shell-
fish live in salt water but need the fresh water that the river brings them
to cut the water's salinity. This discourages conchs and other predators
from invading their territory and brings nutrients downstream from the
river swamps. Domestic and industrial pollutants and heavy loads of
silt from dredging operations upriver inhibit the oysters' growth and can
sicken the people who eat them.

At a public meeting held in 1974 by the Corps on the issue of
modification of the Apalachicola River in Florida, representatives from
the Audubon Club, the Florida Pollution Control Board, the Florida
Game and Fresh Water Fish Commission, the Florida Department of
Commerce, and cities and counties along the lower river—even the beekeepers of Liberty County—all vehemently stated their objections. Their
main point was that the Apalachicola estuary and, therefore, their livelihood would be destroyed by further tampering with their river. Jack Rudloe, a Florida naturalist, asked the Corps to consider that once the estuary was destroyed, it could not be revived. And if more dams and dikes
were built to effectively turn a natural river into a canal, "Apalachicola
would become the receiving end of . . . oil spills, and millions of gallons
of sewage gushing down into our once clean, pristine waters."[3]

Upriver interests, as represented by J. W. Woodruff, Jr., countered
that if the nine-foot depth was not assured, all the previous labor and
money devoted to build the four upriver dams would be for naught, and
soon the "upward trend of waterborne commerce . . . on the tri-rivers
system will . . . turn downward."[4]

The hearing represented the opening salvos in a long and mighty
river war, and the battles between upriver and downriver interests have
continued into the late 1990s. In simplified form the disagreement
amounts to this: Georgia and Alabama require the river to be structurally
changed in order to benefit from it, while Florida can only benefit from
the lower river when it is left in its natural state. It was, and still is, difficult for either side to see the other's point of view. For example, Georgia
state representative Mobley Howell wrote the Corps of Engineers after
the Florida cabinet resolved to object to the dam proposal in 1974, saying,
"It would appear that the Florida objection is more political and emo-
tional than objective."[5]

The controversy heated when Florida decided to take matters into its
own hands by applying for federal protection for the Apalachicola estuary
by having it declared a national estuarine sanctuary (NES). Floridians
saw this action as a defensive one—as saving their economy and their

184   ecosystem from the developers to the north. Georgians and Alabamians viewed Florida's obstruction as provocational. They feared that the Floridians were deliberately trying to ruin them economically in the name of the environment. If the Floridians were hoping to delay Corps action on the river by applying for NES status, they were successful. The application slowed down the paper chase from one government agency to the next, and hamstrung the Corps while upriver interests hounded them to do something to deepen the river, even if it was only emergency dredging.[6]

In retaliation of Florida's move, the Georgia legislature, with the Alabama legislature not far behind, approved a resolution creating a "Tri-Rivers Waterway Compact." The resolution specifically stated that "any two of our states [bordering on the river system] (with the concurrence of Congress) can join in this compact and bind the third state."[7] One can only imagine the furor this proposal caused in Florida. Florida governor Bob Graham wrote Georgia governor George Busbee that the bill was but a "thinly disguised attempt to usurp Florida's role in the management of the Apalachicola River system."[8]

Understanding that the Tri-Rivers Compact was not only unconstitutional but would also block any compromise the three states must eventually make, Governor Busbee vetoed the resolution. But his constituents living along the lower Chattahoochee were, in their words, "stirred up" by the governor's action. "I have always felt that the river would some day save us, but it has to be deep enough to float a barge," wrote a citizen of rural southwest Georgia.[9] "Boardwalks and oysters are fine," another said, "but we have to have the use of that waterway."[10]

Eventually, the government did grant NES status to the Apalachicola estuary, but the Tri-Rivers Development Association and the other upriver interests were comforted by the ruling that "the establishment of the estuarine sanctuary itself cannot prevent the continued operation, maintenance, or enhancement of a Congressionally authorized project."[11] A temporary cease-fire was declared, but an even bigger water-allocation issue was already brewing. This one centered on the other end of the river.

Atlanta, the largest city in the Southeast, ballooned even larger in the 1980s. The city drew 70 percent of its drinking water from the Chattahoochee. As planners looked ahead to the next century, they found the only factor that would inhibit continued growth to be a lack of water. In 1989 Atlanta swallowed thirty-five million gallons of the Chattahoochee

River daily, and planners projected that double that amount would be necessary to sustain growth through the year 2010.[12]

As Atlanta unveiled its plans for guzzling more and more river water, the droughts of the 1980s reminded all river residents that their water source was finite. The year 1988 was especially dry, leaving boat docks at Lake Lanier high and dry. Lawn sprinkling became a criminal offense in Atlanta. Downriver, those dependent on the river for navigation found their barges dragging bottom. Recreation interests that relied on a constant water level for boating and fishing in the man-made lakes of the Chattahoochee worried about a significant loss of revenue. Suddenly people up and down the river saw the Chattahoochee differently. No longer taken for granted, the river had become "liquid gold."[13]

No matter where one lived along the river system, an endangered water supply threatened everyone where it hurt the most—in the pocketbook. Each segment of the region needed Chattahoochee water for its own purposes, and none intended to be denied. "It gets [to be] almost like a classism issue: How do you want to distribute the wealth of water in the basin?" said Steve Leitman, Apalachicola coordinator for the Florida Defenders of the Environment.[14]

From the headwaters to the Gulf of Mexico, every region of the river valley relied on the Chattahoochee for its livelihood. Above Lake Lanier, the river was a popular trout-fishing area, or, as one person has said, a "free grocery store."[15] Downstream at Lake Lanier, million-dollar houses line the shore. Boating-and fishing-related sales underpin the economy of the Gainesville, Georgia, area. Farther downstream at Atlanta, it has been projected that some $127 billion in wages will be lost by the year 2010 if Atlanta does not have the water resources to grow.

People living downstream worry about the quality of their water as more and more people will be flushing toilets their way. Fishermen south of Atlanta have seen cancers growing on the gills of their catches. One sportsman said it had been years since he had eaten anything he caught in the Chattahoochee, but he remembers the flavor of the last bite: "It tasted like creosote, but it was sewage."[16] While Atlanta's interest in the river is to underpin its burgeoning commercial growth, towns and cities downstream simply want as much clean water as they have always had. "We're not looking for extra water [like Atlanta], just for what we were built on," said state senator Pete Robinson of Columbus.[17]

By impounding the river in places, the Corps unintentionally applied new stresses. The man-made lakes that dot the river from Lake Lanier

Fishing at the fall line. *Photo by Ed Ellis. Courtesy of Columbus Ledger–Enquirer.*

Fishing guide Tommy Mike of LaGrange casts for bait on West Point Lake. Photo by Clint Williams. *Courtesy of Columbus Ledger-Enquirer.*

to Lake Seminole were originally intended to ensure sufficient depth in the river channel to support a barge industry. But when the lakes were born, marinas soon lighted on their shores. Campgrounds, picnic areas, and boat ramps invited fishermen, skiers, and sailors to enjoy a day on the water. The lakes became oases in the midst of an economic desert. Instead of the lakes serving the river, many now believe the river should serve the lakes. Those who live nearby do not care so much about the constant depth in the river channel as they do about a stable water level in the lakes.

Below Columbus, in the stretch of the river where steamboats once buzzed around like dragonflies, the days of cotton prosperity had melted into economic decline until the Walter F. George Reservoir revived commerce in the region. But in 1989 annual attendance at Lake Walter F. George topped 324,000 visitors. The impact of West Point Lake above Columbus was even more impressive. In 1989 over eight million people brought their wallets to the river.[18]

On the southernmost stretch of the Chattahoochee, between the Walter F. George Dam and Lake Seminole (formed by the Jim Woodruff Dam), residents value the river as a cheap form of transportation and as a source of water for agricultural irrigation. Southeast Alabama and southwest Georgia are part of the last regions within the South to develop. The recreational industry of the lakes is too distant to affect them directly. Local boosters had hoped to lure industry to the river by promising them a reliable form of cheap transportation in the Chattahoochee. But the droughts of the late 1980s significantly damaged barge traffic on the lower Chattahoochee. The lockmaster at the Walter F. George Reservoir had "maybe one customer a day."[19]

Agricultural interests represent the largest single drain on the water of the lower Chattahoochee. The river runs through farmland as it flows between lakes. Gigantic silver rooster tails spew water into the air to irrigate the peanuts of southwest Georgia and southeast Alabama. It is estimated that farmers will pump from 60 to 80 percent of all future regional water withdrawals into their irrigation systems.[20] And this water does not return to recharge the aquifer. Its spray is lost to the air and topsoil. Already the water table of the nearby Flint River has dropped because of irrigation pumps. If current trends continue, the Chattahoochee will be next.

Below the Jim Woodruff Dam at the corner of the three states, fresh water meets salt and commercial fishermen eke out a living tonging oysters and dragging for shrimp. Their incomes have dwindled with pollu-

The snag boat *Guthrie* in the 1970s. This was the next-to-last steam vessel on the Chattahoochee. *Courtesy of Frank Schnell.*

tion, droughts, and upriver siphoning of the water to other uses. An exploding coastal tourist industry puts other demands on the waters.

Faced with a decision similar to the biblical Solomon when two mothers fought over one baby, we must somehow find among all the competing demands for the river a basin-wide compromise to use the Chattahoochee in the wisest way. Otherwise, the baby may perish in the process of dividing it. Major General Jackson Graham, director of civil works of the Corps of Engineers, may have expressed the dilemma most eloquently back in 1966:

> Let us not devote the resources of our own communities to our own comfort, and then demand that the people of some other community forego the benefits of modern civilization so that we may, when we wish, visit an unspoiled wilderness. Let us not vote down a big reservoir on our own river in our own state, and then expect our essential water storage to be provided in some remote valley whose farmlands may well be the sole support of an entire county. Let us not dump tons of fertilizer on our lawns and gardens, wash our clothes and dishes with deter-

gents, install two bathrooms in every home—all without making proper provision for controlling pollution—and then burst into a rage at someone else because our rivers and lakes are unfit for use.

For centuries humankind has relied on the Chattahoochee. It has fed and watered the people. It has guided their boats to market. Its waterfalls turned the turbines of industry. Its beauty has served as inspiration to poets, nature lovers, novelists, and country-and-western songwriters. It is the region's most important asset. It does not seem fitting that it should die an ignoble death.

It is time for the people who depend on the Chattahoochee to make the sacrifices necessary to preserve it.

NOTES

Abbreviations

BML   Bradley Memorial Library, Columbus, Georgia

CCA   Columbus College Archives, Simon Schwob Memorial Library, Columbus, Georgia

CMA   Cobb Memorial Archives, Valley, Alabama

HAER   Historic American Engineering Record

ORA   *The War of the Rebellion: A Compilation of the Official Records of the Union and Confederate Armies in the War of the Rebellion.* 69 vols. Washington, D.C.: Government Printing Office, 1880–1901.

ORN   *Official Records of the Union and Confederate Navies of the War of the Rebellion.* 30 vols. Washington, D.C.: Government Printing Office, 1894–1927.

SHC   Southern Historical Collection, University of North Carolina, Chapel Hill

Introduction

1. "Heart and Soil," *Charlotte (N.C.) Observer,* February 20, 1994; Thomas W. Hodler and Howard A. Schretter *The Atlas of Georgia* (Athens: The Institute of Community and Area Development/The University of Georgia, 1986), 15.

2. "Heart and Soil," *Charlotte Observer,* February 20, 1994.

3. *LaGrange (Ga.) Reporter,* August 23, 1883.

4. Georgia Mountains Planning and Development Commission, "River Corridor Studies of the Upper Chattahoochee, Chestatee, and Etowah Rivers," 1973, 26, BML.

5. Bill Winn, "Reality, Dreams Flow Together in Chattahoochee," *Columbus (Ga.) Ledger-Enquirer,* April 8, 1990.

6. Tom Sellers, *Valley Echoes* (Atlanta: Davicone, 1986), 3.

Chapter 1. The Ancients

1. For an excellent treatise on the lifestyles of both the prehistoric and historic-period Native Americans of the Chattahoochee River, see William W. Winn, *The Old Beloved Path: Daily Life among the Indians of the Chattahoochee River Valley* (Eufaula, Ala.: Historic Chattahoochee Commission and the Columbus Museum, 1992). Unless otherwise noted, this work is the source of information on the archaeology and anthropology of the Chattahoochee Indians of the prehistoric and protohistoric periods. See especially pp. 6–120.

2. Ibid., 38.

3. [Frank Schnell], "Diversity over Time and Space: Indians of North America," program of the Indian Cultural Festival, 1991.

4. Winn, *The Old Beloved Path*, 48.

5. Jon Gibson et al., "Cultural Investigations in the Apalachicola and Chattahoochee River Valleys in Florida, Alabama, and Georgia: History, Archeology, and Underwater Remote Sensing," typescript, 1980, 123, Frank Schnell Personal Collection, Columbus Museum; [Schnell], "Diversity over Time and Space," n.p.

6. *Columbus Ledger-Enquirer,* April 25, 1982. For extensive analysis of the Cemochechobee site by those who excavated it, see Frank Schnell, Vernon J. Knight, and Gail S. Schnell, *Cemochechobee: Archaeology of a Mississippian Ceremonial Center on the Chattahoochee River* (Gainesville: University Presses of Florida, 1981).

7. Frank T. Schnell, working copy of "A Preliminary Culture History of the Lower Chattahoochee Valley in the Sixteenth Century," typescript, October 27, 1989, 6. In possession of the author.

8. Ibid.

9. Ibid., 7.

10. Ibid., 9.

11. Ibid.

12. The term "Creek" will be used throughout to mean all those Native Americans associated with the Creek Confederation, regardless of what language they spoke.

13. Michael D. Green, *The Politics of Indian Removal: Creek Government and Society in Crisis* (Lincoln: University of Nebraska Press, 1982), 14.

14. Ibid.

15. Ibid., 15.

16. Ibid., 11.

17. Winn, *The Old Beloved Path*, 138–39.

18. Ibid., 140.

19. Ibid.; Green, *Politics of Indian Removal*, 4–6.

20. Green, *Politics of Indian Removal*, 11.

21. David H. Corkran, *The Creek Frontier, 1540–1783* (Norman: University of Oklahoma Press, 1967), 38–39.

22. Ibid., 16.

23. Ibid., 39.

24. Ibid.

25. Winn, *The Old Beloved Path*, 156.

26. James Adair, quoted in John R. Swanton, *Social Organization and Social Usages of the Indians of the Creek Confederacy,* Bureau of American Ethnology Bulletin No. 42 (Washington, D.C.: Government Printing Office, 1928), 366.

27. Winn, *The Old Beloved Path*, 165.

28. Swanton, *Social Organization of the Creek Confederacy*, 492–94.

29. Green, *Politics of Indian Removal*, 3.

30. John R. Swanton, *The Indians of the Southeastern United States,* Bureau of American Ethnology Bulletin No. 137 (1946; reprint, Grosse Pointe, Mich.: Scholarly Press, 1969), 34.

31. Winn, *The Old Beloved Path,* 84–85.

32. J. Leitch Wright, *Creeks and Seminoles: The Destruction and Regeneration of the Muscogulge People* (Lincoln: University of Nebraska Press, 1986), 35.

33. Etta Blanchard Worsley, *Columbus on the Chattahoochee* (Columbus, Ga.: Columbus Office Supply Co., 1951), 43.

34. Alexander B. Meek, *Romantic Passages of the Southwest,* quoted in Anne Kendrick Walker, *Russell County in Retrospect: An Epic of the Far Southeast* (Richmond: Dietz, 1950), 23.

Chapter 2. The Scramble for Muscogee

1. As recorded by the Spanish bishop Calderon of St. Augustine, these towns were Chicahuti, Sabacola el Grande, Oconi, Apalachocoli, Ilapi, Tacusa, Ocmulgui, Ahachito, Cazithto (Cusseta), Colomme, Cabita (Coweta), Cuchiguali, and Usachi. See Mark E. Fretwell, *This So Remote Frontier: The Chattahoochee Country of Alabama and Georgia* (1980; reprint, Eufaula, Ala.: Historic Chattahoochee Commission, 1987), 83–84.

2. Charlton W. Tebeau, *A History of Florida* (Coral Gables: University of Miami Press, 1971), 51.

3. Swanton, *Indians of the Southeastern United States,* 62.

4. Fretwell, *This So Remote Frontier,* 93.

5. Worsley, *Columbus on the Chattahoochee,* 6.

6. Quoted in Fretwell, *This So Remote Frontier,* 97.

7. Corkran, *The Creek Frontier,* 51; Fretwell, *This So Remote Frontier,* 100.

8. Corkran, *The Creek Frontier,* 62.

9. Ibid., 79.

10. Ibid., 61.

11. Ibid., 63–64.

12. Ibid., 64–65.

13. Ibid., 65–81. Brims died between 1730 and 1733. His son Sepeycoffee died of drunkenness in 1726. Brims's brother Chigelley was commissioned by the English as Brims's successor, but in Creek tradition, he held the position only until Brims's underage son Malatchi was mature enough to become "emperor."

14. Ibid., 81–87.

15. Green, *Politics of Indian Removal,* 26.

16. John Walton Caughey, *McGillivray of the Creeks* (Norman: University of Oklahoma Press, 1938), 20.

17. Green, *Politics of Indian Removal,* 28.

18. Ibid.

19. Ibid., 30.

20. Ibid., 31–33.

21. Ibid., 33.

22. James H. O'Donnell III, *Southern Indians in the American Revolution* (Knoxville: University of Tennessee Press, 1973), 125.

23. Corkran, *The Creek Frontier,* 13.

24. Ibid., 131.

25. James H. O'Donnell III, *The Georgia Frontier, 1773–1783* (n.p., 1975), 12–13.

26. O'Donnell, *Southern Indians in the American Revolution,* 139.

27. Green, *Politics of Indian Removal,* 34.

28. Ibid.

29. Caughey, *McGillivray of the Creeks,* 33.

30. "Return of Persons Killed Wounded and Taken Prisoner," in File II, Record Group 4, Subgroup 2, Series 46, Box 76, Georgia Department of Archives and History, Atlanta.

31. Caughey, *McGillivray of the Creeks,* 154.

32. Green, *Politics of Indian Removal,* 35.

33. Ibid.

34. J. Leitch Wright, *William Augustus Bowles: Director General of the Creek Nation* (Athens: University of Georgia Press, 1967), 25.

35. Ibid., 38.

36. Ibid., 39.

37. Ibid., 56–57.

38. Quoted in Caughey, *McGillivray of the Creeks,* 57.

39. Green, *Politics of Indian Removal,* 36.

40. Wright, *William Augustus Bowles,* 149.

41. Green, *Politics of Indian Removal,* 36.

42. Ibid., 37.

43. Mark E. Fretwell, *West Point: The Story of a Georgia Town* (West Point, Ga.: Chattahoochee Valley Historical Society, 1987), 7.

44. Henry DeLeon Southerland, Jr., and Jerry Elijah Brown, *The Federal Road through Georgia, the Creek Nation, and Alabama, 1806–1836* (Tuscaloosa: University of Alabama Press, 1989), 124.

45. Ibid., 22–36; Green, *Politics of Indian Removal,* 39.

46. The speech was pieced together by an early Alabama historian who talked to eyewitnesses. It is quoted in Frank Lawrence Owsley, Jr., *Struggle for the Gulf Borderlands: The Creek War and the Battle of New Orleans, 1812–1815* (Gainesville: University Presses of Florida, 1981), 12–13.

47. Ibid., 13.

48. Ibid.

49. Ibid., 17.

50. Ibid., 39.

51. Angie Debo, *The Road to Disappearance: A History of the Creek Indians* (Norman: University of Oklahoma Press, 1941), 76; Walker, *Russell County in Retrospect,* 94; James C. Bonner, "Journal of a Mission to Georgia in 1827," *Georgia Historical Quar-*

terly 44 (March 1960): 81; "Indian Chiefs," *Alabama Historical Quarterly* 13 (1951): 28–30, 37–45.

52. Owsley, *Struggle for the Gulf Borderlands*, 52.

53. Fretwell, *West Point*, 9–10. Ten boats were ordered. See Montgomery to Jackson, March 20, 1814, reprinted in Franklin M. Garrett, *Atlanta and Environs: A Chronicle of Its People and Events*, 2 vols. (New York: Lewis Historical Publishing Co., 1954), 1:13. The road from this Fort Peachtree to Hog Mountain in present-day Gwinnett County was the original Peachtree Road (ibid., 11).

54. Debo, *The Road to Disappearance*, 82.

55. Owsley, *Struggle for the Gulf Borderlands*, 86.

56. Green, *Politics of Indian Removal*, 43.

57. William S. Coker and Thomas D. Watson, *Indian Traders of the Southeastern Spanish Borderlands: Panton, Leslie & Company and John Forbes & Company, 1783–1847* (Pensacola: University Presses of Florida/University of West Florida Press, 1986), 281–83.

58. Owsley, *Struggle for the Gulf Borderlands*, 175–77.

59. Coker and Watson, *Indian Traders*, 291–99.

60. Ibid., 302.

61. Ibid., 307–8. Debo recorded that McIntosh led five hundred Creeks (*The Road to Disappearance*, 84).

62. Debo, *The Road to Disappearance*, 85.

63. Walker, *Russell County in Retrospect*, 45–46.

64. Antonio J. Waring, ed., *Laws of the Creek Nation* (Athens: University of Georgia Press, 1960), in *A Creek Source Book*, ed. William Sturtevant, Bureau of American Ethnology Bulletin No. 123 (New York: Garland Publishing Co., 1987), 17–27.

65. Ibid., 88.

66. Ibid., 89.

67. Ibid., 90.

68. Ibid., 91.

69. Relevant portions of Levasseur's journal are reprinted in Walker, *Russell County in Retrospect*, 68–71.

70. Ibid., 69.

71. Debo, *The Road to Disappearance*, 95.

72. Quoted in ibid., 96.

Chapter 3. Along the White Frontier

1. From an 1824 letter quoted in Betty Dickinson Ivey, "From River to Rail in Pickens County," *Alabama Review* 7 (1954): 58–59.

2. Edward A. Mueller, *Perilous Journeys: A History of Steamboating on the Chattahoochee, Apalachicola, and Flint Rivers, 1828–1928* (Eufaula, Ala.: Historic Chattahoochee Commission, 1990), 15–16.

3. "An Act to Dispose of and Distribute the Lands Lately Acquired by the United States for the Use of Georgia," *Acts of the General Assembly of the State of Georgia, Passed in May and June, 1825*, 3–16, in "History: Founding of Columbus" vertical file, CCA.

196

4. The river drops 125 feet here within two and a half miles, producing between 66,000 and 99,000 horsepower. Sandra Dixon, "Muscogee County," in "A History of the Chattahoochee Region," typescript for Westville Historic Handicrafts, Inc., June 20, 1987, in "Chattahoochee Region—History" vertical file, CCA; "An Act to Lay Out a Trading Town and to Dispose of the Lands Reserved for the Use of the State Near the Coweta Falls on the Chattahoochee River," in "History: Founding of Columbus" vertical file, CCA.

5. *Columbus (Ga.) Enquirer,* February 25, 1862.

6. John Goff, "The Steamboat Period in Georgia," *Georgia Historical Quarterly* 12 (March 1928): 246.

7. Mueller, *Perilous Journeys,* 16.

8. *Mobile Register,* June 28, 1827, quoted in ibid., 17.

9. Quoted in Mueller, *Perilous Journeys,* 17.

10. Quoted in ibid., 19.

11. Quoted in ibid., 19–20.

12. Report given in *Columbus Enquirer,* June 21, 1828, as reprinted in T. Joe Peddy, "Steamboats on the Chattahoochee River, 1832–1902," hand-bound typescript, BML (hereinafter cited as Peddy, "Steamboats").

13. T. Joe Peddy, "Reminiscences of Columbus by John E. Lamar," hand-bound typescript, BML.

14. *Birmingham (Ala.) News,* March 26, 1922.

15. Sandra Dixon, "A History of the Chattahoochee Region," 11.

16. Quoted in Mueller, *Perilous Journeys,* 20–21.

17. Worsley, *Columbus on the Chattahoochee,* 156.

18. Hoyt M. Warren, *Chattahoochee Trails: Short, Factual, Historical Stories about the Chattahoochee Valley* (Abbeville, Ala.: Henry County Historical Society, 1981), 108; Willis S. Cox, "A Story of the Chattahoochee River as It Has affected Fort Gaines and Clay County Together with Some Articles of Historical Interest," typescript, 1966, 28, in CCA.

19. Warren, *Chattahoochee Trails,* 47.

20. Green, *Politics of Indian Removal,* 142.

21. Anne Kendrick Walker, *Backtracking in Barbour County: A Narrative of the Last Alabama Frontier* (Richmond: Dietz, 1941), 17–18; Warren, *Chattahoochee Trails,* 45.

22. Walker, *Backtracking in Barbour County,* 17–18; Warren, *Chattahoochee Trails,* 45.

23. Clifford L. Smith, *History of Troup County* (Atlanta: Foote & Davies Co., 1933), 54.

24. Both quotes in Mueller, *Perilous Journeys,* 24.

25. C. D. Arwedson's impressions are reprinted in Mills Lane, ed., *The Rambler in Georgia* (Savannah: Beehive Press, 1973), 24–25.

26. Quoted in Green, *Politics of Indian Removal,* 142.

27. Louise Gunby Jones DuBose, *A History of Columbus, Georgia, 1828–1928* (Columbus, Ga.: Historical Publishing Co., 1929), 45–46.

28. Bill Winn, "Reality, Dreams Flow Together in Chattahoochee," *Columbus Ledger-Enquirer,* April 8, 1990.

29. Cox, "A Story of the Chattahoochee River," 3.

30. Solomon F. Smith, *Theatrical Management in the West and South for Thirty Years* (New York: Harper & Brothers, 1868), 79–80.

31. Tyrone Power, *Impressions of America; during the years 1833, 1834, and 1835,* vol. 2 (Philadelphia: Carey, Lea & Blanchard, 1836), 80.

32. Quoted in Green, *Politics of Indian Removal,* 156.

33. Grant Foreman, *Indian Removal: The Emigration of the Five Civilized Tribes of Indians* (Norman: University of Oklahoma Press, 1932), 107.

34. Quoted in ibid., 107–8.

35. Ibid., 110–11.

36. Mary Elizabeth Young, *Redskins, Ruffleshirts, and Rednecks: Indian Allotments in Alabama and Mississippi* (Norman: University of Oklahoma Press, 1961), 75–76, 86.

37. Green, *Politics of Indian Removal,* 176.

38. Ibid., 177.

39. Ibid., 179–80.

40. John H. Martin, comp., *Columbus, Geo., from Its Selection as a "Trading Town" in 1827 to Its Partial Destruction by Wilson's Raid, in 1865* (1874; reprint, Easley, S.C.: Georgia Genealogical Reprints, 1972), 32, 46–47.

41. Ibid., 47.

42. Ibid., 21.

43. *Columbus Enquirer,* December 13, 1834, as reprinted in Peddy, "Steamboats."

44. Ibid.

45. Foreman, *Indian Removal,* 152; Green, *Politics of Indian Removal,* 184; *Columbus Enquirer,* June 9, 16, 1836, as reprinted in Peddy, "Steamboats," ; Sara Robertson Dixon and A. H. Clark, *History of Stewart County, Georgia,* vol. 2 (Waycross, Ga.: A. H. Clark, 1975), 29–32.

46. Army surgeon J. R. Motte is quoted in Richard H. Coss, "On the Trail of Jim Henry," *Muscogiana* 3 (Fall 1992): 55.

47. Undated Resolution of John Fontaine to Governor Schley, in Record Group 4, Subgroup 2, Series 46, Box 76, Folder 12, Georgia Department of Archives and History, Atlanta.

48. Green, *Politics of Indian Removal,* 185.

49. Foreman, *Indian Removal,* 152–54.

50. Ibid., 155.

51. Ibid., 156.

52. Ibid., 159.

53. Debo, *The Road to Disappearance,* 103.

54. Ibid., 104–5.

Chapter 4. A Land of Cotton

1. *Columbus (Ga.) Times,* December 25, 1844, quoted in *Inventory of the County Archives of Georgia,* No. 106: Muscogee County (Atlanta: Georgia Historical Records Survey, 1941), 11; Martin, *Columbus, Geo.,* 162.

198   2. Sandra Dixon, "A History of the Chattahoochee Region," n.p.

3. T. Joe Peddy, comp., *Olden Days in Columbus, Georgia, 1842–1856, as Described in Columns from the "Columbus Enquirer-Sun" during 1895–1898* (privately published, n.d.), 74.

4. Quoted in Martin, *Columbus, Geo.*, 92.

5. John Lupold, J. B. Karfunkle, and Barbara Kimmelman, "Water Power Development at the Falls of the Chattahoochee," HAER Report, GA-22, 4–5, typescript, August 1977, in CCA.

6. Ibid., 5.

7. J. H. Howard to Farish Carter, August 2, 1848, Farish Carter Papers, SHC.

8. Lupold, Karfunkle, and Kimmelman, "Water Power Development at the Falls of the Chattahoochee," 6; Peddy, *Olden Days in Columbus,* 74.

9. Maj. Leighton Morey et al., "Brief History of the Columbus Iron Works, 1853–1865," typescript, March 5, 1957, 2, in "Columbus History" vertical file, CCA.

10. Lupold, Karfunkle, and Kimmelman, "Water Power Development at the Falls of the Chattahoochee," 6; Marjorie W. Young, *Textile Leaders of the South* (Anderson, S.C.: James R. Young, 1963), 454.

11. Lupold, Karfunkle, and Kimmelman, "Water Power Development at the Falls of the Chattahoochee," 6; Richard P. Spencer, "The Empire State in the New South" (Senior thesis, Princeton University, 1988), 38–39.

12. Quoted in John Lupold, J. B. Karfunkle, and Barbara Kimmelman, "The Evolution of Hydro-Power Development at the Falls of the Chattahoochee," typescript overview of other HAER reports prepared by the authors in 1977, 3, in the possession of John Lupold.

13. Ibid., 1.

14. Sandra Dixon, "A History of the Chattahoochee Region," n.p.; Spencer, "The Empire State in the New South," 37.

15. Harry P. Owens, "Apalachicola before 1861" (Ph.D. diss., Florida State University, 1966), 243.

16. See *Apalachicola (Fla.) Commercial Advertiser,* January 8, 1844; Mrs. Marvin Scott, *History of Henry County, Alabama* (Pensacola: Frank R. Parkhurst & Son, 1961), 23, 27, 34, 43, 91, 93; Walker, *Russell County in Retrospect,* 176, 181.

17. Clay County Library, *The History of Clay County* ([Fort Gaines, Ga.]: n.p., 1976), 7–8.

18. Louis C. Hunter, *Steamboats on the Western Rivers: An Economic and Technological History* (1949; reprint, New York: Dover, 1993), 94–100.

19. These were the *Edwin Forest,* built in 1835, and the *Florence* and *Frances,* built in 1837. See Mueller, *Perilous Journeys,* Appendix C, 1–14.

20. Gibson et al., "Cultural Investigations in the Apalachicola and Chattahoochee River Valleys."

21. These were the *America,* the *Catherine,* the *Chewala,* the *Franklin,* the *Indian,* the *Indian No. 2,* the *Laura,* the *Munnerlyn,* the *New Boston,* and the *Retrieve.* See ibid.

22. Ibid.

23. *Columbus Enquirer,* May 6, 1862.

24. Mueller, *Perilous Journeys*, Appendix C, 1–14.

25. Joseph B. Mahan, *Columbus: Georgia's Fall Line "Trading Town"* (Northridge, Calif.: Windsor, 1986), 24.

26. Mueller, *Perilous Journeys*, 28.

27. *Columbus Enquirer*, January 16, 1835, as reprinted in Peddy, "Steamboats."

28. Mahan, *Columbus*, 34.

29. George P. Rawick, gen. ed., *The American Slave: A Composite Autobiography*, Supplement, Series 1, vol. 1, Alabama Narratives (Westport, Conn.: Greenwood Press, 1979), 381.

30. Callie B. McGinnis and Sandra K. Stratford, *Muscogee County, Georgia, 1860 Census Index* (Columbus, Ga.: Yesteryear Research Associates, 1985), x.

31. Worsley, *Columbus on the Chattahoochee*, 216.

32. *Columbus Times*, April 2, 1850.

33. Walker, *Backtracking in Barbour County*, 28.

34. Sellers, *Valley Echoes*, 38.

35. Warren, *Chattahoochee Trails*, 142.

36. John Horry Dent Papers, Microfilm copy, Historic Chattahoochee Commission, Eufaula, Alabama.

37. Rawick, *The American Slave*, Series 2, Georgia Narratives, vol. 13, part 3:185.

38. St. Andrews fishermen peddled their salted fish by wagon as far north as Columbus. See G. M. West, *St. Andrews, Florida* (Panama City, Fla.: Panama City Publishing Co., 1960), 51, 94.

39. Rawick, *The American Slave*, vol. 8, part 2:250.

40. Ibid., Supplement, Series 1, vol. 3 (Georgia Narratives), part 1:6–7.

41. *Eufaula (Ala.) Democrat*, October 24, 1848; *Eufaula (Ala.) Spirit of the South*, January 14, 1851.

42. Hatcher and McGehee Negro Book, *passim*, CCA.

43. James G. Bogle, "Horace King, 1807–1887," *Georgia Life*, Spring 1980, 33.

44. *Columbus Ledger-Enquirer—East Alabama Edition*, July 1, 1982; *LaGrange (Ga.) Daily News*, July 12, 1978; Bogle, "Horace King," 33–35; Horace King vertical file, Troup County Archives, LaGrange.

45. George Rogers Taylor, *The Transportation Revolution, 1815–1860* (New York: Harper & Row, 1951), 71. The steamboat *Champion* set a new speed record for the round trip between Apalachicola and Columbus in 1844, averaging just over ten miles per hour. See *Apalachicola Commercial Advertiser*, February 12, 1844.

46. U. B. Phillips, *A History of Transportation in the Eastern Cotton Belt to 1860* (1908; reprint, New York: Octagon Books, 1968), 17–18.

47. Ibid., 18.

48. Milton Sydney Heath, *Constructive Liberalism: The Role of the State in Economic Development in Georgia to 1860* (Cambridge: Harvard University Press, 1954), 279.

49. *Columbus Times*, November 4, 1846.

50. *Columbus Enquirer*, May 14, 1845.

51. *Columbus Times*, February 1, 1848.

200   52. Heath, *Constructive Liberalism*, 280.

53. *Columbus Enquirer*, May 24, 1853.

54. *Columbus Times*, February 8, 1848.

55. *Albany (Ga.) Patriot*, December 8, 1854; *Columbus Times*, February 22, 1848.

56. *Columbus (Ga.) Times and Sentinel*, January 17, 1854.

57. The Montgomery and West Point Railroad was completed in 1845. See T. D. Clark, "The Montgomery and West Point Railroad Company," *Georgia Historical Quarterly* 17 (March 1933): 297.

58. Harriet E. Amos, *Cotton City: Urban Development in Antebellum Mobile* (Tuscaloosa: University of Alabama Press, 1985), 205.

59. *Columbus Times and Sentinel*, July 8, 1854; *Debow's Review* 29 (November 1860): 670.

60. For Apalachicola cotton receipts during the years 1840 to 1860, see Lynn Willoughby Ware, "The Cotton Trade of the Apalachicola/Chattahoochee River Valley, 1840–1860" (Ph.D. diss., Florida State University, 1989), 235.

61. Owens, "Apalachicola before 1861," 249.

62. *Apalachicola Commercial Advertiser*, December 9, 1848. The Macon and Western was a part of the Western and Atlantic line.

63. Reprinted in the *Columbus Enquirer*, November 14, 1854.

64. Paris J. Tillinghast to Samuel W. Tillinghast, September 22, 1855, William Norwood Tillinghast Papers, William R. Perkins Library, Duke University, Durham, North Carolina.

65. William N. Thurston, "The Apalachicola-Chattahoochee-Flint River Water Route System in the Nineteenth Century," *Georgia Historical Quarterly* 57 (Summer 1973): 204.

Chapter 5. The Civil War Years

1. John Lupold, *Columbus, Georgia, 1828–1978* (Columbus, Ga.: Columbus Sesquicentennial, 1978), 29.

2. Alexander A. Allen to George W. Allen, February 12, 1861, George W. Allen Papers, SHC.

3. Entry of January 5, 1861, Charles Arnold Hentz Diary, SHC.

4. Scarborough to Sissy, April 19, 1861, in Elizabeth F. Smith, ed., *The Civil War Letters of Rabon Scarborough, Apalachicola, Florida, 1861–1862* (Crawfordville, Fla.: Magnolia Monthly Press, 1973), 1.

5. Ibid.

6. H. E. Owens to Hon. L. P. Walker, March 9, 1861, *ORA*, 1:448 (all references to *ORA* are to Series 1).

7. Joseph D. Cushman, Jr., "The Blockade and Fall of Apalachicola," *Florida Historical Quarterly* 41 (July 1962–April 1963): 38.

8. Order of Commander Shaw, June 11, 1861, *ORN*, 16:544 (all references to *ORN* are to Series 1 unless otherwise noted).

9. E. F. Smith, *Civil War Letters of Rabon Scarborough*, 24.

10. Scarborough to Sissy, October 2, 1861, ibid., 6.

11. Milton to Brown et al., October 29, 1861, 8–11, John D. Milton Correspondence, Florida State Archives, R. A. Gray Building, Tallahassee.

12. Milton et al. to Davis, November 4, 1861, John D. Milton Letterbook, vol. 6 of Territorial and State Governors' Letterbooks, Florida State Archives, R. A. Gray Building, Tallahassee.

13. Blocker to Milton, November 11, 1861, Milton Letterbook, 80–82.

14. Milton to Benjamin, November 14, 1861, *ORA*, 6:319.

15. Scarborough to Wife, November 8, 1861, in E. F. Smith, *Civil War Letters of Rabon Scarborough*, 14.

16. Cushman, "Blockade of Apalachicola," 41.

17. Floyd to Milton, December 18, 1861, *ORA*, 6:355.

18. Emmons to W. W. McKean, December 18, 1861, *ORN*, 17:7.

19. E. F. Smith, *Civil War Letters of Rabon Scarborough, passim.*

20. Scarborough to Sissy, October 2, 1861, ibid., 7.

21. Simon Peter Richardson, *The Lights and Shadows of Itinerant Life: An Autobiography of Rev. Simon Peter Richardson, D.D.* (Nashville: Methodist Episcopal Publishing Co., 1901), 174.

22. Milton to Brown, February 20, Milton to Trapier, February 20, and Milton to Trapier, February 22, 1862, Milton Letterbook, 123, 177, 242.

23. Apalachicola City Resolution, n.d., ibid., 188.

24. Young et al. to Benjamin, February 22, 1862, *ORA*, 53:219–20.

25. Floyd to Milton, March 17, 1862, *ORA*, 6:412–13.

26. Stellwagen to W. W. McKean, March 25, 1862, *ORN*, 17:193.

27. Ibid.

28. Ibid, 193–94.

29. *Columbus Enquirer*, March 25, 1862.

30. William R. Boggs, *Military Reminiscences of Gen. Wm. R. Boggs, C.S.A.*, ed. William K. Boyd (Durham, N.C.: Seeman Printery, 1913), 30.

31. Morris to Theodorus Bailey, May 1, 1863, *ORN*, 17:432.

32. Abbot to Stellwagen, March 25, 1862, ibid., 195.

33. Stellwagen to W. W. McKean, April 4, A. J. Drake to W. W. McKean, April 8, 1862, ibid., 201–4, 204–5.

34. Stellwagen to W. W. McKean, April 4, 1862, ibid., 202.

35. Ibid., 203.

36. Catherine Cooper Hopley, *Life in the South, from the Commencement of the War*, 2 vols. (London: Chapman & Hall, 1863), 1:264–65.

37. Ibid., 327–28.

38. Lupold, *Columbus, Georgia*, 31.

39. Spencer, "The Empire State in the New South," 41.

40. Lupold, Karfunkle, and Kimmelman, "Water Power Development at the Falls of the Chattahoochee," 7; Lupold, *Columbus, Georgia*, 31.

41. Lupold, *Columbus, Georgia*, 33; Spencer, "The Empire State in the New South," 42–43.

42. Lupold, *Columbus, Georgia,* 35.

43. *Columbus Enquirer,* March 19, 1862.

44. *Columbus Enquirer,* September 15, 1862, as reprinted in Peddy, "Steamboats."

45. *Columbus Enquirer,* September 27, 1862, in ibid.

46. Maxine Turner, *Navy Gray: A Story of the Confederate Navy on the Apalachicola and Chattahoochee Rivers* (Tuscaloosa: University of Alabama Press, 1988), 53.

47. McLaughlin to J. McC. Baker, June 22, 1862, *ORN,* Series 2, 2:208–9.

48. Ibid.; John Thomas Scharf, *History of the Confederate Navy from Its Organization to the Surrender of Its Last Vessel* (New York: Rogers & Sherwood, 1887), 48. This ship was officially known as the *Jackson.*

49. Milton to Randolph, September 24, 1862, Milton Letterbook, 460; Milton to Davis, October 10, 1862, *ORA,* 53:260; Milton et al. to Davis, November 4, 1862, Milton Correspondence, n.p.

50. *Columbus Enquirer,* August 26, September 16, 1862.

51. G. W. Randolph to J. F. Bozeman, November 5, S. Cooper to Milton, November 27, and Cooper to John Gill Shorter, December 28, 1862, *ORA,* 14:666, 689, 735.

52. Patricia L. Faust, ed., *Historical Times Illustrated Encyclopedia of the Civil War* (New York: Harper & Row), 146.

53. Cobb to G. T. Beauregard, December 9, Thomas Jordan to Cobb, December 18, 1862, *ORA,* 14:703–5, 707–9.

54. Horace Montgomery, *Howell Cobb's Confederate Career* (Tuscaloosa: Confederate Publishing Co., 1959), 85.

55. Morris to Theodorus Bailey, April 24, May 1, 1863, *ORN,* 17:421, 432.

56. Cobb to Beauregard, December 22, 1862, *ORA,* 14:728–31.

57. Cobb to Jones, January 2, 1863, *ORN,* 17:865.

58. Gift to Collier, January 30, 1863, George W. Gift Papers, SHC.

59. Quoted in Turner, *Navy Gray,* 83.

60. Gift to E. Shackleford, February 1, January 31, 1863, Gift Papers.

61. Gift to E. Shackleford, September 13, 1862, ibid.

62. Gift to E. Shackleford, March 15, January 31, 1863, ibid.

63. Gift to E. Shackleford, February 2, 1863, ibid.

64. Entry of June 10, 1862, Laura Beecher Comer Diary, 1862–1863, SHC.

65. Gift to E. Shackleford, February 2, 1863, Gift Papers.

66. Ibid.

67. Moreno's memoir is quoted in Turner, *Navy Gray,* 92.

68. *Register of Officers of the Confederate States Navy, 1861–1865* (Mattituck, N.Y.: J. M. Carroll & Co., 1983), 70, 77.

69. Gift to E. Shackleford, April 7, 1863, Gift Papers.

70. Gift to E. Shackleford, April 11, 1863, ibid.

71. Gift to E. Shackleford, May 4, 1863, ibid.

72. Morris to G. Welles, May 24, 1863, *ORN,* 17:447.

73. Gift to E. Shackleford, May 25, 28, 1863, Gift Papers.

74. Moreno to D. B. Harris, May 28, 1863, *ORA,* 14:954.

75. Gift to E. Shackleford, May 30, March 15, Gift Papers.

76. McLaughlin to Jones, June 15, Morris to Theodorus Bailey, June 18, 1863, *ORN*,
17:869–70, 475.

77. Gift to E. Shackleford, June 17, 1863, Gift Papers; McLaughlin to Jones, June 15, 1863, *ORN*, 17:870.

78. Moreno to D. B. Harris, May 28, 1863, *ORA*, 14:954.

79. Scharf, *History of the Confederate Navy*, 618.

80. McLaughlin to Jones, June 15, 1863, *ORN*, 17:870.

81. Gift to E. Shackleford, May 30, 1863, Gift Papers.

82. McLaughlin to Jones, June 15, 1863, *ORN*, 17:870.

83. Ibid., 871.

84. Ibid.

85. McLaughlin to Jones, December 26, J. K. Mitchell to Gift, May 18, 1863, ibid., 872, 867.

86. Gift's explanation to the Office of Order and Details was deemed "entirely satisfactory under the circumstances." Gift to E. Shackleford, September 10, 1862, Gift Papers.

87. Gift to E. Shackleford, June 3, 1863, ibid. No record of this report was found in naval records.

88. Gift to E. Shackleford, June 17, 1863, ibid.

89. McLaughlin to Jones, December 26, 1863, *ORN*, 17:872.

90. McLaughlin to Jones, June 15, 1862, ibid.; Gift to E. Shackleford, June 17, 1863, Gift Papers.

91. McLaughlin to Jones, December 26, 1863, *ORN*, 17:872.

92. J. Wells to C. K. Stribling, January 29, 1865, ibid., 797–800.

93. C. K. Stribling to G. Welles, March 14, 1865, ibid., 825–26.

94. *Columbus Enquirer*, December 23, 1864.

95. Maxine Turner, "Naval Operations on the Apalachicola and Chattahoochee Rivers, 1861–1865," reprinted in *Alabama Historical Quarterly* 36 (Fall and Winter 1974–75): 65.

96. Brown to Milton, February 18, Ives to Milton, March 9, and Milton to Brown, March 9, 1865, Milton Letterbook, 181–83.

97. Ethelred Philips to James Philips, January 12, 1865, James J. Philips Papers, SHC.

98. Jennie to Annie, January 18, 1864, Ruffin-Roulhac-Hamilton Family Papers, SHC.

99. DuBose, *History of Columbus, Georgia*, 127.

100. Lupold, *Columbus, Georgia*, 38.

101. Colonel LaGrange's report is quoted in Fretwell, *West Point*, 31.

102. Lupold, *Columbus, Georgia*, 43.

103. Sandra Dixon, "A History of the Chattahoochee Region," n.p.

104. A. Asboth to C. T. Christensen, June 6, 1865, *ORN*, 17:856–57.

Chapter 6. Moonlight and Magnolias

1. *Columbus Sun*, January 10, 1867, as reprinted in Peddy, "Steamboats." Unless otherwise noted, all contemporary Columbus newspaper articles used in this chapter came from this source.

2. *Columbus (Ga.) Enquirer-Sun*, June 7, 1878.

204   3. *Columbus Times,* March 27, 1879; *LaGrange Reporter,* February 12, 1885; "Song of the Chattahoochee," special edition of the *Columbus Ledger-Enquirer,* September 6, 1964.

4. *Columbus (Ga.) Times,* March 24, 1879.

5. Ibid.

6. *Columbus Times,* March 15, 1879.

7. Ibid., March 13, 1879.

8. *Columbus (Ga.) Enquirer-Sun,* August 4, 1901.

9. Ibid., October 6, 1886.

10. Ibid., March 30, 1886.

11. Ibid., November 16, 1880.

12. Ibid., December 28, 1885.

13. Ibid.

14. Ibid.

15. Ibid., November 5, 1886.

16. Clason Kyle, *Images: A Pictorial History of Columbus, Georgia* (Norfolk, Va.: Donning, 1986), 126.

17. J. Truman Holland, "Stern Wheeling on the Chattahoochee," *Thomasville (Ga.) Courier,* March 10, 1977.

18. Ibid.

19. Sellers, *Valley Echoes,* 7.

20. Ibid.

21. *Columbus Enquirer,* August 1, 1876.

22. *Columbus Enquirer-Sun,* January 19, 1900, March 19, 1879.

23. Ibid., August 4, 1901.

24. *Columbus Times,* March 26, 1879.

25. *Columbus Sun,* January 10, 1867.

26. *Columbus Enquirer-Sun,* August 4, 1901.

27. *Columbus Sun,* January 10, 1867.

28. *Columbus Enquirer-Sun,* September 9, 1897.

29. "Meddye Tipton Willis' Trip to Alabama," typescript, 5, in Schnell Personal Collection.

30. Hoyt M. Warren, "Henry's Heritage: A History of Henry Co., Ala.," 138, reprinted in appendix of Peddy, "Steamboats."

31. Bill Winn, "Reality, Dreams Flow Together in Chattahoochee," *Columbus Ledger-Enquirer,* April 8, 1990.

32. *Columbus Enquirer-Sun,* December 28, 1885.

33. Warren, "Henry's Heritage," 138.

34. *Columbus Times,* March 19, 1879.

35. Ibid., March 15, 1879.

36. Quoted in Mueller, *Perilous Journeys,* 120.

37. *Columbus Enquirer-Sun,* December 7, 1880.

38. Ibid., July 18, 1878; Mueller, *Perilous Journeys,* 183.

39. *Columbus Enquirer-Sun,* January 19, 1900.

40. Ibid., May 3, 1900.

41. *Report of the Board of Engineers for Rivers and Harbors on Survey: Preliminary Examination of Chattahoochee River, Georgia, and Alabama,* House Document No. 1664, 65th Cong., 3rd sess., 1916, 23.

42. Ibid.

43. Ibid., 23–25.

44. *Columbus Enquirer-Sun,* May, 14, 1878.

45. Ibid., May 22, 1878.

46. Ibid.

47. Ibid., May 30, 1879.

48. The Villa Reich occupied an entire city block in Columbus. Built in the 1880s, this amusement center offered ornamental gardens, a beer garden, a bandstand, and a ballroom measuring fifty by one hundred feet. See Kyle, *Images,* 83.

49. *Columbus Times,* April 17, 1879.

50. Ibid.

51. Ibid., May 29, 1879.

52. Ibid.

53. Ibid., June 7, 1879.

54. Worsley, *Columbus on the Chattahoochee,* 151.

55. *Columbus Enquirer-Sun,* October 24, 1891.

Chapter 7. Workin' the River

1. Bill Winn to the author, [May 1995].

2. Walker, *Russell County in Retrospect,* 302–3.

3. *Columbus Enquirer-Sun,* August 15, 1887, October 13, 1888, or reprinted in Peddy, "Steamboat." Unless otherwise noted, all contemporary Columbus newspapers cited in this chapter come from this source.

4. Cox, "A Story of the Chattahoochee River," 17–18.

5. *Columbus Enquirer-Sun,* January 5, 1886.

6. Ibid., March 25, 1892.

7. Ibid., April 4, 1887.

8. Ibid., December 25, 1888, March 3, 1889.

9. *Columbus Enquirer,* January 9, 1877.

10. Mueller, *Perilous Journeys,* 254–55.

11. *Columbus Enquirer-Sun,* September 26, 1901.

12. Robert H. Flewellen, "The Tavern at Eufaula, Alabama (A Documentary)," typescript, in "Alabama-Eufaula-Tavern" vertical file at Carnegie Library, Eufaula, Alabama.

13. *Columbus Enquirer-Sun,* March 18, 1894.

14. Ibid.

15. *Columbus Times,* March 12, 1879.

16. *Columbus Enquirer-Sun,* August 4, 1901.

17. J. Truman Holland, "Stern Wheeling on Chattahoochee," *Thomasville Courier,* March 20, 1977.

206   18. Frank Schnell, "Life on the Chattahoochee," clipping dated February 7, 1983, in Schnell Personal Collection.

19. Mueller, *Perilous Journeys*, 202.

20. Ibid., 214.

21. *Columbus (Ga.) Daily Enquirer*, September 21, 1867.

22. *Columbus (Ga.) Daily Sun*, January 12, 1873.

23. *Columbus Enquirer-Sun*, April 4, 1884.

24. Tom Sellers, "Ol' Water Nymph Has Boat Fever," undated clipping in Schnell Personal Collection.

25. *Columbus Enquirer-Sun*, August 4, 1901.

26. Hunter, *Steamboats on the Western Rivers*, 457.

27. *Columbus Daily Sun*, September 28, 1865.

28. *Columbus Enquirer-Sun*, June 18, 1899.

29. "Song of the Chattahoochee," *Columbus Ledger-Enquirer*, September 6, 1964.

30. *Columbus Enquirer-Sun*, February 20, 1900.

31. Ibid., November 21, 1900.

32. Ibid., February 19, 1901.

33. Ibid., February 1, 1901.

34. Ibid., February 28, 1901.

Chapter 8. The Business of Steamboating

1. Thurston, "Apalachicola-Chattahoochee-Flint River Water Route," 205.

2. *Columbus Enquirer-Sun*, August 13, 1881, as reprinted in Peddy, "Steamboats." Unless otherwise noted, all contemporary Columbus newspapers cited in this chapter came from this source.

3. Thurston, "Apalachicola-Chattahoochee-Flint River Water Route," 206.

4. Ibid., 206–7.

5. *Columbus Enquirer-Sun*, December 16, 1900; *Report of the Board of Engineers for Rivers and Harbors on Survey*, 14.

6. *Columbus Enquirer-Sun*, May 17, 1878.

7. Mueller, *Perilous Journeys*, 121.

8. *Columbus Daily Sun*, February 19, 1867.

9. *Columbus Enquirer*, October 24, 1868.

10. Ibid., July 9, 1868.

11. Ibid., March 16, 1869.

12. Mueller, *Perilous Journeys*, 129.

13. Ibid.

14. *Columbus Enquirer-Sun*, May 8, 1878.

15. Ibid., November 21, 1878.

16. *Columbus Times*, June 14, 1879.

17. *Columbus Enquirer-Sun*, September 6, 1881, quoting from the edition of June 3, 1879.

18. *Columbus Times*, January 15, 1879.

19. *Annual Report of the Chief of Engineers of the United States Army*, 1876, as quoted 207
in Thurston, "Apalachicola-Chattahoochee-Flint River Water Route," 207.

20. *Columbus Enquirer-Sun*, August 12, 19, 1881.

21. Ibid., August 19, 1881.

22. *Annual Report of the Chief of Engineers of the United States Army*, 1883, as quoted
in Thurston, "Apalachicola-Chattahoochee-Flint River Water Route," 207.

23. *Columbus Enquirer-Sun*, October 4, 1895.

24. Ibid., January 14, 1894.

25. Ibid., September 12, 1897.

26. Ibid., September 29, 1897.

27. Ibid.

28. Ibid., August 27, 1881.

29. Ibid., September 7, 1881.

30. Ibid., September 28, 1881.

31. Ibid., November 24, 1881.

32. Worsley, *Columbus on the Chattahoochee*, 160; *Columbus Enquirer-Sun*, October
1886.

33. *Columbus Enquirer-Sun*, January 19, 1883.

34. Ibid., January 19, 1884.

35. Ibid., October 10, 1886.

36. Ibid., August 2, 1878.

37. *Columbus Enquirer*, March 27, 1881.

38. Ibid., June 19, 1881.

39. Ibid., December 20, 1881.

40. *Columbus Enquirer-Sun*, January 23, 1881.

41. Ibid., April 24, 1886.

42. Ibid., March 20, April 16, 1886.

43. Ibid., October 10, 1886, November 19, 1887, February 26, 1889.

44. Ibid., June 2, 1898.

45. Ibid., June 22, 1898.

46. Ibid., October 12, 1889.

47. Ibid., January 6, 1889.

48. *LaGrange Reporter*, January 4, 1883.

49. *Columbus Enquirer-Sun*, September 5, 1884.

50. *LaGrange Reporter*, August 7, 1884.

51. Joe Barrow, "The Way I Heard It," handwritten account in folder 93 of the
Chattahoochee Valley Historical Society Collection, CMA.

52. *Columbus Enquirer-Sun*, August 25, 1891.

53. Ibid., June 10, 1896.

54. Ibid., September 23, 1897.

55. Ibid., March 23, 1899.

56. Ibid., June 25, 1899.

57. Ibid., February 6, December 18, 1900.

208   58. Ibid., December 18, 1900.

59. Ibid., January 4, April 16, 1901.

60. Ibid., April 16, 1901.

61. Bert Neville, *Directory of Steamboats with Illustrations and List of Landings, on Chattahoochee-Apalachicola-Flint-Chipola Rivers* (Selma, Ala.: privately published, 1975), 31–35.

62. *Columbus Enquirer-Sun,* May 2, 1901.

63. *Report of the Board of Engineers for Rivers and Harbors on Survey,* 23–25.

64. Mueller, *Perilous Journeys,* 237.

65. *Report of the Board of Engineers for Rivers and Harbors on Survey,* 21–22.

66. Ibid., 16.

67. Mueller, *Perilous Journeys,* 212.

68. *Columbus Enquirer-Sun,* May 3, 1900.

69. *Report of the Board of Engineers for Rivers and Harbors on Survey,* 1916, 22.

70. Ibid., 48.

71. Special Sesquicentennial Supplement III, *Columbus Ledger-Enquirer,* April 30, 1978.

72. Mueller, *Perilous Journeys,* 247.

73. Ibid., 248.

74. "River Transit Co. and Its Fleet of Boats, Barges," *Industrial Index,* 31:50, in "Columbus—Riverboats" vertical file, BML; Mueller, *Perilous Journeys,* 251; Frank Schnell to author, July 17, 1995.

Chapter 9. River Power

1. M. W. Young, *Textile Leaders of the South,* 361.

2. Sandra Dixon, "A History of the Chattahoochee Region," n.p.

3. John Lupold, J. B. Karfunkle, and Barbara Kimmelman, "The Eagle and Phenix Mills," HAER Report, GA-30, 5–6, typescript, August 1977, in CCA; Lupold, Karfunkle, and Kimmelman, "Water Power Development at the Falls of the Chattahoochee," 7–8.

4. "Song of the Chattahoochee," special edition of the *Columbus Ledger-Enquirer,* September 6, 1964.

5. Spencer, "The Empire State in the New South," 49.

6. John S. Lupold, "Industrial Archeology of Columbus, Georgia: A Tour for the 8th Annual Conference of the Society for Industrial Archeology," typescript, April 1979, n.p., in CCA.

7. Press release from Mrs. Hugh Smith for Historic Marker Dedication at Langdale, Alabama, on April 24, 1964, in Janie Lovelace Heard Collection, CMA.

8. M. W. Young, *Textile Leaders of the South,* 359.

9. William Warren Rogers et al., *Alabama: The History of a Deep South State* (Tuscaloosa: University of Alabama Press, 1994), 445. West Point Manufacturing Company merged with Pepperell Manufacturing Company of Maine in 1965.

10. Ibid., 363.

11. Worsley, *Columbus on the Chattahoochee,* 396.

12. Lupold, Karfunkle, and Kimmelman, "Water Power Development at the Falls of the Chattahoochee," 10.

13. Lupold, Karfunkle, and Kimmelman, "The Evolution of Hydro-Power Development at the Falls of the Chattahoochee," 6.

14. Ibid., 11.

15. Lupold, "Industrial Archeology," n.p.

16. Ibid.

17. These mills were the Columbus Manufacturing Company, Swift Spinning Company, Perkins Hosiery, and Topsy Mill. See Lupold, *Columbus, Georgia,* 90.

18. Lupold, Karfunkle, and Kimmelman, "Water Power Development at the Falls of the Chattahoochee," 12.

19. *Report of the Board of Engineers for Rivers and Harbors on Survey,* 13–14.

20. Quoted in Lupold, Karfunkle, and Kimmelman, "Water Power Development at the Falls of the Chattahoochee," 16.

21. Ibid., 20.

22. Ibid., 21.

23. Ibid.

24. "A Brief History of Electric Power in Columbus and Surrounding Area. Taken from the Records of the Power Company," typescript, n.d., 5, in CCA.

25. Quoted in *Atlanta Constitution,* May 20, 1934, clipping in George S. Cobb Collection.

26. U.S. District Engineer, "Survey of Chattahoochee River, Ga. and Ala.," 1918, in *Report of the Board of Engineers for Rivers and Harbors on Survey,* 30–47.

27. *West Point (Ga.) Press,* April 10, 1886, in Cobb Collection.

28. Joe Barrow Account of 1886 flood, in "Georgia–Troup County–West Point Flood, First-Hand Accounts" vertical file, CMA.

29. William H. Scott Account of 1886 flood, ibid.

30. "Chattahoochee River Levels at West Point, Georgia," in Cobb Collection. While there were other years when the river spilled slightly over its banks, the years listed here were those in which the waters exceeded flood stage by at least three and one-half feet.

31. Ibid.

32. Undated clipping in Cobb Collection.

33. *Opelika-Auburn (Ala.) News,* June 6, 1993.

34. Ibid.

35. Undated clipping in Chattahoochee Valley Historical Society Collection, CMA.

36. Worsley, *Columbus on the Chattahoochee,* 424–25.

37. *Columbus Ledger-Enquirer,* August 1, 1993.

38. *Columbus Ledger-Enquirer, East Alabama Friends* edition, July 20, 1989.

39. Ibid.; undated article circa late 1930s from *Chattahoochee (Fla.) Valley Times,* in Janie Heard Collection.

210   40. *Annual Report of R. M. Harding, Pres., and J. Ralston Cargill, Sec.-Treas. & Traffic Manager, Columbus Chamber of Commerce, for Fiscal Year Ending September 30, 1927,* in J. Ralston Cargill Collection, CCA; *Columbus (Ga.) Ledger,* March 28, 1928.

41. *Columbus Ledger,* August 15, 1928.

42. *Columbus Enquirer,* November 28, 1929.

43. Worsley, *Columbus on the Chattahoochee,* 391; *Atlanta Journal-Constitution,* March 29, 1953.

44. U.S. Army Corps of Engineers, map entitled "Apalachicola, Chattahoochee, & Flint Rivers, Ala., Ga., & Fla."; "Water Resources Development by the U.S. Army Corps of Engineers in Georgia," March 1977, 29–32. Copies of both documents are found in Jack T. Brinkley Collection, CCA.

45. Sidney Lanier is said to have visited his relatives in West Point frequently. For his kinswoman, Mrs. W. C. Lanier, he composed "The Song of the Chattahoochee" to be published in her hometown newspaper in the late 1870s. See "Remarks by J. L. Lanier" in Janie Heard Collection.

46. Ibid.

47. *Columbus Ledger-Enquirer,* March 17, 1957.

48. *Columbus Ledger,* October 5, 1951.

49. *Columbus Ledger-Enquirer,* March 17, 1957. The papers of James W. Woodruff, Sr., and of the Three Rivers Association are being processed at the Columbus College Archives and will be available to researchers in the future.

50. "Water Resources Development by the U.S. Army Corps of Engineers in Georgia," 29–32.

51. Georgia Power Company, "Oliver Dam: Dedication," November 12, 1959, pamphlet found in "Oliver Dam" vertical file, BML.

52. *Atlanta Journal-Constitution,* July 8, 1951.

53. *Valley (Ala.) Times-News,* March 25, 1957.

54. *Atlanta Constitution,* November 6, 1958.

55. *Valley Times-News,* February 1, 1959.

56. Ibid., November 4, 1959.

57. *Atlanta Journal,* February 27, 1961, and *LaGrange Daily News,* March 5, 1961, in R. Shaefer Heard Collection, CMA.

58. Senate Resolution No. 81, in Middle Chattahoochee River Development Association Collection, CMA.

59. *Atlanta Journal-Constitution,* April 17, 1966; Fretwell, *West Point,* 61.

60. *LaGrange Daily News,* February 12, 1970.

Chapter 10. Troubled Waters

1. Frank Schnell, "A Cultural Resource Assessment of the Proposed Site of the River Club, Columbus, Georgia," typescript, 1989, in "Chattahoochee River" vertical file, CCA.

2. *Inventory of the County Archives of Georgia,* Number 106: Muscogee County, 30.

3. *Columbus Ledger-Enquirer,* December 3, 1989.

4. Ibid., December 3, 1989.

5. J. Arch Avary, Jr., to Joe Barrow, July 8, 1981, in Arch Avary Collection, CMA.

6. Stuart Galishoff, "Paying for the Cost of Growth: The Environmental Engineering Debate in Atlanta, 1877–1914," *Essays in Public Works History* 18 (Winter 1994/1995): 30.

7. Ibid., 37.

8. *Columbus Ledger-Enquirer,* September 6, 1964.

9. U.S. Department of the Interior, *Proceedings: Conference In the Matter of Pollution of the Interstate Waters of the Chattahoochee River and Its Tributaries, from Atlanta, Georgia, to Fort Gaines, Georgia,* vol. 2 (n.p., 1966), 179–80.

10. "Song of the Chattahoochee," special edition of the *Columbus Ledger-Enquirer,* September 6, 1964.

11. U.S. Army Corps of Engineers, "Draft Environmental Impact Statement: Walter F. George Lock, Dam and Lake, Alabama and Georgia: Operation and Maintenance," 1979, 21, in Brinkley Collection.

12. *Atlanta Constitution,* November 6, 1963.

13. U.S. Army Corps of Engineers, "Draft Environmental Impact Statement," 23.

14. Ibid., 31.

15. Ibid., 32.

16. *Atlanta Journal-Constitution,* June 26, 1994.

17. *Columbus Ledger-Enquirer,* December 3, 1989.

18. *Atlanta Journal-Constitution,* June 26, 1994.

19. Ibid.

20. *Columbus Ledger-Enquirer,* June 26, 1989.

21. *Atlanta Journal-Constitution,* June 26, 1994.

22. Undated clipping circa 1989 in "Chattahoochee River" vertical file, CCA.

23. Ibid.

24. *Columbus Ledger-Enquirer,* November 15, 1992.

25. *Atlanta Journal-Constitution,* July 3, 1994.

26. Ibid., October 15, 1993.

27. Ibid., April 24, July 3, 1994.

28. Ibid., May 18, 1994.

29. Ibid., July 3, 1994.

30. Ibid.

31. Ibid.

32. *Congressional Digest,* vol. 74, no. 12, December 1995, 299.

Chapter 11. Will the Water Last?

1. *Columbus Ledger-Enquirer,* August 19, 1990.

2. Ibid.

3. Jack Rudloe Statement before the U.S. Army Corps of Engineers, Appendix 33, "Minutes of the Public Meeting on Apalachicola River Below Jim Woodruff Lock and Dam," Marianna, Florida, June 27, 1973, in Brinkley Collection.

212   4. Statement of J. W. Woodruff, Jr., Appendix 25 in ibid.

5. Mobley Howell to Col. Drake Wilson, District Engineer, May 20, 1974, in Brinkley Collection.

6. George Busbee to Lt. Gen. J. W. Morris, May 23, 1979; U.S. Army Corps of Engineers, "Navigation Bulletin No. 79-44," May 24, 1979; George Busbee to Clifford Alexander, June 8, 1979; all in Brinkley Collection.

7. Don Fuqua to Jack Brinkley, April 5, 1979, in Brinkley Collection.

8. Unidentified clipping in Box 197, Brinkley Collection.

9. *Cuthbert (Ga.) Times,* May 10, 1979.

10. *Tallahassee Democrat,* May 3, 1979.

11. Draft Environmental Impact Statement, "Apalachicola River and Bay Estuarine Sanctuary," 1979, in Brinkley Collection.

12. *Columbus Ledger-Enquirer,* June 8, 1988; "River Rivalry," *Economist,* March 30, 1991, 26.

13. *Columbus Ledger-Enquirer,* June 8, 1988.

14. *Atlanta Journal-Constitution,* August 19, 1990.

15. Ibid.

16. Ibid.

17. *Columbus Ledger-Enquirer,* August 23, 1991.

18. Ibid., February 25, 1990.

19. *Atlanta Journal-Constitution,* August 19, 1990.

20. Ibid., July 13, 1994.

BIBLIOGRAPHY

PRIMARY SOURCES

MANUSCRIPTS

Bradley Memorial Library, Columbus, Georgia
    "Columbus—Riverboats" vertical file.
    "Oliver Dam" vertical file.
Carnegie Library, Eufaula, Alabama
    "Alabama-Eufaula-Tavern" vertical file.
Cobb Memorial Archives, Valley, Alabama
    Avary, Arch. Collection.
    Chambers, Nella Jean. Collection.
    Chattahoochee Valley Historical Society. Collection.
    Cobb, George S. Collection.
    Fretwell, Mark. Collection.
    "Georgia–Troup County–West Point Flood, First-Hand Accounts" vertical file.
    Heard, Janie Lovelace. Collection.
    Heard, R. Shaefer. Collection.
    Howard, Lois. Collection.
    Middle Chattahoochee River Development Association. Collection.
Columbus College Archives, Simon Schwob Memorial Library, Columbus, Georgia
    "Bridges" vertical file.
    Brinkley, Jack T. Collection.
    Cargill, J. Ralston. Collection.
    "Chattahoochee Region—History" vertical file.
    "Chattahoochee River" vertical file.
    "Columbus Industry" vertical file.
    Hatcher and McGehee Negro Book.
    "History: Founding of Columbus" vertical file.
    Kroeglin Collection.
    Peddy, Thomas J. Collection.
    Petre, Marjorie Cargill. Collection.
    Petre, Marjorie Cargill, and Louisa Cargill. Collection.

214   Schnell, Frank. Collection.

Woodruff Collection.

Columbus Museum, Columbus, Georgia

    Schnell, Frank. Personal Collection.

Florida State Archives, R. A. Gray Building, Tallahassee, Florida

    Milton, John D. Correspondence.

    Milton, John D. Letterbook. Vol. 6 of Territorial and State Governors' Letterbooks.

Georgia Department of Archives and History, Atlanta

    Creek Indians. Collection. File II, Record Group 4, Subgroup 2, Series 46, Box 76.

    Goff, John. Collection.

    Hays, Louise Frederick, comp. and ed. "Unpublished Letters of Timothy Barnard, 1784–1820." Typescript, 1939.

Historic Chattahoochee Commission, Eufaula, Alabama

    Dent, John Horry. Papers. Microfilm copy.

Southern Historical Collection, University of North Carolina, Chapel Hill

    Allen, George W. Papers.

    Carter, Farish. Diary.

    Comer, Laura Beecher. Diary, 1862–1863.

    Gift, George Washington. Papers.

    Hentz, Charles Arnold. Papers.

    Philips, James J. Papers.

    Ruffin-Roulhac-Hamilton Family. Papers.

Troup County Archives, LaGrange, Georgia

    Horace King vertical file.

William R. Perkins Library, Manuscript Department, Duke University, Durham, North Carolina

    Tillinghast, William Norwood. Papers.

PUBLISHED SOURCES

"An Act to Dispose of and Distribute the Lands Lately Acquired by the United States for the Use of Georgia." In *Acts of the General Assembly of the State of Georgia, Passed in May and June, 1825*, 3–16. In "History: Founding of Columbus" vertical file, Columbus College Archives.

"An Act to Lay Out a Trading Town and to Dispose of the Lands Reserved for the Use of the State Near the Coweta Falls on the Chattahoochee River, December 24, 1827." Photocopy in "History, Founding of Columbus" vertical file, Columbus College Archives.

Banks, John. *A Short Biographical Sketch of the Undersigned by Himself.* Austell, Ga.: E. Leonard, 1936. In John Banks Collection, Columbus College Archives.

Bartram, William. *Travels through North and South Carolina, Georgia, East and West Flor-*

ida, the Cherokee Country, the Extensive Territories of the Muscogulges, or Creek   215
Confederacy, and the Country of the Chactaws [sic]. Philadelphia: James & Johnson,
1771.

Boggs, William R. *Military Reminiscences of Gen. Wm. R. Boggs, C.S.A.* Edited by William
K. Boyd. Durham, N.C.: Seemann Printery, 1913.

Bossu, Jean-Bertrand. *Travels in the Interior of North America, 1751–1762.* Translated and
edited by Seymour Feiler. Norman: University of Oklahoma Press, 1962.

Columbus, Georgia, City Directory. 1873–1908. N.p., n.d. In Bradley Memorial Library, Columbus, Georgia.

Dow, Peggy. *Vicissitudes, or the Journey of Life.* Philadelphia: Joseph Rakestraw, 1815.

Facts in Favor of Deepening the Chattahoochee, Apalachicola, and Flint Rivers. Columbus,
Ga.: Thomas Gilbert, Printer, 1901.

Georgia: The WPA Guide to Its Towns and Countryside. 1940. Reprint, Columbia: University
of South Carolina Press, 1990.

Halbert, H. S., and T. H. Ball. *The Creek War of 1813 and 1814.* Edited by Frank L. Owsley,
Jr. Southern Historical Publications No. 15. Tuscaloosa: University of Alabama
Press, 1969.

Hall, Basil. *Travels in North America in the Years 1827 and 1828.* 3 vols. Edinburgh: printed
for Cadell and Co., Edinburgh; and Simpkin and Marshall, London by Ballan-
tine & Co., 1829. Vol. 3:280–288.

Hall, Margaret Hunter. *The Aristocratic Journey; Being the Outspoken Letters of Mrs. Basil
Hall Written During a Fourteen Months' Sojourn in America, 1827–1828.* Edited by
Una Pope-Hennessey. New York: Putnam, 1931.

Harper, Francis, ed. *The Travels of William Bartram: Naturalist's Edition.* New Haven,
Conn.: Yale University Press, 1958.

Hawkins, Benjamin. *Letters, Journals, and Writings of Benjamin Hawkins.* Edited by C. L.
Grant. 2 vols. Savannah: Beehive Press, 1980.

Hopley, Catherine Cooper. *Life in the South, from the Commencement of the War.* 2 vols.
London: Chapman & Hall, 1863.

Lane, Mills, ed. *The Rambler in Georgia.* Savannah: Beehive Press, 1973.

Latham, Henry. *Black and White: Journal of a Three Months' Tour in the United States.*
Philadelphia: Lippincott, 1867.

Milfort, Louis LeClerc. *Memoirs, or a Quick Glance at My Various Travels and My Sojourn
in the Creek Nation.* Translated and edited by Ben C. McCary. Savannah: Beehive
Press, 1972.

Official Records of the Union and Confederate Navies of the War of the Rebellion. 30 vols.
Washington, D.C.: Government Printing Office, 1894–1927.

Peddy, Thomas J., comp. *Olden Days in Columbus, Georgia, 1842–1856, as Described in Columns from the "Columbus Enquirer-Sun" during 1895–1898.* Privately published, n.d.

———. "Reminiscences of Columbus by John E. Lamar." Hand-bound typescript. In
Bradley Memorial Library, Columbus, Georgia.

———. "Steamboats on the Chattahoochee River, 1832–1902." 27 hand-bound volumes.
1980–81. In Bradley Memorial Library, Columbus, Georgia.

216   Pope, John. *A Tour through the Southern and Western Territories of the United States of America.* Facsimile reproduction of the 1792 edition. Gainesville: University of Florida Press, 1979.

Posey, Walter Brownlow, ed. "Alabama in the 1830s as Recorded by British Travellers." *Birmingham-Southern College Bulletin* 31 (December 1938).

Power, Tyrone. *Impressions of America; during the years 1833, 1834, and 1835.* 2 vols. Philadelphia: Carey, Lea, & Blanchard, 1836.

Register of Officers of the Confederate States Navy, 1861–1865. Mattituck, N.Y.: J. M. Carroll & Co., 1983.

Report of the Board of Engineers for Rivers and Harbors on Survey: Preliminary Examination of Chattahoochee River, Georgia, and Alabama. House Document No. 1664. 65th Cong., 3rd sess., 1916.

Report on Navigation on the Chattahoochee River to Columbus, Georgia. Report to the Mayor and City Commissioners of Columbus, Georgia, by the firm of Thomas and Hutton, 1958.

Report Upon the Improvement of Rivers and Harbors in the Montgomery, Alabama, District. Washington, D.C.: Government Printing Office, 1915.

Report Upon the Improvement of Rivers and Harbors in the Montgomery, Alabama, District. Washington, D.C.: Government Printing Office, 1927.

Richardson, Simon Peter. *The Lights and Shadows of Itinerant Life: An Autobiography of Rev. Simon Peter Richardson, D.D.* Nashville: Methodist Episcopal Publishing Co., 1901.

Smith, Elizabeth F., ed. *The Civil War Letters of Rabon Scarborough, Apalachicola, Florida, 1861–1862.* Crawfordville, Fla.: Magnolia Monthly Press, 1973.

Smith, Solomon F. *Theatrical Management in the West and South for Thirty Years.* New York: Harper & Brothers, 1868.

Swan, Caleb. "Position and State of Manners and Arts in the Creek, or Muscogee Nation in 1791." In *History of the Indian Tribes of North America*, edited by Henry Rowe Schoolcraft, 5:251–83. Philadelphia: Lippincott, 1855.

"Table of Distances on Apalachicola, Chattahoochee and Flint Rivers: Presented by Steamer Shamrock." Columbus, Ga.: Columbus Sun Printers, n.d. In "Bridges" vertical file, Columbus College Archives.

U.S. Army Corps of Engineers, Mobile District. "Minutes of the Public Meeting on Apalachicola River below Jim Woodruff Lock and Dam." Marianna, Florida. June 27, 1973. In Bradley Memorial Library, Columbus, Georgia.

U.S. Department of the Interior. *Proceedings: Conference in the Matter of Pollution of the Interstate Waters of the Chattahoochee River and its Tributaries, from Atlanta, Georgia to Fort Gaines, Georgia.* Vol. 2. N.p., 1966.

The War of the Rebellion: A Compilation of the Official Records of the Union and Confederate Armies in the War of the Rebellion. 69 vols. Washington, D.C.: Government Printing Office, 1880–1901.

Willett, William M. *A Narrative of the Military Actions of Colonel Marinus Willett, Taken Chiefly from His Own Manuscript.* New York: G. & C. & H. Carvill, 1831.

Woodward, Thomas S. *Woodward's Reminiscences of the Creek, or Muscogee Indians Con-*   217
tained in Letters to Friends in Georgia and Alabama. Montgomery, Ala.: Barrett &
Wimbish, 1859.

NEWSPAPERS

Albany (Ga.) Patriot
Apalachicola (Fla.) Commercial Advertiser
Atlanta Constitution
Atlanta Journal
Atlanta Journal-Constitution
Birmingham (Ala.) News
Charlotte (N.C.) Observer
Columbus (Ga.) Daily Enquirer
Columbus (Ga.) Daily Sun
Columbus (Ga.) Enquirer
Columbus (Ga.) Enquirer-Sun
Columbus (Ga.) Ledger
Columbus (Ga.) Ledger-Enquirer
Columbus (Ga.) Sun
Columbus (Ga.) Times
Columbus (Ga.) Times and Sentinel
Cuthbert (Ga.) Times
Eufaula (Ala.) Democrat
Eufaula (Ala.) Spirit of the South
LaGrange (Ga.) Daily News
LaGrange (Ga.) Reporter
Opelika-Auburn (Ala.) News
Tallahassee (Fla.) Democrat
Thomasville (Ga.) Courier
Valley (Ala.) Times-News
West Point (Ga.) Press

SECONDARY SOURCES

BOOKS

Amos, Harriet E. *Cotton City: Urban Development in Antebellum Mobile.* Tuscaloosa: Uni-
versity of Alabama Press, 1985.
Ballard, W. L. *The Yuchi Green Corn Ceremonial: Form and Meaning.* Los Angeles: Uni-
versity of California American Indian Studies Center, 1978.
Braund, Kathryn Holland. *Deerskins and Duffels: The Creek Indian Trade with Anglo-
America, 1685–1815.* Lincoln: University of Nebraska Press, 1993.

218   Caughey, John Walton. *McGillivray of the Creeks.* Norman: University of Oklahoma Press, 1938.

Chapman, George. *Chief William McIntosh: A Man of Two Worlds.* Atlanta: Cherokee Publishing Co., 1988.

Clay County Library. *The History of Clay County.* [Fort Gaines, Ga.]: n.p., 1976.

Coleman, Kenneth. *Georgia History in Outline.* Athens: University of Georgia Press, 1960.

———. *A History of Georgia.* Athens: University of Georgia Press, 1977.

Coker, William S., and Thomas D. Watson. *Indian Traders of the Southeastern Spanish Borderlands: Panton, Leslie & Company and John Forbes & Company, 1783–1847.* Pensacola: University Presses of Florida/University of West Florida Press, 1986.

Corkran, David H. *The Creek Frontier, 1540–1783.* Norman: University of Oklahoma Press, 1967.

Crane, Verner W. *The Southern Frontier, 1670–1732.* 1929. Reprint, Ann Arbor: University of Michigan Press, 1956.

Debo, Angie. *The Road to Disappearance: A History of the Creek Indians.* Norman: University of Oklahoma Press, 1941.

Dixon, Sara Robertson, and A. H. Clark. *History of Stewart County, Georgia.* Vol 2. Waycross, Ga.: A. H. Clark, 1975.

DuBose, Louise Gunby Jones. *A History of Columbus, Georgia, 1828–1928.* Columbus, Ga.: Historical Publishing Co., 1929.

Faust, Patricia L., ed. *Historical Times Illustrated Encyclopedia of the Civil War.* New York: Harper & Row, 1986.

Foreman, Grant. *Indian Removal: The Emigration of the Five Civilized Tribes of Indians.* Norman: University of Oklahoma Press, 1932.

Fretwell, Mark E. *This So Remote Frontier: The Chattahoochee Country of Alabama and Georgia.* 1980. Reprint, Eufaula, Ala.: Historic Chattahoochee Commission, 1987.

———. *West Point: The Story of a Georgia Town.* West Point, Ga.: Chattahoochee Valley Historical Society, 1987.

Fundaburk, Emma Lila, ed. *Southeastern Indians: Life Portraits: A Catalogue of Pictures, 1564–1860.* Birmingham, Ala.: Birmingham Printing Co., 1958.

Garrett, Franklin M. *Atlanta and Environs: A Chronicle of Its People and Events.* 2 vols. New York: Lewis Historical Publishing Co., 1954.

Gatschet, Albert S. *A Migration Legend of the Creek Indians with a Linguistic, Historic, and Ethnographic Introduction.* Vol. 1. 1884. Reprint, New York: AMS Press, 1969.

Georgia: The WPA Guide to Its Towns and Countryside. 1940. Reprint, Columbia: University of South Carolina Press, 1990.

Green, Michael D. *The Politics of Indian Removal: Creek Government and Society in Crisis.* Lincoln: University of Nebraska Press, 1982.

Griffith, Benjamin W. *McIntosh and Weatherford, Creek Indian Leaders.* Tuscaloosa: University of Alabama Press, 1989.

Heath, Milton Sydney. *Constructive Liberalism: The Role of the State in Economic Development in Georgia to 1860.* Cambridge: Harvard University Press, 1954.

Hodler, Thomas W., and Howard A. Schretter. *The Atlas of Georgia.* Athens: The Institute of Community and Area Development/The University of Georgia, 1986.

Hudson, Charles. *The Southeastern Indians.* Knoxville: University of Tennessee Press, 1976.

Hunter, Louis C. *Steamboats on the Western Rivers: An Economic and Technological History.* 1949. Reprint, New York: Dover, 1993.

Inventory of the County Archives of Georgia. Number 106: Muscogee County. Atlanta: Georgia Historical Records Survey, 1941.

Jackson, Harvey H., III. *Rivers of History: Life on the Coosa, Tallapoosa, Cahaba, and Alabama.* Tuscaloosa: University of Alabama Press, 1995.

Jordan, Weymouth T. *Antebellum Alabama: Town and Country.* 1957. Reprint, Tuscaloosa: University of Alabama Press, 1986.

Kyle, Clason. *Images: A Pictorial History of Columbus, Georgia.* Norfolk, Va.: Donning, 1986.

Littlefield, Daniel F., Jr. *Africans and Creeks: From the Colonial Period to the Civil War.* Westport, Conn.: Greenwood Press, 1979.

Lupold, John S. *Chattahoochee Valley Sources and Resources: An Annotated Bibliography.* Vol. 1, *The Alabama Counties.* Eufaula, Ala.: Historic Chattahoochee Commission, 1988.

———. *Chattahoochee Valley Sources and Resources: An Annotated Bibliography.* Vol. 2, *The Georgia Counties.* Eufaula, Ala.: Historic Chattahoochee Commission, 1993.

———. *Columbus, Georgia, 1828–1978.* Columbus, Ga.: Columbus Sesquicentennial, Inc., 1978.

Mahan, Joseph B. *Columbus: Georgia's Fall Line "Trading Town."* Northridge, Calif.: Windsor, 1986.

Major, Glenda, and Clark Johnson. *Treasures of Troup County: A Pictorial History of Troup County.* LaGrange, Ga.: Troup County Historical Society, 1993.

Martin, John H. *Columbus, Geo., from Its Selection as a "Trading Town" in 1827 to Its Partial Destruction by Wilson's Raid, in 1865.* 1874. Reprint, Easley, S.C.: Georgia Genealogical Reprints, 1972.

McGinnis, Callie B., and Sandra K. Stratford. *Muscogee County, Georgia, 1860 Census Index.* Columbus, Ga.: Yesteryear Research Associates, 1985.

Milanich, Jerald, and Charles Hudson. *Hernando De Soto and the Indians of Florida.* Gainesville: University Press of Florida, 1993.

Mitchell, George. *In Celebration of a Legacy: The Traditional Arts of the Lower Chattahoochee Valley.* Columbus, Ga.: Columbus Museum of Arts and Sciences, 1981.

Montgomery, Horace. *Howell Cobb's Confederate Career.* Tuscaloosa: Confederate Publishing Co., 1959.

Mueller, Edward A. *Perilous Journeys: A History of Steamboating on the Chattahoochee, Apalachicola, and Flint Rivers, 1828–1928.* Eufaula, Ala.: Historic Chattahoochee Commission, 1990.

Neville, Bert. *Directory of Steamboats with Illustrations and List of Landings, on Chattahoochee-Apalachicola-Flint-Chipola Rivers.* Selma, Ala.: privately published, 1961.

220   O'Donnell, James H., III. *The Georgia Frontier, 1773–1783.* N.p., 1975.

———. *Southern Indians in the American Revolution.* Knoxville: University of Tennessee Press, 1973.

Owsley, Frank Lawrence, Jr. *Struggle for the Gulf Borderlands: The Creek War and the Battle of New Orleans, 1812–1815.* Gainesville: University Presses of Florida, 1981.

Perry, Joel W., comp. *Some Pioneer History of Early County, 1818–1871.* N.p., n.d.

Phillips, U. B. *A History of Transportation in the Eastern Cotton Belt to 1860.* 1908. Reprint, New York: Octagon Books, 1968.

Pound, Merritt. *Benjamin Hawkins, Indian Agent.* Athens: University of Georgia Press, 1951.

Prehistory of the Middle Chattahoochee River Valley: Findings of the 1989–1990 West Point Archaeological Survey and Site Testing Project. Stone Mountain, Ga.: New South Associates, 1991.

Rawick, George P., gen. ed. *The American Slave: A Composite Autobiography.* Westport, Conn.: Greenwood Press, 1979.

Rogers, N. K. *History of Chattahoochee County, Georgia.* N.p.: N. K. Rogers, 1933.

Rogers, William Warren, et al. *Alabama: The History of a Deep South State.* Tuscaloosa: University of Alabama Press, 1994.

Scharf, John Thomas. *History of the Confederate Navy from Its Organization to the Surrender of Its Last Vessel.* New York: Rogers & Sherwood, 1887.

Schnell, Frank, Vernon J. Knight, and Gail S. Schnell. *Cemochechobee: Archaeology of a Mississippian Ceremonial Center on the Chattahoochee River.* Gainesville: University Presses of Florida, 1981.

Scott, Mrs. Marvin. *History of Henry County Alabama.* Pensacola: Frank R. Parkhurst & Son, 1961.

Sellers, Tom. *Valley Echoes.* Atlanta: Davicone, 1986.

Smith, Clifford L. *History of Troup County.* Atlanta: Foote & Davies Co., 1933.

Southerland, Henry DeLeon, Jr., and Jerry Elijah Brown. *The Federal Road through Georgia, the Creek Nation, and Alabama, 1806–1836.* Tuscaloosa: University of Alabama Press, 1989.

Standard, Diffee William. *Columbus, Georgia, in the Confederacy: The Social and Industrial Life of the Chattahoochee River Port.* New York: William-Frederick Press, 1954.

Sturtevant, William, ed. *A Creek Source Book.* Bureau of American Ethnology Bulletin No. 123. New York: Garland, 1987.

Swanton, John R. *Early History of the Creek Indians and Their Neighbors.* Washington, D.C.: Government Printing Office, 1922.

———. *The Indians of the Southeastern United States.* Bureau of American Ethnology Bulletin No. 137. 1946. Reprint, Grosse Pointe, Mich.: Scholarly Press, 1969.

———. *Social Organization and Social Usages of the Indians of the Creek Confederacy.* Bureau of American Ethnology Bulletin No. 42. Washington, D.C.: Government Printing Office, 1928.

Taylor, George Rogers. *The Transportation Revolution, 1815–1860.* New York: Harper & Row, 1951.

Tebeau, Charlton W. *A History of Florida.* Coral Gables: University of Miami Press, 1971.   221

Turner, Maxine. *Navy Gray: A Story of the Confederate Navy on the Apalachicola and Chattahoochee Rivers.* Tuscaloosa: University of Alabama Press, 1988.

Usner, Daniel H., Jr. *Indians, Settlers, and Slaves in a Frontier Exchange Economy.* Chapel Hill: University of North Carolina Press, 1992.

Walker, Anne Kendrick. *Backtracking in Barbour County: A Narrative of the Last Alabama Frontier.* Richmond: Dietz, 1941.

———. *Russell County in Retrospect: An Epic of the Far Southeast.* Richmond: Dietz, 1950.

Warren, Hoyt M. *Chattahoochee Trails: Short, Factual, Historical Stories about the Chattahoochee Valley.* Abbeville, Ala.: Henry County Historical Society, 1981.

West, G. M. *St. Andrews, Florida.* Panama City, Fla.: Panama City Publishing Co., 1960.

Willoughby, Lynn. *Fair to Middlin': The Antebellum Cotton Trade of the Apalachicola/Chattahoochee River Valley.* Tuscaloosa: University of Alabama Press, 1993.

Winn, William W. *The Old Beloved Path: Daily Life among the Indians of the Chattahoochee River Valley.* Eufaula, Ala.: Historic Chattahoochee Commission and the Columbus Museum, 1992.

Woodall, W. C. *Home Town and Other Sketches.* Privately printed, 1935.

Worsley, Etta Blanchard. *Columbus on the Chattahoochee.* Columbus, Ga.: Columbus Office Supply Co., 1951.

Wright, J. Leitch. *Creeks and Seminoles: The Destruction and Regeneration of the Muscogulge People.* Lincoln: University of Nebraska Press, 1986.

———. *William Augustus Bowles: Director General of the Creek Nation.* Athens: University of Georgia Press, 1967.

Young, Marjorie W. *Textile Leaders of the South.* Anderson, S.C.: James R. Young, 1963.

Young, Mary Elizabeth. *Redskins, Ruffleshirts, and Rednecks: Indian Allotments in Alabama and Mississippi.* Norman: University of Oklahoma Press, 1961.

ARTICLES

Bell, Amelia Rector. "Separate People: Speaking of Creek Men and Women." *American Anthropologist* 92 (June 1990): 332–45.

Bogle, James G. "Horace King, 1807–1887." *Georgia Life,* Spring 1980, 33–35.

Bolton, Herbert E. "Spanish Resistance to the Carolina Traders in Western Georgia (1680–1704)." *Georgia Historical Quarterly* 9 (June 1925): 115–30.

Bonner, James C. "Journal of a Mission to Georgia in 1827." *Georgia Historical Quarterly* 44 (March 1960): 74–84.

Boyd, Mark F. "Events at Prospect Bluff on the Apalachicola River, 1808–1818." *Florida Historical Quarterly* 16 (October 1937): 55–96.

Brannon, Peter A. "Russell County Place Names." *Alabama Historical Quarterly* 21 (1959): 96–103.

———, ed. "Indian Treaties." *Alabama Historical Quarterly* 12 (1950): 245–50.

———. "Journal of James A. Tait for the Year 1813." *Georgia Historical Quarterly* 8 (March 1924): 229–39.

222 Braund, Kathryn E. Holland. "The Creek Indians, Blacks, and Slavery." *Journal of Southern History* 57 (November 1991): 601–36.

———. "Guardians of Traditions and Handmaidens to Change: Women's Roles in Creek Economic and Social Life during the Eighteenth Century." *American Indian Quarterly* 14 (Summer 1990): 239–58.

Brown, Jane Lightcap. "From Augusta to Columbus: Thackeray's Experiences in Georgia, 1853 and 1856." *Georgia Historical Quarterly* 67 (Fall 1983): 315–20.

Bunyan, Hadley Andrew, "Georgia's Chattahoochee River Bank Boundry [*sic*]: A Recapitulatory Note." *Georgia Historical Quarterly* 48 (March 1964), 74–77.

Campbell, John Archibald. "The Creek Indian War of 1836." *Transactions of the Alabama Historical Society* 3 (1898–99): 162–66.

Chambers, Nella J. "The Creek Indian Factory at Fort Mitchell." *Alabama Historical Quarterly* 21 (1959): 15–71.

Chase, David W. "Fort Mitchell: An Archaeological Exploration in Russell County, Alabama." Special Publication No. 1 of the Alabama Archaeological Society, February 1974.

Clark, T. D. "The Montgomery and West Point Railroad." *Georgia Historical Quarterly* 17 (March 1933): 273–99.

Coley, C. J. "Creek Treaties, 1970–1832." *Alabama Review* 11 (1958): 163–76.

Coss, Richard H. "On the Trail of Jim Henry." *Muscogiana* 3 (Fall 1992): 55–63.

Cushman, Joseph D., Jr. "The Blockade and Fall of Apalachicola." *Florida Historical Quarterly* 41 (July 1962–April 1963): 38–43.

Fretwell, Mark E. "Benjamin Hawkins in the Chattahoochee Valley: 1798." *Chattahoochee Valley Historical Association Bulletin No. 1*, May 1954.

Galishoff, Stuart. "Paying for the Cost of Growth: The Environmental Engineering Debate in Atlanta, 1877–1914." *Essays in Public Works History* 18 (Winter 1994/95).

Goff, John. "The Steamboat Period in Georgia." *Georgia Historical Quarterly* 12 (March 1928): 236–56.

Haas, Mary R. "Creek Inter-Town Relations." *American Anthropologist* 42 (1940): 479–89.

Hageman, H. A., and T. B. Parker. "The Bartlett's Ferry Hydroelectric Development." *Journal of the Boston Society of Civil Engineers* 13 (March 1926): 93–95.

Hardaway, B. H. "Remarks on the Recent Failures of Masonry Dams in the South." *Engineering News*, January 6, 1902, 107–9.

"Indian Chiefs." *Alabama Historical Quarterly* 13 (1951): 5–91.

"Indian Tribes and Towns in Alabama." *Alabama Historical Quarterly* 12 (1950): 118–241.

Ivey, Betty Dickinson. "From River to Rail in Pickens County." *Alabama Review* 7 (1954): 53–66.

Justus, Lucy. "Chattahoochee: A Metro River Park." *Outdoors in Georgia*, June 1978, 2–10.

Nunez, Theron A., Jr. "Creek Nativism and the Creek War of 1813–1814." *Ethnohistory* 5 (Winter 1958): 1–47, 131–75, 292–301.

"Oglethorpe's Treaty with the Lower Creek Indians." *Georgia Historical Quarterly* 4 (March 1920): 3–16.

Paredes, J. Anthony. "Some Creeks Stayed: Comments on Amelia Rector Bell's 'Separate

People: Speaking of Creek Men and Women.'" *American Anthropologist* 93 (Sep-   223
tember 1991): 697–99.

Proctor, William G. "Slavery in Southwest Georgia." *Georgia Historical Quarterly* 49 (March 1965): 1–22.

Schnell, Frank T. "The Beginnings of the Creeks: Where Did They First 'Sit Down'?" *Early Georgia* 17, nos. 1 and 2 (1989): 24–29.

Searcy, Martha Condray. "The Introduction of African Slavery into the Creek Indian Nation." *Georgia Historical Quarterly* 66, no. 1 (Spring 1982): 21–32.

Slack, Searcy B. "Building Concrete Bridge around an Old Steel Bridge." *Engineering News,* December 23, 1902, 870–73.

Stephen, Walter W. "The Sunken Guns of the Chattahoochee River." *Alabama Historical Quarterly* 20 (1958): 619–22.

Thurston, William N. "The Apalachicola-Chattahoochee-Flint River Water Route System in the Nineteenth Century." *Georgia Historical Quarterly* 57 (Summer 1973): 200–212.

Turner, Maxine. "Naval Operations on the Apalachicola and Chattahoochee Rivers, 1861–1865." Reprinted from *Alabama Historical Quarterly* 36 (Fall and Winter 1974–75).

"White Men Associated with Indian Life." *Alabama Historical Quarterly* 13 (1951): 140–55.

Wood, Susan K. "Covered Bridges." *Outdoors in Georgia,* June 1977, 22–25.

Woodall, W. C. "Columbus: A Brief History." *Georgia Magazine,* February–March 1963, 21–24.

Worsley, Etta Blanchard. "Columbus." *Georgia Review* 1 (Fall 1947): 366–77.

UNPUBLISHED

"A Brief History of Electric Power in Columbus and Surrounding Area. Taken from the Records of the Power Company." Typescript, n.d. In Columbus College Archives.

Cox, Willis S. "A Story of the Chattahoochee River as It Has Affected Fort Gaines and Clay County Together with Some Articles of Historical Interest." Typescript, 1966. In Columbus College Archives.

Dixon, Sandra. "A History of the Chattahoochee Region." Typescript for Westville Historic Handicrafts, Inc., June 20, 1987. In "Chattahoochee Region—History" vertical file, Columbus College Archives.

Fryman, Robert J. "The Last Redoubt: Archaeological Investigations at Fort Tyler, Troup County, Georgia." Hand-bound typescript, March 1933. In Troup County Archives, LaGrange, Georgia.

Georgia Mountains Planning and Development Commission. "River Corridor Studies of the Upper Chattahoochee, Chestatee, and Etowah Rivers." 1973. In Bradley Memorial Library, Columbus, Georgia.

Gibson, Jon, et al. "Cultural Investigations in the Apalachicola and Chattahoochee River Valleys in Florida, Alabama, and Georgia: History, Archeology, and Underwater Remote Sensing." Typescript, 1980. In Schnell Personal Collection, Columbus Museum.

224   Karfunkle, J. B., John S. Lupold, and Barbara A. Kimmelman. "Hydroelectric Power Development at North Highlands." Historic American Engineering Record, GA-26. Typescript, August 1977. In Columbus College Archives.

Lupold, John S. "Industrial Archeology of Columbus, Georgia: A Tour Guide for the Eighth Annual Conference of the Society for Industrial Archeology." Typescript, April 1979. In Columbus College Archives.

Lupold, John S., J. B. Karfunkle, and Barbara Kimmelman. "The Columbus Iron Works." Historic American Engineering Record, GA-28. Typescript, 1977. In Columbus College Archives.

———. "Columbus Manufacturing Company." Historic American Engineering Record, GA-29. Typescript, 1977. In Columbus College Archives.

———. "The Eagle and Phenix Mills." Historic American Engineering Record, GA-30. Typescript, August 1977. In Columbus College Archives.

———. "The Evolution of Hydro-Power Development at the Falls of the Chattahoochee." Typescript, 1977. In the possession of John Lupold.

———. "Muscogee Manufacturing Company." Historic American Engineering Record, GA-23. Typescript, 1977. In Columbus College Archives.

———. "Water Power Development at the Falls of the Chattahoochee." Historic American Engineering Record, GA-22. Typescript. August 1977. In Columbus College Archives.

McDonald, Cecil Ward. "The Economic History of Columbus, Georgia, to the Civil War." Master's thesis, Alabama Polytechnic Institute, 1940.

Morey, Maj. Leighton, et al. "Brief History of the Columbus Iron Works, 1853–1865." Typescript, March 5, 1957. In "Columbus Industry" vertical file, Columbus College Archives.

Owens, Harry P. "Apalachicola before 1861." Ph.D. diss., Florida State University, 1966.

Schnell, Frank T. "The Chattahoochee Promenade: A Heritage Park for Tomorrow." Typescript, n.d. In Schnell Personal Collection, Columbus Museum.

———. "A Cultural Resource Assessment of the Proposed Site of the River Club, Columbus, Georgia." Typescript, 1989. In "Chattahoochee River" vertical file, Columbus College Archives.

Spencer, Richard P. "The Empire State in the New South: Georgia's Industrial Development from the 1840s to the 1890s." Senior thesis, Princeton University, 1988.

U.S. Army Corps of Engineers. "Draft Environmental Impact Statement: Walter F. George Lock, Dam, and Lake, Alabama and Georgia: Operation and Maintenance." 1979. In Jack T. Brinkley Collection, Columbus College Archives.

Ware, Lynn Willoughby. "The Cotton Trade of the Apalachicola/Chattahoochee River Valley, 1840–1860." Ph.D. diss., Florida State University, 1989.

Watts, Gordon P., Jr., William N. Still, Jr., James Lee Cox, Jr., and Wesley K. Hall. "A Reconnaissance Survey of the Chattahoochee River at Columbus, Georgia." 1982. Prepared for the James W. Woodruff, Jr., Confederate Naval Museum, Columbus, Georgia.

INDEX